This erudite, eloquent and immensley thought-provoking work is indispensable ready for anyone who wants to understand the principles of glory and the prophetic concept of the Day of Jehovah Tsaba and how this revelation affects your relationship with God. This is a profound authoritative work which spans the wisdom of the ages and yet breaks new ground in its approach to understanding the keys to understanding a unique perspective of the divine. This book will possibly become a classic in this and the next generation.

This exceptional work by Dr. Pickney is one of the most inspiring, practical and principle-centered approaches to this subject I have read in a long time. The author's approach to this timely issue brings a fresh breath of air that captivates the heart, engages the mind and inspires the spirit of the reader.

The author's ability to leap over complicated theological and metaphysical jargon and reduce complex theories to simple practical principles that the least among us can understand is amazing.

Enjoy this book and let its pages of wisdom inspire you and expand your faith.

—Dr. Myles Munroe
Pastor and Best-selling Author

A
PROSPERITY
PHENOMENON

DR. DON G. PICKNEY

CREATION
HOUSE

A Prosperity Phenomenon by Dr. Don G. Pickney
Published by Creation House
A Charisma Media Company
600 Rinehart Road
Lake Mary, Florida 32746
www.charismamedia.com

Unless otherwise noted, all Scripture quotations are from the King James Version of the Bible.

Scripture quotations marked AMP are from the Amplified Bible. Old Testament copyright © 1965, 1987 by the Zondervan Corporation. The Amplified New Testament copyright © 1954, 1958, 1987 by the Lockman Foundation. Used by permission.

Scripture quotations marked THE MESSAGE are from *The Message: The Bible in Contemporary English*, copyright © 1993, 1994, 1995, 1996, 2000, 2001, 2002. Used by permission of NavPress Publishing Group.

Scripture quotations marked TLB are from The Living Bible. Copyright © 1971. Used by permission of Tyndale House Publishers, Inc., Wheaton, IL 60189. All rights reserved.

Scripture quotations marked JB are from *The Jerusalem Bible*. Garden City, New York; London: Doubleday; Darton, Longman & Todd, 1966, 1967, 1968.

Scripture quotations marked RSV are from the Revised Standard Version of the Bible. Copyright © 1946, 1952, 1971 by the Division of Christian Education of the National Council of the Churches of Christ in the USA. Used by permission.

Scripture quotations marked LITV are from the Literal Translation of the Holy Bible by Jay P. Green Sr. Copyright © 1976, 2000 by Jay P. Green Sr. Used by permission of the copyright holder.

Scripture quotations marked BECK are from The Holy Bible: An American Translation by William F. Beck. Copyright © 1976. Used by permission of Leader Publishing Company, New Haven, MO. Used by permission.

Scripture quotations marked THOMPSON are from the *Thompson® Chain-Reference Bible* by Dr. Frank C. Thompson. Copyright © 2010. Used by permission of B.B. Kirkbride Bible Co.

Scripture quotations marked BERKELEY are from *The Modern Language Bible: The New Berkeley Version in Modern English*. Copyright © 1959. Used by permission of Zondervan. All rights reserved.

Scripture quotations marked MOFFATT are from The Bible: James Moffatt Translation, Copyright © 1922, 1924, 1925, 1926, 1935 Harper Collins San Francisco, Copyright © 1950, 1952, 1953, 1954 James A. R. Moffatt.

Design Director: Bill Johnson
Cover design by Nathan Morgan

Visit the author's Website: www.donpickneyministries.org

Library of Congress Cataloging-in-Publication Data: 2011943896
International Standard Book Number: 978-1-61638-880-5
E-book International Standard Book Number: 978-1-61638-881-2

First edition

12 13 14 15 16 — 9 8 7 6 5 4 3 2 1
Printed in Canada

DEDICATION

This book is dedicated to the friends of this ministry who have supported us for the past thirty-seven years of full-time ministry and especially to those who have taken this journey with us for the past decade as we have given ourselves to a special assignment: to proclaim A Prosperity Phenomenon—the Day of Jehovah Tsaba.

Special thanks is also given to the Lord Jesus Christ for those who gave special support for this publishing.

And, behold, the angel that talked with me went forth.... [and said] For thus saith the LORD of hosts [Jehovah Tsaba]; After the glory hath he sent me unto the nations [Gentile world] which spoiled [plundered] you: for he that toucheth you toucheth the apple of his eye. For, behold, I will shake mine hand upon them, and they shall be a spoil to their servants: and ye shall know that the LORD of hosts [Jehovah Tsaba] hath sent me.

—ZECHARIAH 2:3, 8–9

CONTENTS

PREFACE

IT IS NOW 2012. What in the world is going on? Stock markets are teetering on the brink, while everyone holds their breath daily with major national banks going under and still more showing signs of possible failure. Governments and regimes have fallen, leaving a void of leadership. Countries are financially defaulting, with riots and demonstrations in their streets over economic failures. National legislative bodies sit paralyzed, unable to pass any meaningful legislation. The debt of all nations continues spiraling far beyond any ability to recover. China is now holding captive unbelievable amounts of U.S. securities. We find unemployment at crisis levels. Housing markets have gone so far under that no one dares forecast a successful outcome. The world is held in a grip of terror, with only a matter of time until another terrorist succeeds in making the world headlines. *Everything is shaking all over the world!*

But wait a minute. What if all of this could be *happening just for your benefit as Christian believers*? What if this is to be a great, global orchestration of God's ability, plan, and purpose to bring a blessing to you by shaking everything that can be shaken in the whole earth? And what if this was all forecasted in the Scriptures, all surely to come to pass in some future time that *happens to be now*? What if it was all designed to bring a prosperity phenomenon to a people especially marked by God as the recipients of all of the plunder of earth's riches?

It is our intent for *A Prosperity Phenomenon* to clearly define the "glory of the world." We do not believe that immense wealth, placed into the hands of the righteous, will be used for the same purposes as it was by the evil, wicked, Gentile world. We will reveal that God's plan is for His people to ultimately use the world's riches for His righteous cause. The purpose of this book is only partly to reveal "the glory of the world," and then to bring into revelation a connection between the immediate, current global events described earlier and scriptures detailing the transfer of God's created glory to the church.

My promise is to never take you where the Word of God doesn't go! But what if there is an event, clearly overlooked by prominent eschatologists and end-time pundits, revealed in Scripture that must take place before the end of the Gentile age and the Rapture of the church? Imagine a special occasion designed to advance a great end-time harvest of souls into Christ's kingdom. What if this book is the only one of its kind in the world with knowledge from God's Word never previously totally explored as it is in these pages? And what if the first portion of this event is already well under way?

All the Way Back to Adam!

The Deuteronomy 4 connection—and you ain't never seen nothin' like this before!

> Ask questions. Find out what has been going on all these years before you were born. From the day God created man and woman on this Earth, and from the horizon in the east to the horizon in the west—as far back as you can imagine and as far away as you can imagine—has as great a thing as this ever happened? Has anyone ever heard of such a thing? Has a people ever heard, as you did, a god speaking out of the middle of the fire and lived to tell the story? Or has a god ever tried to select for himself a nation from within a nation using trials, miracles, and war, putting his strong hand in, reaching his long arm out, a spectacle awesome and staggering, the way God, your God, did it for you in Egypt while you stood right there and watched?
> —Deuteronomy 4:32–34, The Message

An even greater event is here!

You will find in these pages a revelation of one of the greatest events since God created Adam on the earth. God spoke through Moses that the Israelites' deliverance from Egypt and the event of spoiling an entire nation of its personal wealth (the Egyptians' heavy gold and silver jewels and their finest apparel) was the greatest event up to that point in history.

Imagine the miracle that occurred within a single day for Israel, God's ancient people. With no edict from Pharaoh, no mandate to any Egyptian household, yet every household in perfect unison, without any knowledge that all the other households were responding the same as they, handed over their personal heavy gold and silver jewels, and their finest apparel to their Hebrew slaves. It was an orchestrated event, a greater manifestation than anything God had ever planned since His act of creation. He spoiled a nation en masse of their individual wealth in a single day, and gave it to His people Israel.

What would you say if I showed you an even greater event, one not restricted to what God did to only one nation, for His people, but a worldwide, global event that would make His deliverance of the Israelites from Egypt look minuscule? Hard to believe, isn't it? But I am going to prove from the Scriptures such an event and show you that it is even now underway. Humanity all over the earth is wondering, What in the world is happening across the nations of the globe? We will reveal that what is happening was prophesied in Scripture. We will show you that the Scriptures compare this event with Moses's event and declares this event greater. "Pastor, do you mean an event greater than the event that God declared to be the greatest event since creation of mankind?" *Yes*! This event is so much greater than the Moses event that it is almost incomparable in terms of its greatness. And it's happening *now*! It is already underway. It began on September 11, 2001, after I publicly, in my own church and as a guest speaker at other churches, began prophesying and preaching this event from the Scriptures beginning in May 2000, over a year before 9/11.

Later in these pages you will read of an angel visiting my room as I was preparing to be a guest speaker at a church in Memphis, Tennessee. The angel spoke to me of the shaking that would begin with the destruction of the World Trade Center towers and the subsequent economic turmoil that has accelerated up to the time of this writing.

THE DEUTERONOMY 4–HAGGAI 2 CONNECTION

The lessor and the greater events

The Book of Haggai, chapter 2, addresses the prior event of Moses and the deliverance of Israel from Egyptian slavery, plundering their gold and silver jewels, the very event referenced in a staggering description by God as the greatest thing He had ever done since creating mankind. But Haggai boasts of an even greater event to occur in some distant future time that would dwarf the Moses event, an event that would plunder the gold and silver and wealth of all nations of the world on behalf of a single nation (the church, God's holy New Testament elect people). Here is Haggai's prophetic depiction of this event:

> For I am with you, declares Jehovah of Hosts [Jehovah Tsaba], with the Word by whom I covenanted with you when you came out of Egypt, so My Spirit stands among you [power and anointing remains]; do not fear. For so says Jehovah of Hosts [Jehovah Tsaba]: Yet once [one more time], it is a little while [in a distant time], and I will shake the heavens and the earth and the sea and the dry land. And I will shake all the nations; and the desire ["the desirable things," RSV] of all nations shall come. And I will fill this house with glory, says Jehovah of Hosts. The silver is Mine, and the gold is Mine, says Jehovah of Hosts [Jehovah Tsaba].
>
> —Haggai 2:4–9, LITV

Did you catch that? Do you think you could embrace such an unimaginable thing that God insists upon doing at some future time in Haggai's prophecy? We will show you that Haggai's prophetic time has come. It is *now*! You will need to gather all the information you can about this event. We invite you to take the journey with us in these pages. You will surely find opportunity to rejoice and celebrate this dramatic event. It is God's blessing for His church in this end-time period.

You will read the story of how God planned in His covenant with Abraham to demonstrate His power at two distinct distant points in the future. He said to Abraham, "Know of a surety that thy seed shall be a stranger in a land that is not theirs, and shall serve them; and they shall afflict them four hundred years; And also that nation, whom they shall serve, will I judge: and afterward shall they come out with great substance" (Gen. 15:13–14).

When God sent Moses to lead Israel out of Egyptian slavery, He included this judgment in His instructions to Moses: "And I will stretch out my hand…And I will give this people favour…and it shall come to pass, that, when ye go, ye shall not go empty. But every woman shall borrow of her neighbour, and of her that sojourneth in her house, jewels of silver, and jewels of gold, and raiment: and ye shall put them upon your sons, and upon your daughters; and ye shall spoil the Egyptians.…and they borrowed of the Egyptians jewels of silver, and jewels of gold, and raiment: And the LORD gave the people favour in the sight of the Egyptians, so that they lent unto them such things as they required. And they spoiled the Egyptians" (Exod. 3:20–22; 12:35–36).

As you read, we will show you that as God planned this event, and as He revealed it to Moses, there was a great anointing released to accomplish and fulfill a special promise to Abraham.

It is so important for you to comprehend the revelation spoken of, in which God identifies that the anointing that brought Israel out of Egypt, plundering the wealth of the Egyptians, was not spent up entirely in their deliverance but was retained for a second event patterned after the first one but meant to accomplish something so much greater. That promise, found later in the Scriptures, declares, "According to the word that I covenanted with you when ye came out of Egypt, so my spirit [anointing and power] remaineth among you" (Hag. 2:5).

We will reveal to you that Jehovah Tsaba, the Lord of hosts, is right now sending His angels out among the wicked rich Gentile world system to cause this same thing to occur once again prior to the Rapture of the church. We reveal the meaning of the Hebrew scholar James Moffatt's translation of Isaiah 60:5: "The rich sea trade and the wealth of nations shall be converted unto thee."

If you are a Christian who is bewildered about what is happening regarding the economic chaos and financial upheaval throughout the world, you will find real, biblical answers in these pages. We will weave, interweave, and reweave Scriptural evidence to convince you that what looks like it is "out of control" is really God taking into His divine hand the wealth system of the entire earth, shaking it, and bringing it to plunder in order to get it out of the hands of the wicked and into the hands of His people.

Nowhere in the world, not in any bookstore, nor from the pulpit of any church, not even in any message you have ever heard, will you have been given the comprehensive insight that you will have by the time you close the final pages of this book. It is a one-of-a-kind message never before heralded in its entirety, taken straight from God's Word but delivered by an angel of God's glory to this author. It is incomparable to any other end-time revelation, unmatched by any other writing in the world. Get ready to receive revelation of an anointing to take hold of the abundance reserved for God's end-time generation of His people.

Chapter One

THE REVELATION

T HIS BOOK IS a revelation taken directly from Bible scriptures. No matter the depth of your spiritual walk with God, the things contained in this book will thrill and astonish you as you reach into unsearchable truths. It reveals a glory unsurpassed by any event in history including the Cross of Christ. While Jesus "endured the cross, despising the shame" (Heb. 12:2), it was all about this global revival-event, planned for Him to "see his seed" and have His pleasure (Isa. 53:10). Jesus likened His Cross event as a seed going into the ground (John 12:24). Jesus said also in that verse, "It produces many others and yields a rich harvest" (AMP). Ask any farmer, and he will tell you the celebration is in the harvest not in the planting. This book is about God giving the church the rich ability to go get His precious harvest.

It is a message about money, gold, silver, and other materially precious things. Often when I share this important message someone will attempt to divert attention back to the purely spiritual aspects of God's goodness. The moment that we begin preaching on earthly riches, many are conditioned to feel the need to justify it, as if it needs defending. Yet the Scriptures state that if He "spared not his own Son, but delivered him up for us all, how shall he not with him also freely give us all things?" (Rom. 8:32). Jesus declared to His disciples, "Freely ye have received, freely give" (Matt. 10:8). God does bless those who walk in wisdom. But you will see that you can be less than perfect in these areas and still get in on this prophetic event—a prosperity phenomenon. It is one of God's planned blessings upon this final generation of believers at the end of this age. It is for every segment of the body of Christ who will receive it. With respect to God's great harvest of souls, it is God's most important promised blessing to those who will make Jesus Lord of their lives. I want to make clear that this is not a message about sowing and reaping, although I am a firm believer in and practice those scriptural principles. This is a message about mercy and compassion. It is a revelation of a planned event, a fixed occasion by the Father to give us a blessing out of His great love for the church and then to enlist us into His great harvest of souls.

You will learn the role that angels will play in God's plan. You will find almighty God rising up as Jehovah Tsaba, His name that has gone virtually unheralded since Old Testament times! This book is a revelation of this great Jehovah name! The events of this prophetic word include everything that will make the body of Christ glorious and filled with victory just prior to His coming! He will manifest Himself as Jehovah Tsaba in order to give the body of Christ (in mass) a promised blessing: the wealth of the wicked Gentile world!

The promise of wealth is not a new message for many who have taken hold of God's Word. Prosperity has and always will be available through faith in God's promise. Seed faith, sowing and reaping, and other principles concerning godly prosperity have always been available to all in Christ. (See my booklet *What You Need to Know About Seed Faith*.) But it is obvious that many have fallen short of the glory of the provision found in God's seed-faith promises. God is about to show His glory in a new way through an abundant access of the wealth of the wicked Gentile world.

While all of the world's financial institutions will shake with great acceleration, the church (not just its institutions and ministries) will shine in the area of great prosperity. While "darkness shall cover the earth, and gross darkness the people: but the LORD shall arise upon thee, and his glory shall be seen" upon us (Isa. 60:2)!

As you read keep in mind that what we are sharing with you is contained wholly in the Word of God. We have taken nothing out of its context. In fact, we have gone to great distances in preserving the accuracy of this message. The Father made you for this day. You can expect to go from one level of financial blessing to another as symptoms of great prosperity soon begin to appear in your life. You will go from strength to strength—from glory to glory! You will "suck the milk [Heb., 'the richness'] of the Gentiles" (Isa. 60:16).

JOHN WESLEY, FOUNDER OF THE METHODIST CHURCH, FORESAW AND PREACHED THIS EVENT!

From *John Wesley's Explanatory Notes*, we have this commentary about Isaiah 60:16: "That the church shall draw, or receive the wealth of nations, and the riches, and power of kings, and whatever is most excellent, and that it shall come freely, and affectionately, as milk flows from the breast of the mother." Additionally, Robert Jamieson, A. R. Fausset, and David Brown's commentary gives details of the word *suck* used in the verse: "Thou shalt draw to thyself and enjoy all that is valuable of the possessions of the Gentiles." God says, "For brass I will bring gold, and for iron I will bring silver, and for wood brass, and for stones iron" (Isa. 60:17). He is saying, "No matter where you are right now, *up* is where you will be headed!"

You will get to know Jehovah Tsaba, the King of glory! You will find that Jehovah Tsaba has sent His angelic armies out into the wicked, proud, and ungodly Gentile world system in pursuit of their glory—their gold, silver, and all desirable and precious things. His angel will shake them and cause them to be plundered. As their worldwide empire of wealth and influence disintegrates, it will come into the hands of those who favor God's righteous cause. It will be converted from the world into the power of the church, the believers in Christ! You can be a part of the blessing or not, but you cannot just sit it out on the sidelines. The choice of receiving will be yours. All you have to do to get in on this phenomenon will be to open your heart wide and say yes! Personally, I have already proclaimed it for my family and me!

In Isaiah 60 there is a wonderful messianic prophecy for the church. This revelation is written primarily for those who have already been celebrating the first two verses of that chapter, "Arise, shine; for thy light is come, and the glory of the LORD is risen upon thee. For, behold, the darkness shall cover the earth, and gross darkness the people: but the LORD shall arise upon thee, and his glory shall be seen upon thee." Maybe you are in a church that in the past sang the charismatic chorus taken from that scripture. For several years we celebrated and danced as we sang those words, "Arise, shine, for the light is come!" But we had little understanding of what we were singing. We were looking for goosebumps, a holy aura, or feelings of spiritual ecstasy! We believed that this wave of the glory of God would surely produce a spiritual power that could be translated into tangible help and benefits for the church.

We didn't realize that this particular scripture, kept within its context, was speaking about a glory coming upon believers, causing them to spoil (plunder) the evil Gentile world in a great pre-Rapture wealth phenomenon. During this period of glory, God says, "The rich sea trade . . . and the wealth of nations shall be converted unto thee, the forces [Heb., *chayil*: 'forces, wealth, riches, goods, substance, means, men and other resource'] of the Gentiles shall come unto thee" (Isa. 60:10, MOFFATT).

This prophetic word goes on to say, "Therefore thy gates shall be open continually; they shall not be shut day nor night; that men may bring unto thee the forces [forces, wealth, riches, goods, substance, means, men and other resources] of the Gentiles, and that their kings may be brought" (Isa. 60:11).

As these pages unfold, we will take you into God's great plan for the church in this hour. God knew that you would be born into this last generation, a generation destined by Him to walk in total victory just prior to the end of this age! His plan includes you in a great transfer of wealth from the world. He can use your abundant prosperity (instead of evangelism's begging and pleading and sometimes scheming) for funds to spread the gospel. Certainly, God is pleased that His people, though financially weak as a whole, have been willing to make the mass sacrifices necessary to see great strides in furthering the cause of the gospel ministry. But that is not His final plan for this hour.

He must move us into quantum ministry, so to speak. I am speaking of a leap of ability that may stagger your imagination at this moment. But if you are willing to give yourself and everything you have to God, then God, as Jehovah Tsaba, will send His angelic hosts of heaven to the nations (the rich, wicked Gentile world) to bring back for you their riches—their gold, their silver, their money, and all of their great resources. By making almighty God your source while devoting yourself to the support of the gospel of the Lord Jesus Christ, just the runover of your prosperity will allow you to live in a very wealthy place as you give the vastness of your riches for the sake of the gospel. You will see God's great strategic plan for this final harvest call to the world. It is not a new message but an ancient message with a fresh revelation given by the Spirit of God for this end-time harvest of souls!

CAN YOU BE CERTAIN THIS BOOK IS FOR YOU?

As you continue turning these pages, the most challenging thing for you may be that it appears too good to be true. But think: all of God's promises are in that realm. When He speaks, it is in a class of its own. Not one word will return to Him void. He watches over His word to perform it! It is so astounding, it is the only way it could happen. The question you will have to answer in reading this book is, *Are the Scriptures* that are referenced really applicable to me personally and to the church in general at this time? You will not be able to dispute the existence of the Scriptures in reference but only their validity with regard to you right now—today!

In order to set your mind at ease so that you can enjoy the freshness of revelation as you read, I will answer that question at this time and put your mind to rest. There are three main portions of Scripture that we will use to unveil the promise of this great prosperity phenomenon. They are found in Isaiah, Haggai, and Zechariah. Here is a summary of them in that order.

The Isaiah references are chapters 2, 13, 23, and 60–62. These chapters have been widely accepted by the church as messianic prophecies given primarily to encourage the church. That's us!

For more than forty years I have studied from a *Thompson Chain-Reference Bible*. It is held in Christian circles to be a very valuable study source. At the heading of Isaiah 60 it reads, "Glory of the church in the abundant access of the Gentiles, and her great blessings after a short affliction." Of Isaiah 61 it states, "Office of Christ, restoration and blessedness of the Church." Then concerning Isaiah 62 it reads, "The prophet's fervent zeal for the accomplishment of God's promises to His Church." I am not alone in my understanding of why these scriptures were given. Many Bible scholars readily agree that the material contained herein is written for the benefit of the church.

I know how important it is for you as you go further into this book to be certain of the validity of it for you and for the church at this hour, but no more so than all of the other promises too wonderful for words. It is no wonder that we have sung so fervently, "Arise, shine, for thy light is come!"

In Haggai 2:3–9, we will refer to a prophecy that, as you study it out, will prove clearly to be for this end-time period. In Haggai 2:9, God makes reference to the latter house as being greater than the former house. The word *house* in the Hebrew denotes "in the greatest variation, especially a family." The scholars go on to say, "…as in the house [family] of David." In this writing, God is making reference to two families. One (the former) is making reference to ancient Israel, and the other (the latter) is speaking of the church. Remember, there have only been [two] "families" ordained of God since Adam sinned: the Abrahamic or Jewish family (the natural seed of Abraham) and those born of God through

Christ Jesus who make up God's family (the church). In this context, as we will later provide evidence, Haggai is speaking of the church as the "latter house."

The next major portion of Scripture that makes up this revelation is found in Zechariah. An angel appeared to Zechariah and gave him a prophetic word. It is interesting how God hides what He is going to do in latter times through the process of "mirroring" one prophecy but revealing that it is actually for two separate time periods. In other words, it will come to pass in two phases, or in some cases it may come to pass twice but perhaps with and through the same anointing and for a separate purpose. A little later on in this book we will cover the application of what the New Testament has to say about Zion as the church. For now I am merely going to ask you to make the assumption with the understanding that we will clarify it later on. Zechariah 1:14 speaks about God being "jealous for Jerusalem and for Zion with a great jealousy."

These words make this prophecy twofold. It is for Jerusalem (or Israel) eventually and also for Zion (God's dwelling place, the church), as you will see with His next statement, quoted from Zechariah 2:10–11: "Sing and rejoice, O daughter of Zion: for, lo, I come, and I will dwell in the midst of thee, saith the LORD. And many nations shall be joined to the LORD in that day, and shall be my people [2 Corinthians 6:16 confirms this to be the church]: and I will dwell in the midst of thee, and thou shalt know that the LORD of hosts [Jehovah Tsaba] hath sent me unto thee." I encourage you to keep these thoughts in your mind as you continue to explore with me this revelation.

THE POWER TO GET WEALTH!

> And thou say in thine heart, My power and the might of mine hand hath gotten me this wealth. But thou shalt remember the LORD thy God: for it is he that giveth thee power to get wealth, that he may establish his covenant which he sware unto thy fathers, as it is this day.
> —DEUTERONOMY 8:17–18

Do you understand, with righteousness in your heart, what you could do for God with untold riches and favor? I promise you that your church pastor, with his vision of what God has called him to do, knows all too well what you could do! The ministries that are being called across the globe with exceptionally colossal assignments know what you could do! We'll show you that God wants

His people wealthy! He needs you to take this seriously and exercise faith for it. He also wants you void of covetousness in order to get you into position to be used for His purpose. God will separate you from the idea that "things" are bad for you. You will see that the same sins exist in mansions, moderate neighborhoods, and in the most poverty stricken homes. Don't ever look down your nose at someone else, no matter what his or her position is in life. Always remember, as someone has said, "Money may make your 'better off,' but it does not make you 'better'!" You will come to understand that money and wealth are morally neutral. They are neither for nor are they against you. If you are willing to link yourself up with almighty God as your source, all the wealth of the world may be placed at your unlimited disposal! It will be positioned into your hands in order that you may become a greater influence in the world for goodness and God's righteous cause.

God has sent me to bring you into a place of faith that has a relevance for only this final generation upon earth! God has insight for you that you would find impossible to believe if it were any book other than the Bible. Get ready to enter a life of total victory—a life of previously inconceivable supernatural abundance and spiritual power! There is so much for you to learn about God's name Jehovah Tsaba. You will come to understand the avenues by which He will gather the wealth of the world and bring it to you because you will know His great name!

Perhaps you have wondered why many of God's ministers today are proclaiming the message of supernatural prosperity for Christian believers. An ever-expanding presence of preaching concerning the principles of giving and receiving and of sowing and reaping is found. But we will unveil a scriptural prophecy, occurring now as an end-time event during which God is arising as Jehovah Tsaba. The change for you will astound you.

One key to this revelation is to be aware that God has not declared Himself as Jehovah throughout the New Testament church period. It is relevant that only once does the Scripture break precedent in the New Testament and speak in any Jehovah name. It is that reference that will change everything for this great chapter of the church.

God is now sending His angelic armies out to the wicked Gentile nations to bring back the glory of the world and put it into the right hands. They will put it into your hands if you are favoring God's righteous cause! Oh yes, you will have to use your faith for it if you want in on the cutting edge of this event! You will need to take your focus off of a "paycheck to paycheck" kind of faith for living. You will want to turn loose of any "bill to bill" kind of faith mentality. And you will also need to take what you have learned about walking by faith and use it with a grandeur that is worthy of what God has planned for you. His plan calls for the gold and silver of the world, their precious things, and their immense wealth to be taken from their hands. It will be placed into the hands of God's people to enjoy and to use for His glory. I trust you are ready to get into position for this prosperity phenomenon as God unfolds this great wealth conversion!

There will be a great spiritual battle for the goods of this world! But you will not fight in this battle! As He reveals Himself to you as Jehovah Tsaba, you will find that the battle is the Lord's. We will show you that you are not His army (except in the sense of a large mass); you are His family! I know that many have been told that they are in the army of the Lord. If you have been under the impression that you are called to fight, please don't get out of sorts with me! I believe before we are through, if you open your heart to Scripture, you'll understand where I'm coming from on this. It is from God!

YE SHALL NOT NEED TO FIGHT!

I have a radical, even revolutionary message from God for you! You do not have to fight the world, the flesh, or the devil. Early in my ministry, I was listening to one of God's great teachers. He said, "Some folks always greet you with, 'How goes the battle?' I always reply, 'It's victory that I'm in.' You see, I've found the devil is defeated!"

What a great revelation that was for me as a believer thirty-seven years ago when I first heard it! You see, any battle you might have engaged in is the one you might have with yourself, in your mind or your own reasoning. Once you've learned to yield to the principle of placing your thought processes under subjection to God's Word, then you will find rest.

The fight of faith mentioned in 1 Timothy 6:1 is not fighting to win but rather using your faith to enter into rest.

For we which have believed do enter into rest.

—HEBREWS 4:3

Let us labour therefore to enter into that rest.

—Hebrews 4:11

The Word of God reveals God's intentions regarding how His family would live as sons and daughters of the Most High. His vast eternal resources require no aid from His kids. He has His armies in heaven to do battle for Him and His family. He would never send His own sons and daughters into battle. Unfortunately, many of God's children have insisted on going into battle for themselves thinking that it is God's plan.

In Exodus 14:10, 13–14, the Word declares, "The Egyptians marched after them; and they were sore afraid: and the children of Israel cried out unto the Lord....And Moses said unto the people, Fear ye not, stand still [maintain your current position; you have fulfilled what needs to be done; you have trusted in me, says God], and see the salvation of the Lord, which he will shew to you to day: for the Egyptians whom ye have seen to day, ye shall see them again no more for ever. The Lord shall fight for you, and ye shall hold your peace."

Again, in Exodus 23:27, 31 we read, "I will send my fear before thee, and will destroy all the people to whom thou shalt come, and I will make all thine enemies turn their backs unto thee....I will deliver the inhabitants of the land into your hand." Later on Moses speaks to Israel in Deuteronomy 1:29–30 and says, "Dread not, neither be afraid of them. The Lord your God which goeth before you, he shall fight for you, according to all that he did for you in Egypt before your eyes." As Israel moved on through the land, God spoke through Moses to them again in Deuteronomy 3:22, "Ye shall not fear them: for the Lord your God he shall fight for you."

To make the plan entirely clear, God instructed Moses to declare the following to Israel in Deuteronomy 20:1–4:

> When thou goest out to battle against thine enemies, and seest horses, and chariots, and a people more than thou, be not afraid of them: for the Lord thy God is with thee...And it shall be, when ye are come nigh unto the battle, that the priest [Soldiers? *No!* The priest!] shall approach and speak unto the people, And shall say unto them, Hear, O Israel, ye approach this day unto battle against your enemies: let not

your hearts faint, fear not, and do not tremble, neither be ye terrified because of them; For the Lord your God is he that goeth with you, to fight for you against your enemies, to save you.

In the days of King Jehoshaphat, Israel learned to allow God's angelic armies to fight their battles. In 2 Chronicles 20:17, 22–25, 27, 29–30 we see what God's angelic army can do for those who will accept their help:

Ye shall not need to fight in this battle: set yourselves, stand ye still, and see the salvation of the Lord with you…for the Lord will be with you.…And when they began to sing [not fight, but sing!] and to praise, the Lord set ambushments against the children of Ammon, Moab, and mount Seir, which were come against Judah; and they were smitten. For the children of Ammon and Moab stood up against the inhabitants of mount Seir, utterly to slay and destroy them: and when they had made an end of the inhabitants of Seir, every one helped to destroy another. And when Judah came toward the watch tower in the wilderness, they looked unto the multitude, and, behold, they were dead bodies fallen to the earth, and none escaped. And when Jehoshaphat and his people came to take away the spoil of them, they found among them in abundance both riches with the dead bodies, and precious jewels, which they stripped off for themselves, more than they could carry away: and they were three days in gathering of the spoil, it was so much. [Praise God!] Then they returned…for the Lord had made them to rejoice over their enemies.…And the fear of God was on all the kingdoms of those countries, when they had heard that the Lord fought against the enemies of Israel. So the realm of Jehoshaphat was quiet: for his God gave him rest round about.

Then, in the days of King Hezekiah, at a time when Judah was being threatened, we read, "Be strong and courageous, be not afraid nor dismayed for the king of Assyria, nor for all the multitude that is with him: for there be more with us than with him: With him is an arm of flesh; but with us is the Lord our God to help us, and to fight our battles. And the people rested themselves upon the words of Hezekiah king of Judah" (2 Chron. 32:7–8).

You might ask, But didn't Israel have to do a lot of fighting for themselves?

In fact, did they not meet with some great defeats in battle? The answer, of course, is yes. The same is true today in spite of the fact that God has made His angelic armies available to the church. Still there are many Christians who are busy fighting, fighting, fighting! You ask, Why? Listen to these words in 1 Samuel 8:19–20, "Nevertheless the people refused to obey the voice of Samuel; and they said, Nay; but we will have a king over us; That we also may be like all the nations; and that our king may judge us, and go out before us, and fight our battles."

God spoke a message in Psalm 81:10–11, 13–16 concerning this matter:

> I am the LORD thy God, which brought thee out of the land of Egypt: open thy mouth wide, and I will fill it. But my people would not hearken to my voice; and Israel would none of me. Oh that my people had hearkened unto me, and Israel had walked in my ways! I should soon have subdued their enemies, and turned my hand against their adversaries. The haters of the LORD should have submitted themselves unto him. . . . He should have fed them also with the finest of the wheat: and with honey out of the rock should I have satisfied thee.

I pray for the body of Christ that we will wake up and allow God to fight our battles for us in this great last time of harvest!

Jacob looked up one day and saw an angelic army. He immediately declared, "This is God's host!" You must learn how to cooperate with this great angelic army as they go to battle to get your goods from the wicked Gentile world. They will open up gates of opportunity for you and literally send men to lay riches at your feet as you concentrate the direction of your resources toward God's righteous cause in the earth. God will do it to keep His covenant, which He swore on your behalf!

Are you tired of fighting spiritual battles all of the time? I can help you. Let me share my understanding of two vital passages of Scripture. Of course, you can receive or reject this, but I am personally convinced of its scriptural integrity. It is also in complete harmony with the scriptures we've already shared.

The first scripture is found in 2 Corinthians 10:3–4, "For though we walk in the flesh, we do not war after the flesh: (For the weapons of our warfare are not carnal, but mighty through God to the pulling down of strong holds)."

This is the scripture that hangs most Christians up and gets them on the wrong track. Many use this scripture to teach a kind of constant warfare for the believer. In my studies, however, I have seen a totally different message. Reading from the King James Version text we see the word *war* (e.g., "We do not war after the flesh"). In the Greek manuscript it is the word *strateuomai*. The Greek Dictionary states that speaking literally this word means "war." In other words, if we are speaking to a soldier, that is what it means. The dictionary goes on to say, however, that if used figuratively (as Paul is speaking in these verses) it means "to execute the apostleate [apostleship] with its duties."

In verse 4, we deal with two words *weapons* and *warfare*. In the Greek Dictionary the word *weapons* is the Greek word *hoplon*. Used literally it also means "a weapon for warfare." The dictionary goes on again to say, however, that when used figuratively (as Paul was doing here) it means "a utensil or tool of trade." So what is Paul's trade in context to this writing? He is an apostle! He is not a Roman soldier; he is an apostle of the Lord Jesus Christ!

Now let's move on to the word *warfare*. The Greek dictionary states that *warfare* is translated from *strateia*, which means "the apostolic career with its hardships and dangers."

Let's just take a few moments and translate these verses, using their figurative meanings: "For though we walk in the flesh [Notice the figurative use of the word *walk* in this context], we do not [execute the apostleship with its duties] after the flesh: (For the [utensils or tools of trade] of our [apostolic career with its hardships and dangers] are not carnal…)."

Let me share this passage with you from Eugene Peterson's The Message translation of the Bible: "The tools of our trade aren't for marketing or manipulation, but they are for demolishing that entire massively corrupt culture. We use our powerful God-tools for smashing warped philosophies, tearing down barriers erected against the truth of God, fitting every loose thought and emotion and impulse into the structure of life shaped by Christ" (2 Cor. 10:3–4). Wow! That is far from the warrior manner of some cultures within Christianity.

I believe it is time for us to take our position in the family and begin enjoying the complete victory already won for us through the conquest of the Lord Jesus Christ! With God's Word as your foundation you can start in victory and then use your faith in God's Word to stay in victory and live in a divine rest.

We also need to deal with another misused reference that often comes up to try and justify the "Christian soldier" concept of life. It is found in Ephesians 6:10–17, and it deals with the armor of God. This verse is used to teach some Christians that they are going to have to fight the devil. They teach that this is God's call for us to take an aggressive position in warfare. I have often heard people say, "You have to get your armor on if you want to get the victory in your life." Again, God has given me a wonderful, revolutionary understanding of this passage of Scripture. One thing is certain! You are not going to convince me to use this scripture to go to war and spend my time fighting! Why should I? Jesus has already gained the victory over the world, the flesh, and the devil! By accurately using your faith, you can move into a complete and lasting spiritual rest. Once you capture the meaning of the finished work of Jesus you can rest in who you are in Him, what you have received through Him, and what you can do because of your place in Him.

Israel was never able to enter in because of unbelief. They refused to accept and believe that God had already declared victory for them and would fight for them. The Seventy-eighth Psalm states, "[They] forgat his works, and his wonders that he had shewed them. Marvellous things did he in the sight of their fathers, in the land of Egypt" (vv. 11–12). They were a "generation that set not their heart aright, and whose spirit was not stedfast with God" (v. 8). They "believed not in God, and trusted not in his salvation" (v. 22). They "turned back and tempted God, and limited the Holy One of Israel" (v. 41). Interestingly, He makes a judgment of them later in that chapter: "Yet they tempted and provoked the most high God, and kept not his testimonies: But turned back, and dealt unfaithfully like their fathers: they were turned aside like a deceitful bow" (vv. 56–57). Let's look at the Amplified Bible for the last part of that verse: "They were twisted like a warped and deceitful bow [that will not respond to the archer's aim]."

Let me share how many become a "warped bow" in the hands of God's Word. They take God's already-declared victory and change it into their trying to get the victory! (That's warped!) They use verses that are written in the past tense ("strengthened with all might, according to his glorious power" [Col. 1:11]) and they turn it into a future-tense promise, something like, "Oh God, give us strength. Please fill us with Your power." What is the correct "position of the bow that will respond to the archer's aim"? It is this: "Father, I thank You that You have strengthened me with all might, according to Your glorious power!" Now, the bow is not warped and deceitful. Now the archer (almighty God) can shoot His arrows (His Word), and they will hit their mark—*you*!

As you can see, God expects us to trust in Him completely and not take the battle into our own hands. So what about the armor in Ephesians 6:10–17?

First, this is not an armor that we are to take on to win battles and victories! Rather, it is an armor awarded to us as a part of the spoils of God's victory through the Lord Jesus! Ephesians does not say "put on your armor." I heard someone say, "I'm getting my sword." They were speaking of the Word of God mentioned in Ephesians 6:17. But it is not your sword! It is the sword *of the Spirit*. You can see that individual inadvertently became a "warped and deceitful bow," not responding accurately to the Archer's aim!

Let me repeat myself: This is not armor handed out to you as a soldier to fight battles and win victories. Rather, it is your reward from spoils of war, from a war and a battle already fought and won by the Lord Jesus Christ. He has made His victory available to you by awarding you with His own armor for your protection against all of the wiles of the wicked one. It guarantees protection for all who will wear it.

The sword of the Spirit in Ephesians is the written, spoken Word of almighty God. When you read and speak it, it (not you) goes to work for you, allowing you to rest in it! I believe that you are getting hold of this revelation! It works, and you rest! Hallelujah! Revolutionary, isn't it? But I am preaching God's Word, not my ideas, to you! Always remember this important point: If your stand is not a position of completed victory, it is the wrong stand!

As you read Ephesians 6:10–17 from this standpoint of victory, holding on to and standing in the conquest already won and afforded you by Jesus's victory, then you will see it in the proper perspective. You will not be a "warped bow," unable to respond to the Archer's aim.

Never speak of Satan's power but rather of his "wiles" (Eph. 6:11). The word *wiles* means "trickery and deception." If Satan can't get you to give up God's Word, he'll try to get you to misunderstand the correct position to take with it. He'll attempt to get you to warp it. He'll make an effort to move you away from God's intended purpose of what He has spoken, just a little push, just a little variance from what the Word actually says. Remember, in the Garden of Eden, God spoke with great simplicity, but Satan moved Adam and Eve just a nudge away from what God actually said. The apostle Paul, in 2 Corinthians

11:3, wrote, "I fear, lest by any means, as the serpent beguiled Eve through his subtilty [deceitfulness], so your minds should be corrupted from the simplicity that is in Christ."

You will notice that none of this is aggressive behavior, but rather it is God's armor resting upon us, putting Him in control of maintaining our defenses against Satan. Notice the defensive stand in these verses found in Ephesians 6:11, 13, 16: "That ye may be able to stand against the wiles of the devil. . . . that ye may be able to withstand in the evil day. . . . wherewith ye shall be able to quench [stop or snuff out] all the fiery darts of the wicked [one]." Praise God for an ironclad defense system!

I wrote a song many years ago that says, "I use the Spirit's sword, and now the battle is the Lord's, the battle is the Lord's. I've learned to use the Spirit's sword!" The first verse of that song begins with teaching I heard early in my ministry on this subject: "Some folks greet you with, 'How goes the battle?' I reply, 'It's victory that I'm in.' You see, I've learned the devil is defeated. The back of the Book declares we win!" The chorus continues, "So ask me why I'm happy and contented. Ask me why I will not have a care. Ask me why I only speak of victory. The answer that I give is very clear. I use the Spirit's sword, and now the battle is the Lord's!"

I have walked in the blessedness of this for over thirty-seven years now, and I still say, "Wow! What a revelation from God for this life!"

> Now thanks be unto God, which always causeth us to triumph in Christ. . . . thanks be to God, which giveth us the victory through our Lord Jesus Christ.
> —2 Corinthians 2:14, 1 Corinthians 15:57

Since Ephesians 6:10–17 is a defensive armor, it is important to grasp the significance of what it really means to "stand" in the context of these verses. The word *stand* here was used to denote "a victory already gained." When Paul wrote in Galatians 5:1 saying, "Stand fast therefore in the liberty wherewith Christ hath made us free," he wasn't suggesting warfare but rather maintaining the current position of victory already obtained—in this case through Christ's victory for us!

Remember what you've learned about "the warped or deceitful bow that will not respond accurately to the Archer's aim"? The word *truth* in Ephesians

6:14—"having your loins girt about with truth"—is, in the Hebrew, the word *aletheuo,* which means "to be accurate in doctrine and profession." Perhaps the closest modern word to fit that description would be *integrity.* In this case we are speaking of the integrity of the position we are taking in God's Word. If you don't get your "belt" on right, none of the other armor will work accurately.

Understanding this concept is vital in order for God to go out for us and shake loose what the enemy has possessed. An accurate stand on the Word will release His angelic armies to go forth and fight all of the battle for us! As this great wealth conversion event occurs, the wicked rich will "weep and howl" for the miseries coming upon them! Their abuse of riches and power has "entered into the ears of the Lord of Sabaoth." (*Sabaoth* is the Greek transliterated word in James 5:4 for the Hebrew: Jehovah Tsaba, Lord of Hosts.)

I have an assignment from God! As you study this out with me, you may discover many scriptures that you have never understood in the Bible. Even if you are among those who teach "prosperity" (you may be one of many "prosperity teachers" that God has raised up) you will discover wonderful new and exciting truths of God's Word as the Holy Spirit uses this message to unfold to you the "exceeding riches of his grace in his kindness toward us through Christ Jesus" (Eph. 2:7). Throughout this writing, chapter by chapter, I will weave and interweave connective scriptures. Together they will bring a full revelation of God's will for you in this End Time. To accomplish this, we will revisit many scriptures, using them repeatedly as we connect them again and again with diverse parts of the Scriptures to show you their harmonious context.

The body of Christ in masses are going to enter into a wealthy place before the coming of the Lord. If you are a believer, you are included in this great prosperity phenomenon!

Humility, meekness, and gentleness should always be the hallmarks of your walk as a believer, and especially as you enter into a wealthy place! The apostle Peter spoke of our appropriate life-attire as believers when he wrote, "And be clothed with humility: for God resisteth the proud, and giveth grace to the humble" (1 Pet. 5:5). True Spirit-filled Christianity is necessary for God to be glorified in you as you possess this world's glory. The apostle Paul also wrote, "With all lowliness and meekness, with longsuffering, forbearing one another in love; Endeavouring to keep the unity of the Spirit in the bond of peace " (Eph. 4:2–3).

It's time we came out from among the world and walked in our Christianity.

In Ephesians 4 and 5 we read, "Let all bitterness, and wrath, and anger, and clamour, and evil speaking, by put away from you...And be ye kind one to another, tenderhearted, forgiving one another....And walk in love, as Christ also hath loved us....But fornication, and all uncleanness, or covetousness, let it not be once named among you...neither filthiness, nor foolish talking, nor jesting, which are not convenient [appropriate]" (Eph. 4:31–32; 5:2–4). The Living Bible paraphrases that last part as "dirty stories, foul [base] talk, and coarse jokes—these are not for you." There is never a place for believers to be rude, unmannerly, or unbecoming.

Likewise, it is never appropriate for you to present yourself as lofty or high-minded. Sometimes money, position, or influence will tempt someone to become more demanding of others. By the way, ministers are not exempt from this premise. No matter how great the platform of service that has been given, meekness and humility represent the real beauty of Christ. As God blesses you, you should become more tolerant of those around you. You may be placed in the position to make heavier demands upon those serving you. This very fact places upon you a greater responsibility to be long-suffering and gentle. Your wealthy influence will not sparkle as greatly, and your support of the gospel will not glorify God nearly as much if you do not clothe yourself with meekness. Allow the fruit of the recreated spirit to come forth as you yield to the Holy Spirit to do great things!

You will not be perfect. None of us is! Some people will expect you to be perfect just because of your position of wealth and influence as a Christian. Just remain humble and submissive to the Word of God and open to those who may challenge you! What God will hold you accountable for, along with the rest of us making this journey, will be to walk in love, joy, peace, long-suffering, goodness, gentleness, faithfulness, meekness, and temperance. God is raising up a generation of believers who will take hold of great end-time benefits of wealth, honor, and life. They will use them to serve and glorify Him in every area of their existence.

In your personal life, as you move into this wealthy place, it is important that you walk, talk, and act with the integrity, dignity, and grace becoming a believer. In your calling as a Christian you will need to focus your resources primarily to further the work of God. Don't ever forget to bring your tithe to your pastor in a humble manner! Remember that the tithe (10 percent of your increase) is the initial door God will use to pour out His blessings in your life.

You might ask, But is the tithe for the New Testament Christian? For faith to be operative in our lives it is important that questions be answered. We find a foundation for our answer in Hebrews 7:8: "And here men that die receive tithes; but there he receiveth them, of whom it is witnessed that he liveth." Keep in mind, this is written to the church, not to the Jews. He is comparing the Old Testament plan of giving the tithe to the priest, who then gave a portion to the High Priest according to the Jewish Law.

But now, while we do give our tithe to men here on earth, yet "there He receives them, of whom it is witnessed that He lives." Only Jesus holds that title, exclusive of the New Testament period—"it is witnessed that he liveth." In the Old Testament period Jesus was not in the High Priesthood to receive the tithe. But today, He is our Great High Priest. Revelation 1:18 identifies Jesus exclusively as, "I am he that liveth, and was dead; and, behold, I am alive for evermore." Hebrews 7:25 says, "Wherefore he is able also to save them to the uttermost that come unto God by him, seeing he ever liveth to make intercession for them."

The institution of the tithe, along with many other things, was not unique to the Law. For example, murder and stealing were mentioned in the Jewish Law, but they were not unique to it; therefore, just as they preceded Moses and the Jewish Law, even so they continue to be relevant in the church period as well. The tithe was instituted by Abraham, Isaac, and Jacob as God's plan long before a Jewish Law was given. The tithe holds relevance today, as demonstrated in the Hebrews 7:8 passage. No tithe? No blessing of the tithe. (We cover this more fully in Chapter 11.)

Also, be certain to remember the poor and needy (those who are in any trouble), especially your brothers and sisters in the body of Christ.

> And let us not be weary in well doing: for in due season we shall reap,
> if we faint not. As we have therefore opportunity, let us do good unto
> all men, especially unto them who are of the household of faith.
> —GALATIANS 6:9–10

Together, we will usher in this great "generation of victory"! Together we will be those who are alive and remain at the coming of the Lord Jesus for His church!

Chapter Two

THE PROSPERITY PHENOMENON

A s PREVIOUSLY STATED, we are about to experience a great prosperity phenomenon for Christian believers. We are witnessing a convergence of spiritual forces and principles at the very end of this age. God is a master planner, and nothing takes Him by surprise. You can believe that!

When He made Adam and declared, "Be fruitful, and multiply" (Gen. 1:28), He knew the masses that would accumulate at the end of this age.

When He put the gold and potential for wealth in the earth—"that is...which compasseth the whole land of Havilah, where there is gold; And the gold of that land is good" (Gen. 2:11–12)—He divinely knew that men would hoard it up from generation to generation, culminating in a conglomeration of wealth in the hands of powerful men.

When He proclaimed, "O Daniel...shut up the words...even to the time of the end: many shall run to and fro, and knowledge shall be increased" (Dan. 12:4), He knew that the very expensive technology would be invented and marketed with the ability to be used for the church and evangelism.

When He covenanted that "the wealth of the sinner [finds its way eventually] into the hands of the righteous, for whom it was laid up" (Prov. 13:22, AMP), and when He declared, "This [which I am about to tell] is the portion of a wicked man with God, and the heritage which oppressors shall receive from the Almighty.... Though he heaps up silver like dust and piles up clothing like clay; He may prepare it, but the just will wear it, and the innocent will divide the silver" (Job 27:13, 16–17, AMP), He knew He would need those hoarded-up treasures to be handed over to the body of Christ to fund His end-time strategic climax.

When He said, "Go to now, ye rich men, weep and howl for your miseries that shall come upon you.... Ye have heaped treasure together for the last days...and the cries of them which have reaped are entered into the ears of the Lord of sabaoth [Jehovah Tsaba]. Be patient therefore, brethren, unto the coming of the Lord. Behold, the husbandman waiteth for the precious fruit of the earth, and hath long patience for it, until he receive the early and latter rain" (James 5:1, 3–4, 7), He knew that His plan would work and that the body of Christ would receive the ability to take back what Satan had stolen.

Let me outline my case that I will prove through Scripture:

1. The masses of people living at this time have reached a huge potential for a full harvest of souls, which God calls "the precious fruit of the earth" (a bumper crop). If He lost this generation to hell, He would be losing the majority of mankind to the devil's devices. His plan will almost immediately saturate the earth with evangelism in order to get this "precious fruit."

2. The nations have devised financial systems to heap up the treasures of the earth over many generations to hold a stronghold of its wealth through their conglomerate central banks, international trading houses, the International Monetary Fund (IMF), and World Bank.

3. An explosion of knowledge has occurred, allowing for industrial, mechanical, and technological breakthroughs that, if used, will enable us to reach the earth's huge final harvest of souls with the gospel.

4. A righteous seed has been raised up in the earth willing to walk in, be obedient to, and dedicate vast personal resources toward furthering God's plan. They favor His righteous cause and are willing even to sacrifice their own plans to get what is needed into the hands of the ministry.

5. Finally, for this purpose, God is moving to convert and transfer the great wealth of the nations into the hands of those favoring His righteous cause.

It is now time for a great inversion of wealth through which God is going to turn things inside out, outside in, upside down, rightside up! He is raising Himself up to give the wealth of the world to the body of Christ. Zechariah 2:13 declares, "Be silent, O all flesh, before the LORD: for he is raised up out of his holy habitation."

UNDERSTANDING MY SPIRITUAL JOURNEY

I have been in full-time ministry since 1974, living and preaching God's Word. God has sent me to you to bless and to help you. I have a message from God for you! But, it is important that you receive me as God's messenger to get the fullest blessing from my assignment.

I have served the Lord Jesus for almost all of my life. I accepted Jesus at eight years of age. I received the baptism of the Holy Spirit and began utterances in tongues at the age of nine. I was raised in a Pentecostal Christian home. We were in church several times each week. My folks were not in the ministry. Dad worked at a shoe factory and built houses. Mother managed the family mercantile store. The very first sound I remember hearing in the mornings, however, would be the sound of my parents praying together before beginning their day. They were faithful each evening to gather us together for family Bible reading and prayer (except those evenings when we went to church). It was not a little "Now I lay me down to sleep" prayer but a time of real prayer and worship. Often the evening Bible study and prayer time would last for an extended period. The admonishment of 1 Timothy 2:1–2 (LITV)— "First of all then, I exhort that petitions, prayers, supplications, and thanksgivings be made on behalf of all men, for kings and all the ones being in high position"—was not widely preached and taught in many spiritual circles. Somehow, though, my dad and mom had already come to understand it! I never recall a single evening when we failed to have this time together all the years of being at home.

By age eleven, I was leading the Sunday morning, Sunday evening, and Wednesday evening congregational singing in my home church. At age twelve, I began helping in the leadership of children's church during the Sunday morning worship. Beginning in 1966, as a very young adult, I served as choir director for Berea Temple Assembly of God church, a large congregation at the time in south St. Louis, Missouri. It was during this period that my eyesight began to fail, resulting in my becoming legally blind in my right eye, with my left eye also becoming progressively worse. I continued to serve in my church in every way possible. I taught a young boys' Sunday school class, drove a church bus, and helped lead home-to-home witnessing groups on Saturday mornings. During these earlier years of my life, I did all I knew to do to serve God in lay church positions!

During one period of about a year, at age sixteen, I went through a time of spiritual and personal rebellion. I missed being with my family for devotions. It did not take God very long, however, to get me back on track spiritually! I would come home at a very late hour (sometimes after midnight) and pull into the driveway. As I would get out of my car, Mom and Dad's bedroom window would be open for fresh air. I could hear my mother praying, "No, devil! You can't have him! You can't have our son! We dedicated him to the Lord when he was a baby. He belongs to God, and you can't have him!" Praise God for praying, Christian parents. I am today built upon the foundation of their faith of yesterday!

Shortly after, God began dealing with me to go back to my home state of Arkansas. I moved my business to Jonesboro, Arkansas, in the spring of that year. Shortly after that, I was appointed area director of youth for the Assemblies of God, of which I was a member. I was responsible for coordinating several churches and pastors together as I scheduled and directed youth rallies. This was a position almost exclusively held by an area pastor, although at that time I had not acknowledged any calling to the ministry. I held that position until about a year after I did enter full-time ministry of the gospel.

In 1973, after returning to Arkansas, I had my first notable encounter with God. It was on a Sunday night in the church where I was a member. After completing a week of revival services, at the close of the last night's service, the evangelist was standing in the foyer of the church bidding the people farewell and fellowshiping with them. Suddenly he stopped and said, "Someone here has experienced deafness, and God wants to restore your hearing before I leave tonight! God wants to heal you!"

I had been totally deaf in my left ear since early childhood. In the autumn of 1964, my parents took me to Memphis, Tennessee, to see Dr. John J. Shea, a world-renowned surgeon at the Shea Ear Clinic, who was known for his discovery of a method of surgically restoring the inner ear. He examined me as a possible candidate for his technique. However, after consultation, he advised us that I was a hopeless case. He told my parents that there was nothing medical science could do for me. I lost all hope of ever hearing out of that ear.

Shortly after that my mother wrote to Oral Roberts Ministries asking for prayer. She received a prayer cloth in response to her request, instructing me to carry it on my person until I had experienced my miracle. Although I was hopeless about the situation, to please my mother I carried it in my wallet from 1966 until the miracle did occur.

Now, suddenly, in this revival service, God was speaking to me with a word of knowledge through this evangelist. He caught me by surprise! I had learned to compensate for my deafness. Since the left side of my head was dead to sound, I would hold conversations with those at my right hand. I would turn my head, when necessary, to position my right ear toward whoever was speaking. I made certain the telephone was always to my right, and most of the time I hardly noticed any difficulty. I did not consider myself deaf because I had good hearing in my right ear. I was neither expecting nor seeking my healing.

When no one responded to the evangelist's prophetic announcement, he repeated more specifically, "The Lord has shown me that someone here tonight is deaf in one ear." About that time I looked across the church sanctuary. Someone was pointing toward me and gesturing to their left ear. I was the one! I went to the minister and said something spiritually dumb, like, "I am deaf in my left ear, but you can't be talking about me, because I have no inner ear parts remaining." He responded, "Son, if you're deaf in one ear, it's you!" Almost before I could object, he swung me around and stuck his finger in my left ear. He said, "You spirit of deafness, come out! Now! In Jesus's name, I command you to come out of him and let him hear!" Instantly, sound flooded my ear and I could hear perfectly. I left the service and shared it with everyone I knew. Soon I was asked to give my testimony at different area churches within my denominational membership. I became so excited about this encounter with the almighty God and His power!

A few weeks later I awakened one morning and knew immediately that I was deaf again in that ear! I went to the phone and picked it up. I put it to that ear. There was no sound. I tried so hard to hear something but could not do so. That side of my head was again dead to sound. What had I done,

I wondered, to lose my healing? I knew that I had not mistakenly heard. The doctors had said I would never be able to hear. They had shown through test results that there were no inner ear parts. I had endured countless hearing tests in school, for the selective service board, at employment medical exams, and so on. Yet, for many days I had heard perfectly. My testimony was out there as a witness to many people. I suddenly felt ashamed and embarrassed as a Christian. How would I explain to people what had happened?

I called my pastor and arranged to go by that morning to see him on my way to the office. I was momentarily so stunned that I did not know what to do. When I explained to him what had occurred, he wilted right in front of me. His countenance took on the appearance of shock and dismay. Then he did me the greatest favor he could have done. He gave an explanation that I knew could not be truth! He said, "Don, there are just some things that we'll never understand in this life. Perhaps God just wanted to receive glory by displaying His power, but maybe it's not in His will for you to continue hearing out of that ear. Perhaps His plan is for you to be deaf. You'll understand it better when you get to heaven."

When he spoke those words to me, I could not buy into it. I loved my pastor and respected him. But this just didn't ring true in my heart. I thought to myself, "That would be a cheap carnival trick. I just don't believe that God, my heavenly Father, would pull something like that. Why would He want to spiritually destroy, shame, and embarrass me before others with whom I have shared my testimony? Why would He want to confuse me?" I went away from there not accepting the pastor's lame traditional reasoning. I resolved that I would begin a prayer meeting in my home every Tuesday and Friday evening (the only two evenings that I was free of other responsibilities).

For almost a year I spent all of my free time seeking to make contact again with the almighty God. I would go to the altar at church and remain there, sometimes for lengthy periods. Everyone else would be gone, and the pastor would have to wait around to lock up when I was through. I am sure that I became a real nuisance. It seemed like the heavens were brass and that no one was listening to my prayers. I cried out continually to God. In spite of my determination to seek God, I remained deaf for almost another year.

In 1974, I had my second and most powerful encounter with almighty

God! After almost a year of prayer, I had become very sensitive to my spiritual need for more of God in my life.

My pastor, who had grown weary after many months of my incessant need to pray for extended periods, was getting concerned about me. Friends in the church were accustomed to my meeting them after church at the local "afterglow" spot (usually the pizza place). They knew that I no longer had time to join them because I was lingering at the church altar. It concerned them that I was having some type of emotional breakdown. Isn't it interesting that when you start seeking God more than what is normal people think there is something wrong with you?

Then one Sunday evening in April 1974 things made a dramatic turn. The pastor told me that a couple of ministers were going to be conducting a faith-teaching seminar locally. He said that one of them, a young man named Jerry Savelle, had traveled with a minister by the name of Kenneth Copeland. He explained that Brother Copeland was known for his teaching on the principles of faith. Brother Savelle had recently launched out into his own ministry and would be conducting a faith-teaching seminar in our town.

I had not heard of either of these ministers. The pastor said that his wife was healed of a back injury many years ago while in a meeting sponsored by Kenneth E. Hagin and that these men had been influenced by his ministry. He felt strongly that I should attend. He also mentioned that the second speaker was Charles Capps, a farmer who God was using to bring a message of faith to believers. It seemed strange to me that a farmer would be coming to minister in a faith seminar. The pastor went on to say that he felt this meeting might be a help to me. I informed him that I had a busy schedule at the office but agreed to try to get away for at least the first morning session. My pastor did not take a chance on my forgetting. At 9:00 a.m. that Thursday he was at my office encouraging me to break away and get to the morning session.

The first session was different than anything I had ever attended. Brother Savelle commanded an air of joy and power unlike anyone I had known. He was on fire with faith! He preached from Joshua 1:8 and Mark 4:14–20 and declared repeatedly, "You don't have to be sick; you don't have to be poor any longer. If you'll meditate in God's Word day and night and not let the devil steal the Word, you'll make your way prosperous and have good success!"

I was not accustomed to hearing anyone speak so positively. No one I had known had ever commanded the devil with such certainty and authority. His much assured manner offended me. I sat through the service angry with those who had allowed him to come into my Pentecostal, denominational church to preach. I did not connect it to God responding to my yearlong spiritual search. I sat in the audience at this seminar (in fact, I played the organ for the worship in the evening services) greatly offended because I was suffering with several incurable diseases. It offended me that they were telling me I did not have to be sick! I was sick! It offended my traditional doctrinal beliefs.

I had almost died at birth. For many years no one discussed it with me. I was not aware of the severity of it until just after my high school graduation. I had just given myself more completely to God and His service in my life and was getting ready to leave home. My mother told me that she felt spiritually compelled to write down on paper the events surrounding my birth. She told me that she had felt a greater need to stay in prayer before God for me during all of my growing-up years because she believed the devil would attempt to distract me concerning God's call on my life. She said that shortly after my birth she was visited by an angel. She had not talked of her experience much because once she had tried to tell someone, and they treated her so strangely, she decided not to mention it after that.

She explained that at the time of my birth I had some type of sleeping sickness. She did not know the formal term for it. Doctors did not allow their patients to be as conversant in medical terms back then. She only knew that I remained in a kind of coma for several days. She remained with me at Dr. Fairthcloth's medical clinic, where I was born. She said that late one evening the nurse brought me to her. The doctor did not expect me to be alive until daybreak. He thought Mom might want to hold me in her room until the end came. My body was blue from lack of oxygen, and she began to cry. As she sat there holding me in the darkened room, suddenly it lit up with the most beautiful bright light. Standing in front of her was an angel. The angel said to her, "Your son will not die but live because God has a work for him to do." She said as suddenly as the angel had appeared, he was gone. The room was dark again. When the nurse came in some time later, I was a beautiful pink (at least she thought I was beautiful).

Over the next few days, the doctor pronounced me well, and my mother was able to take me home. She said she had often pondered the event.

Interestingly, I was born at the same day and hour of the evening that the United Nations voted to create the state of Israel (November 26, 1947). Do you think that might make me a member of the "shall not pass until all is fulfilled" generation?

In spite of this angelic message, until 1974 I suffered with several incurable diseases. At the time of this faith-teaching seminar, besides being totally deaf in my left ear, I was legally blind in my right eye. As previously stated, my eyesight was rapidly getting worse. It required me to wear glasses with very thick lenses to see. As a child, I had also contracted an incurable skin disease that plagued me. Without daily medication, a liquid would pour out of my skin. Blisters and very painful scales would form on the top of my head, my face, and other parts of my upper body. Twenty-four hours without the prescription medication and I would look like some kind of monster. The pain would be excruciating. Even with daily medication, it would not stay totally in check. I also had a chronic sinus infection that required me to carry three to five handkerchiefs on my person every day. Furthermore, from the age of seventeen I had suffered with bleeding hemorrhoids and broken arches in my feet. At the time of the seminar I was obese (75 lbs. overweight), and I suffered with extreme hypertension. Of course, I was a wreck, but I was trying to serve God in every way that I knew.

I decided as I left that first morning's teaching service with Brother Savelle that I would take off work the rest of the day. I planned to go home for lunch and spend that time with my Bible, disproving all the things I had heard that morning. I felt that I knew many scriptures that would repudiate the "heresy" taught. Much to my surprise, when I looked up the verses of Scripture they did not say what had been originally taught me.

So, I returned for the afternoon session with Charles Capps. (They alternated sessions throughout the seminar.) He took his text from Proverbs 4:20–22 and taught, "If you will attend to God's Word, incline you ears to His sayings, let them not depart out of your mouth, keep them in the midst of your heart, and they will become life and health to all your flesh—and you'll never have to be sick or poor again!"

He referred to himself as a farmer but spoke with a plain kind of eloquence and the authority of a great man of faith. Again, I was unaccustomed to this demeanor of certainty in the pulpit. I had not been around much of

God's anointing, and I mistook it for arrogance. This resulted in my leaving that service in the same manner as that morning. I was upset and angry! I thought I would go home and spend the time between the afternoon and evening services getting together the scriptures that I was certain would prove the teaching to be wrong. I planned to go back that evening and confront them with "the truth."

As I searched out the scriptures again, I saw them in a new light, and they did not say what I thought they did! The Bible did not say, "God will never put more trials and tests on you than you can bear." It did not say, "The trial of your faith came from God to test you or teach you something." What it did say was, "Let no man say when he is tempted [tested or tried], I am tempted [tested or tried] of God: for God cannot be tested with evil, neither tests he any man" (James 1:13).

Things I thought to be in the Bible were just not there, like, "God moves in mysterious ways His wonders to perform," or "Eye has not seen nor ear heard what God has in store for us, but over on the other side we'll understand it better by and by." Instead it said, "But as it is written, Eye hath not seen, nor ear heard, neither have entered into the heart of man, the things which God hath prepared for them that love him. But God hath revealed them unto us by his spirit: for the Spirit searcheth all things, yea, the deep things of God" (1 Cor. 2:9).

I went back that first evening more open to hear what they had to say. I attended that and every service for three days, and each time I would become offended again. Each service I returned ready to hear, and each service I left offended.

After the final meeting, I went home with my life changed by the Word of God. I stayed up all night until after daybreak. I sat quietly in my office deciding that a choice in my Christian experience had to be made—that night! I was now convinced that what they had taught was true. I had to make a choice! I either had to walk away from serving God and purposefully become a hypocrite or make the decision to walk and live by faith and patience in God's Word from that day forward. I agonized as I reasoned with God. I told Him that I would probably lose all of my Christian friends and church family, who would think that I had gone off the deep end. I told Him that once I had made the decision to walk by faith, there would be no turning back. I contended with God that either His healing power would have to miraculously come, or I would go down in history as the biggest idiot in town. I wrestled with it all night long.

I can honestly say that after three agonizing days and nights, Don Pickney, as he had previously lived, died there in that office in the very early hours of that Sunday morning. As the sun arose I began a brand new life. It would be a life of faith and patience, a life of learning how to walk in love, a life that would prove to be free of sickness and disease and of poverty! Hallelujah!

Within three and one-half days miracles began to occur. First, at about 11:30 a.m. of the fourth day (the Wednesday following the seminar), I received a miracle in both of my eyes. I went from being legally blind to having perfect vision in one moment. I was driving my car. I had been to the post office and was returning home. As I turned into my subdivision, I looked out across the rolling hills and realized God's presence upon me. Suddenly, like a thick plastic sheet melting from my sight, my vision returned perfectly. I had not known how beautiful colors could be as I looked out across the rolling hills of that subdivision and saw the greenest greens and the bluest blues. Today, after almost thirty-eight years, my vision remains perfect without any natural aid. I see perfectly and read even the smallest print legible to the human eye. I have shared this testimony everywhere I've gone in ministry since 1974.

The second miracle occurred later that same day in the midafternoon. I had told God that I would never again put the phone to my right ear until I could hear again out of the left one. I had great confidence because of the experience a year earlier when I had temporarily heard out of my left ear, which doctors declared had no inner ear parts. Brother Savelle had taught us that Satan comes to steal the Word. He had explained from Mark 4:17 that there are those who "have no root in themselves, and so endure but for a time [for me the healing of my ear had only lasted a few weeks]: afterward, when affliction or persecution arises for the word's sake, immediately they are offended" (Matt. 4:17). He explained in the teaching that the reason Satan brings these attacks is to get us to become confused, bewildered, and disappointed and to doubt the Word of God. He said, "Stand on God's Word!"

By this time I was convinced that God had healed me of deafness, but because of a lack of teaching I had not known what to do when Satan returned to attack me again with deafness. Now I could make my stand that I had received healing and would be victorious!

So, during the same midafternoon after receiving my sight I needed to make a phone call. For three days I had been making calls or answering the phone by placing it to my left ear. Although I could not hear a sound, I would say something like this, "Father, I believe I receive my healing. I thank You that I hear perfectly out of this ear!" Then I would thank whoever it was that called. If I made the call, I would speak of why I was calling, Then I would hang up! I did this consistently for three days. I would go to the office and conduct my business in that manner. At home, I remained just as steadfast in my insistence upon that plan of action!

In old-time Pentecostal circles after the turn of the twentieth century, there were great miracles stemming from the believers' willingness to step out and explore faith actions. In a published copy of the official Assemblies of God history, *Suddenly From Heaven*, accounts are given of special actions of faith that produced many outstanding miracles. During this period, I was especially inspired by these written historical events.

On that afternoon, when I went to make a phone call something was different. As I began rotary dialing the phone (there were no push buttons back then), it was as if someone took hold of a volume knob. Suddenly I heard a sound, and then in quick succession it increased up to normal volume. I had been made whole, this time never to lose it again.

Today, after all these years, I continue to hear perfectly. Mom's persistent faith in God, along with Oral Roberts's prayer cloth, were collectively making God's power available for a miracle to occur in my life. I did not know at the time, but I was acting in agreement with their faith by submitting myself to carry the cloth. All it took to complete it was for me to exercise my faith on a higher level. There is sometimes controversy around faith teaching. The faith teaching seminar, however, simply taught me principles of how to act on the Word of God!

That first Sunday morning after making my decision I took my prescription medication to church with me. I had previously known the agony of accidentally leaving it at home when going somewhere overnight. The unsightly condition of my skin, coupled with the intense pain, was almost unbearable. That morning as I sat down at the church organ to play for the Sunday worship service, I slipped that medication into the organ bench. I have not seen it to this day, and I have not needed it once since then! Praise God for His faithfulness to His Word!

Every disease disappeared without exception! I had been extremely overweight during all of my adult life. During the next six weeks I lost seventy-five pounds, eleven inches off my waist, and two shoe sizes. I have not had a weight problem since then and have consistently maintained the same range of weight to this day. Still, there are those who will try to tell me that the principles taught in the Faith movement don't work! As the blind man responded to Jesus, "One thing I know, whereas I was blind, now I see!" Sometimes as human Christians we are prone to fear what we don't understand. I have made it my mission in ministry to bring principles of faith to as many as will open their hearts to receive it.

For all of these years since I received my healings, I have preached and taught the Word of God faithfully and consistently. God has used me to write and publish over 160 songs celebrating faith and patience and declaring His goodness to His people. Songs like "I Believe I'm Good Ground," "Fighting the Good Fight of Faith," "The Blood Covenant," "The Word Is So Good," "In the Spirit of Wisdom and Revelation Knowledge," "Father God, Sir," and "The Righteousness of Faith," have been recorded and receive regular airplay across the nation and continue to be a blessing.

From 1975 until 1983 I traveled into southeast Missouri once a week to conduct a teaching service on Monday nights with participation from throughout that region. I did this fifty weeks out of the year for nine years. Then, in August 1982 God spoke to me at the Kenneth Copeland Southwest Believers' Convention in Fort Worth, Texas. He instructed me to found a church, and for almost twenty years we pastored in southeast Missouri. Our first service was in January 1983. Three months later Rev. Jerry Savelle came at my request to give an impartation of the Spirit in my pastoral ministry. He laid his hands upon me before many that day. He spoke prophetically that I was to bring the Faith message to the southeast Missouri region. He spoke by the Spirit and said, "This man has been called and proven himself faithful to the ministry of the gospel to this region. It is now time that this region show that same faithfulness to God by giving due honor to this servant of the Lord

Jesus Christ." During these many years since, I have walked in the strength of that impartation to this very day!

The world learned long ago to intimidate through the use of slogans and name-calling. I tell people when someone makes reference to "those faith teachers," you know, the "name-and-claim-it bunch," I always instantly throw both hands into the air and declare, "You found one of them. I'm one of them. Attempts at intimidation do not find any lodging in this "faith-walkin' preacher"!

Shortly after beginning my pastorate at the church in southeast Missouri, I was married to my wife, Olene Welch, who is my most precious gift from God and my greatest treasure for this life. Together we have walked by faith and seen many victories. Ministers have been raised up under our covering. Over the years we have been blessed with many Rhema Bible Training Center graduates who have worked and served under our ministry. Some have gone on out in various fields of ministry, some founding their own church ministries. Today God is training a new crop who will also go forth at the right time.

Jesus told the religious leaders of His day, "I have not lived in, nor ministered in secret. I have ever been among you in the synagogues and in public ministry." Like Jesus, every minister knows in his own heart his faithfulness to his calling. I know that I have been faithful to God's calling. With what God has instructed me I have remained faithful. I have on occasion stretched myself farther than my level of faith would carry me. Often we have prayed, used our faith when there was no known possibility, and stood and shouldered the results, at times alone, until we would see the answer come.

Sometimes I would come up short for a while, but I would always recover and keep going forward. Ministering in southeast Missouri, with a record of being one of the poorest regions in the state of Missouri (and the country), with lack and want always so apparent, required diligence, discipline, and determination. It has sometimes saddened us when some became offended by either our message or our imperfections and left following our ministry. My most sincere desire is that I may be found faithful to the calling of the Lord Jesus and that He might continue to perfect that which is in me until the day of the Lord Jesus. Yet, we have always prospered. I have, along with others with me, remained faithful to the Lord Jesus and to His calling. I can testify that God, in His goodness, is rolling off of His people all of the reproach of lack and want. I can tell you that God is setting His family into a wealthy place. I am blessed! But, to use an Arkansas boyhood expression, "We ain't seen nothin' yet!"

I have spent the vast majority of my time during these years waiting before God for His people. Countless hours of study and meditation in God's Word have produced a harvest of understanding. God blessed me with a special teaching gift, and I have always brought forth fresh revelation from God's Word. I also praise God for the formal education and training He has provided, but that could never take the place of the fresh anointing of the Holy Spirit, which continues to strengthen my assignment from Him. I am blessed to have a part of Jesus's ministry in the earth. Nothing, however, could compare to the overflowing of anointing that began to come in May 2000.

THE ANOINTING!

My lady and I had just come out of one of the hardest periods of our ministry. In 1998, our church had suffered a split. In spite of everything we could do, we were unable to bring peace to a few offended people who momentarily seemed bent on destroying our ministry. Some made it their goal to discredit us due to misunderstandings. A concerted effort was made to drive us out of the ministry. But through it all, God's grace and goodness sustained us. In spite of the difficulties presented to us, our days were good, filled with the warmth of love and peace and much fulfillment. To this very day, we miss their love toward us and pray for some day of eventual reconciliation. Each one is very precious, and we know their true hearts. But, during this difficult period, every service continued to be filled with the anointing of God, as much revelation of God's Word flowed out to the congregation.

Then in May 2000, while spending a great deal of time in prayer, God spoke to us and said, "Go get an anointing that I have for you." We had heard that one of the leading men of God teaching prosperity, Dr. Leroy Thompson, would be in Little Rock, Arkansas, at a meeting hosted by Pastor Happy Caldwell and Agape Church. God said to us, "Go!"

We went to the meeting and received what God had for us! I owe a great debt to God's servant for being obedient to pioneer God's great message, "Money Cometh!" to the body of Christ. It is not my message, but I have benefited greatly from his anointing.

Immediately after that time of ministry, with that anointing providing the "prime," new revelation began pouring out of the Scriptures. Some who had left our services returned with a new vehemence to get in on what God was doing. I have had to run just to keep up with the insight that is flowing concerning this great pre-Rapture event that is now ready to take place in the earth. I am excited about the opportunity to bring that information and this anointing to you! I often say to those under my ministry, "Thank God for the knowledge and information, but what we're taking is the anointing!"

I have received from many of our national ministries who have been faithful to hold up the Word of Faith message. God has been using them for some time to herald prophetic news regarding a supernatural move of God for prosperity. I am not spearheading anything! What I have received from God, however, can add to that anointing! While God has recently revealed many prophetic Scripture passages of this writing to me, many other truths mentioned have been studied out and taught for many years. I promise that this message will change your life if you will get it into your heart and act upon it. I am currently living in the manifestation of God's great move to bring about this prosperity phenomenon.

While most people who don't know me would disbelieve this statement, I have not had one "down" day in all of these years since beginning to walk by faith and patience. I will make my boast in the Lord!

> My soul shall make her boast in the LORD: the humble shall hear thereof, and be glad. O magnify the LORD with me, and let us exalt his name together....O taste and see that the LORD is good: blessed is the man that trusteth in him.
>
> —PSALM 34:2–3, 8, KJV

I have not been discouraged, despondent, depressed, burdened, burned out, defeated, or been tempted to quit or go backward—not in thirty-eight years of full-time ministry. Ask my closest friends and ministers, or just hang around and watch for yourself. I do not just preach victory. It is a reality in my life. I am not perfect in many areas of my life, to say the least! But I walk by faith in total victory in this life! I cannot be defeated! God has said, "I will not in any way fail you nor give you up nor leave you without support. [I will] not, [I will] not, [I will] not in any degree leave you helpless nor forsake nor let [you] down (relax My hold on you)!—[Assuredly not!]" (Heb. 13:5, AMP). Praise God—if He is for us, no one can successfully be against us!

What God Said to Me About Valleys and Burdens

Do not believe or accept valleys or valley-type experiences! Many believe in valley experiences. The word *valley* is only in the New Testament once. In Luke 3:5, John the Baptist preached a sermon. He said, "Every valley shall be filled, and every mountain and hill shall be brought low; and the crooked shall be made straight, and the rough ways shall be made smooth." This is the last time the subject is mentioned in the Bible! End of the story!

In Christianity, valleys represent the low places in a believer's emotional life. They represent the times when people become despondent, depressed, and vulnerable to the attacks of the enemy. Valleys may have filled many pulpits, sermons, and gospel songs, but valley experiences are not referenced in the New Testament for the church. The psalmist David declared, "Blessed (happy, fortunate, to be envied) is the man whose strength is in You, in whose heart are the highways to Zion. Passing through the Valley of Weeping (Baca), they make it a place of springs; the early rain also fills [the pools] with blessings. They go from strength to strength [increasing in victorious power]" (Ps. 84:5–7, AMP). In effect, the psalmist was saying, "If one went into a valley of weeping, she would just turn it into a resort paradise because all she knows how to do is go from strength to strength, constantly increasing in victorious power. No up-and-down valleys for her. Up is the only way she knows to go!" Praise God, the only way I know to go is *up*!

Do not believe or accept "burdens from God"! In Jeremiah 23:33–40, God spoke through His prophet about this subject. Before we look at that passage of Scripture, let me suggest a scenario to you. Imagine that, as a pastor, I went to a member of my congregation and asked him to help me receive the offering or help me welcome someone to the service or asked him to sing a song. Then imagine how I would feel if every time I asked him to do something for me I would overhear him saying to someone, "The pastor has given me a heavy burden!" I think before too long I would probably quit asking him to help me if he always called it a burden. I want folks to help me who consider it a joy!

God spoke through Jeremiah and said:

And when these people, or a prophet or a priest, ask you, What is the burden of the Lord [the thing to be lifted up now]? then you shall say to them, What burden [indeed]! [You are the burden!] And I will disburden Myself of you and I will cast you off, says the Lord. And as for the prophet, the priest, or [any of these] the people, whoever [in mockery calls the word of the Lord a burden and] says, The burden of the Lord, I will even visit in wrath and punish that man and his house. [For the future, in speaking of the utterances of the Lord] thus shall you say every one to his neighbor and every one to his brother: What has the Lord answered? or, What has the Lord spoken? But the burden of the Lord you must mention no more, for every man's burden is his own response and word [for as they mockingly call all prophecies burdens, whether good or bad, so will it prove to be to them; God will take them at their own word]; for you pervert the words [not of a lifeless idol, but] of the living God, the Lord of hosts, our God! Thus shall you [reverently] say to the prophet: What has the Lord answered you? Or, What has the Lord spoken? But if you say, The burden of the Lord, therefore thus says the Lord: Because you said these words, The burden of the Lord, when I sent to you, saying, You shall not say, The burden of the Lord, Therefore behold, I, even I, will assuredly take you up and cast you away from My presence, you and the city [Jerusalem] which I gave to you and to your fathers. And I will bring an everlasting reproach upon you and a perpetual shame which will not be forgotten.

—Jeremiah 23:33–40

Believe me, since learning this truth I have always walked in victory!

Chapter Three

THE GREAT WEALTH CONVERSION

AS PREVIOUSLY REFERENCED, in Charismatic churches and groups we have often sung a prophetic chorus. It is taken from Isaiah 60:1, "Arise, shine; for thy light is come, and the glory of the LORD is risen upon thee." We sang this chorus without realizing all that it held for us. In some of the succeeding Scripture verses, Isaiah says, "For, behold, [Note: whenever you see the word *behold* in this or any other scripture it is alerting you to "an event." Something is going to occur, and this word, *behold*, means "put your attention upon what He says about it"!] the darkness shall cover the earth, and gross darkness the people: but the LORD shall arise upon thee, and his glory shall be seen upon thee. And the Gentiles shall come to thy light, and kings to the brightness of thy rising."

Let me give a word of explanation here about two expressions that we will use often in our Scripture passages. These two expressions are *Zion* and *the Gentiles*. The word *Zion* is from the Hebrew word *tsiyown* or the Greek transliterated word *sion*, both of which mean "a hill of Jerus (upon which the city of Jerusalem was built), or the church, militant and triumphant." In the Hebrew mind it represents the dwelling place of God. Often, when God revealed Old Testament prophecies, He would mirror prophecies for both the Jewish people and the New Testament church. In our reference of these two words, He would do it by mentioning both Jerusalem and Zion in the same sentence or context. This is always a "hot button" for you to pay attention to, a double reference concerning how it may apply to the church in these last days!

In Ephesians 2:20, we are told that God's Word today is "built upon the foundation of the apostles and prophets." The word *foundation* in reference to the prophets in this verse is referring to those times in the Old Testament when God mirrored the same promise in prophecy to either Jerusalem or

Judah (a prophecy to occur in that day) and Zion (a promise for, "a founda-tion" that would later be applicable for the body of Christ).

God's purpose for doing it this way was to hide in a mystery the things that were for the last days, so that Satan, men, and demonic ploys would not foil His plans. First Corinthians 2:7–8 says, "But we speak the wisdom of God in a mystery, even the hidden wisdom, which God ordained…Which none of the princes [of darkness] of this world knew: for had they known it, they would not have crucified the Lord of glory."

Then we have the word *Gentiles* to deal with in Old Testament prophe-cies. In these messianic prophecies the world at large is referenced as either *nations* or *heathen* or *Gentiles* and sometimes *strangers* or *aliens*. Usually, whichever of these expressions are used, they are the same Hebrew word, *gowy*, meaning "nations, strangers, aliens, heathen, or Gentiles." In Old Testament times, all non-Jewish people were considered Gentiles, or heathens. The Jews viewed their nation as God's elect people, and the world consisting of all other non-Jewish people were Gentiles. In the New Testament, if you have accepted Jesus as Lord of your life, you are no longer a Gentile! This is a very important point to fully understand the references to the church in the messianic prophe-cies of Isaiah and the other prophets.

In 1 Corinthians 10:32, the apostle Paul wrote, "Give none offence, nei-ther to the Jews, nor to the Gentiles, nor to the church of God." You will notice that he distinguished a difference among these three groups of people! Speaking to you as a believer, you are no longer a Gentile.

Paul helped to lay the foundation for the identification of this third class of people. The following scripture becomes the cornerstone of this truth. He states in 1 Corinthians 12:13 (THE MESSAGE), "By means of his one Spirit, we all said good-bye to our partial and piecemeal lives…but then we entered into a large and integrated life in which he has the final say in everything. (This is what we proclaimed in word and action when we were baptized.) Each of us is now a part of his resurrection body, refreshed and sustained at one fountain— his Spirit—where we all come to drink. The old labels we once used to identify ourselves—labels like Jew or Greek, slave or free—are no longer useful. We need something larger, more comprehensive."

Ephesians 2:11–13, 19–20 states in part, "Wherefore remember, that ye being in time past Gentiles…at that time ye were without Christ, being aliens from the commonwealth of Israel, and strangers from the covenants of promise, having no hope, and without God in the world. But now in Christ Jesus…therefore ye are no more strangers and foreigners [Gentiles], but fellowcitizens with the saints, and of the household of God; And are built upon the foundation of the apostles and prophets, Jesus Christ himself being the chief corner stone."

Perhaps I should also use this occasion to show how this verse connects to the word *Zion* as used in the Old Testament messianic prophecies. Notice how the previous scripture ends: "Jesus Christ himself being the chief corner stone." I want to put one other connective scripture in place right here. It is found in 1 Peter 2:6, 9–10, which says, "Wherefore also it is contained in the scripture, Behold, I lay in Sion a chief corner stone, elect, precious: and he that believeth on him shall not be confounded…But ye are a chosen generation, a royal priesthood, an holy nation, a peculiar [set apart and elect] people…Which in time past were not a people, but are now the people of God." Again, in Hebrews 12:22–23 we read, "But ye are come unto mount Sion, and unto the city of the living God…To the general assembly and church of the firstborn, which are written in heaven." As you continue to study out the meaning of these Old Testament prophecies in relation to the church, you will make the connection of the importance of the New Testament explanation of Zion in order to understand what God is saying concerning the great transference of wealth from the secular Gentile world.

Isaiah Speaks of a Deluge of Wealth for God's People: Isaiah's Opening Statement

Arise, shine; for thy light is come, and the glory of the LORD is risen upon thee. For, behold, the darkness shall cover the earth, and gross darkness the people: but the LORD shall arise upon thee, and his glory shall be seen upon thee. And the Gentiles shall come to thy light, and kings to the brightness of thy rising.

—ISAIAH 60:1–3

Now that we have some understanding of who the Gentiles are and what Zion represents in the messianic scriptures, we can go further with our revelation of a prosperity phenomenon. Remember, in Isaiah's opening remark we learned that the glory of the Lord is to come upon the church, and His glory will be seen upon us. Additionally, we found that the Gentile world and even their kings will see the "brightness of our rising" (v. 3). Now, beginning in Isaiah 60:5, we see the word *then:* "Then [When? When the glory of the Lord rises upon us!] thou shalt see, and flow together, and thine heart shall fear, and be enlarged: because the abundance of the sea shall be converted unto thee, the forces of the Gentiles shall come unto thee."

You will need to take an extensive look into the Hebrew dictionary as we read these verses in Isaiah 60. In verse 5 we come across the phrase *flow together* ("Then thou shalt see, and flow together"). In the Hebrew it is one word, *nahar.* It means "sparkle; be cheerful; like the sheen of a running stream, hence 'to flow'; be lightened." Later we will paraphrase this verse using these definitions found in our Hebrew dictionary. For example, when we do so, we will use the phrase *sparkle and be cheerful*, speaking figuratively.

Let's also examine the word *enlarged* in verse 5 ("and thine heart shall fear, and be enlarged"). The Hebrew means "to broaden; open up wide, make room for more." You can see that God has to open our hearts to make room for many new things that will transform us into His glorious people. You must keep in mind that this is not for heaven. It is for while "darkness covers the earth, and gross darkness the people [of the earth]" (Isa. 60:2).

Next, take a closer look at the phrase *abundance of the sea* ("because the abundance of the sea shall be converted unto thee"). These words in the Hebrew text consist of two words: *hamown* and *yam* (or *yawm*). The meaning of the word *hamown* consists of several expressions, including "wealth, abundance, many, multitude, multiply, riches and store." In other words, *hamown*, as translated, speaks of riches in abundance! Next is the word *yam*. *Yam* simply means "the sea (best known for the Mediterranean Sea)." The Hebrew scholars can help us out some on this point. James Moffatt denotes that the Mediterranean Sea represented most of the wealth of that part of the world. Almost all wealth was connected to it. Moffatt's Translation of the Bible renders this part of the verse, "The rich sea trade...and the wealth of nations." So later on we will settle on that rendering when we go to form our own paraphrase of this verse.

We are now going to look at the word *converted* ("the abundance of the sea shall be converted unto thee"). In the Hebrew it is the word *haphak.* This word literally means "to turn about or over; to overturn, change, be converted, overthrow, tumble; to turn back again." What is He going to convert? The "rich sea trade and the wealth of the nations." Who is He going to convert it to? "Unto thee." That's *you*!

Psalm 35:27 declares, "Let those who favor my righteous cause shout for joy and be glad and say continually, 'Let the Lord be magnified, who takes pleasure in the prosperity of His servants.'" He tells us to "let the Lord be magnified"! The word *magnified* in the Hebrew means "to boast of, brag or loudly declare. To cause to make large in various senses, as in mind, estate, or honor; also to advance, boast, bring up, exceed, be greater, lift up, magnify, promote, be proudly spoken of." God is going to take the wealth of the nations and bring about a supernatural wealth conversion. He is going to turn it all about. He is going to overturn the wealth of the wicked, rich Gentile world, and it is going to tumble, tumble, tumble—*to us*! Praise God for this great wealth conversion!

That is something to shout about! But let's enhance it with the study of yet another word in verse 5: the word *forces* ("the forces of the Gentiles shall come unto thee"). In the Hebrew it means "a force, whether of men, means or other resources; wealth, strength, goods, riches, substance, etc."

Let's turn a page in our Bible to Isaiah 61:6, where we read, "But ye shall be named the Priests of the LORD: men shall call you the Ministers of our God: ye shall eat [Heb., "consume"] the riches [this is the same as the word translated "forces" in Isaiah 60:5] of the Gentiles, and in their glory shall ye boast yourselves." So *forces* in Isaiah 60:5 is the same as *riches* in Isaiah 61:6!

I hope that you are finding it difficult to contain yourself. It's OK. Your neighbors are so busy working to pay their bills, they won't even notice anyway! But if you haven't caught on yet, just hold on, because before we are through you will see it! I believe it!

Now I want to take you to the next verse, Isaiah 60:6: "The multitude of camels shall cover thee, the dromedaries of Midian and Ephah; all they from Sheba shall come: they shall bring gold and incense; and they shall shew forth the praises of the LORD."

I am sure when you saw that word *camels* you pictured some hump-backed, long-legged creature crossing the desert. You might find it difficult to identify with that. But, I am going to change that picture in your mind, and I believe you'll never be the same again! In the Hebrew, that word *camels* is the word "gamal" ("gaw-mawl"). It refers to "any burden bearing labor to bring goods." Can you see the significance of that? He says these *gamals* will "cover us"! The word translated "cover" means *kacah,* "to overwhelm." Do you get it? ("Any burden bearing labor to bring goods"!) We don't use camels in our culture today to bring goods to us. We use eighteen wheelers! We use transport planes! We use railroad cars! We use FedEx and UPS! We use Brinks Security and Wells Fargo trucks! Are you catching on? These "burden bearing labor to bring goods" will "overwhelm us"! Remember, the word *multitude* preceded that word *camels.* In other words, "a multitude of burden bearing labor to bring goods" has now entered the picture. And they will "overwhelm" us! What are they going to bring? "They shall bring gold and incense." They are going to bring things that represent wealth to you! How many of you could handle being overwhelmed with a multitude of eighteen wheelers bringing goods to you? Or a multitude of Wells Fargo trucks bringing money to you? But we're not through yet, so hang on!

The Word goes on to say in Isaiah 60:9, "Surely the isles shall wait for me, and the ships of Tarshish bring...their silver and their gold with them, unto the name of the LORD thy God, and to the Holy One of Israel, because he hath glorified thee"! Notice the connection between "the glory" ("and the glory of the Lord is risen upon thee...but the Lord shall arise upon thee, and his glory shall be seen upon thee") in Isaiah 60:1–2 and "the gold" ("to bring...their silver and their gold with them unto the name of the Lord thy God...because he hath glorified thee") in Isaiah 60:9!

They will bring their gold and silver to us because God's glory has come upon us! The glory of the Lord upon you will bring the glory of the world to you! Say with me right now. Say, "The glory of the Lord upon me will bring the glory of the world to me!" Say it again now, "The glory of the Lord upon me will bring the glory of the world to me!" One more time: "The glory of the Lord upon me will bring the glory of the world to me!"

On August 2, 2000, in one of our services, the Spirit of God came upon Olene, my wife. She prophetically exclaimed, "God is going to give the world's glory to us, so that we can take His glory to the world!" Immediately after she spoke those words, I heard this in my spirit: "God will give us the world's goods (wealth) so that we may go to the world to get His goods (souls)!" That is what is really the thrust of this "prosperity revival." You will see that what is really behind so many of the ministries majoring on the subject of supernatural wealth is this very fact. God's harvest of the precious fruit of the earth must be harvested prior to the end of this age, which is upon us! Let's review our convergence of end-time forces and principles:

1. Mass population;

2. A stronghold of wealth laid up in store by the wicked Gentile world's global elite;

3. An explosion of knowledge in mechanical, industrial, and technological fields;

4. A righteous seed longing to get the gospel to the vast reaches of the earth's globe;

5. God's conversion of the world's wealth into the hands of the righteous ones (for whom it was intended), since God has already declared it would eventually find its way into their hands (Prov. 13:22, AMP);

6. And all of this equals an ability to gather the "precious fruit" (harvest of souls of the earth) for which God has waited and had "long patience" (James 5:7).

We also need to cover one other verse in Isaiah 60:11: "Therefore [because of what we have shown you in Isaiah 60:1–9] thy gates shall be open continually; they shall not be shut day nor night; that men may bring unto thee the forces [remember our prior definition of *forces*: "wealth, riches, goods, means, substance, and resources"] of the Gentiles, and that their kings may be brought." That word *continually* in the Hebrew is the word *tamiyd*. It means "to stretch; indefinite extensions; constantly, regularly; continual employment, ever."

Get ready! I am going to prophesy to you! But first, stretch your arm out and upward into the air right now with your hand open. Then suddenly pull it back down to you as you close your hand into a fist (as if you were grabbing hold of something tightly and pulling it to you)! As you do this, say, "I am reaching for the anointing to take back what's been stolen!" Do it again and say now with me, "Father, I thank You for the knowledge. I thank You for the information. But I am reaching for the anointing!" Now stretch your arm out and upward again and bring it back toward you as you close your fist as an expression of what you are taking. Take that anointing! I will prophesy to you! I hope your heart is open and ready to receive it *now*! If you will receive it, you are going to have to hire twenty-four-hour shifts of employment! Your doors will be open continually. They will not be shut day nor night, that men may bring to you the forces, wealth, riches, goods, means, substance, men, and other resources of the wicked Gentile world! You will not have to go after them! Men will bring them to you!

Now, let me give you my complete paraphrase of what we have been reading from Isaiah 60:1–11:

> First he tells us that His glory will arise and be seen upon us. Then he tells us that the "Gentile world will see the brightness of our rising." Everyone will be talking about the Christians everywhere. "How did they become so wealthy and influential?" We will begin to be cheerful and sparkle like the sheen of a running stream. What God is doing will literally cause our hearts to shake and tremble in awe, and He will enlarge our hearts and open it wide to make room for His great abundance. The rich merchant trade and the wealth of nations will be converted (transferred), they will be turned about (right-side up), they will be overturned or overthrown, they will be turned back again, and they will tumble to us! And the forces, riches, goods, means, substance, men, and other resources of the wicked Gentile world will come to us! God will loose the wealth (as He did with Egypt) from all over the world to be brought to us because he has glorified us. And finally, our gates (the doors of our businesses) will be open continually. They shall not be shut day nor night, that men may bring unto us the forces, wealth, riches, means, substance, men, and other resources of the Gentiles.

In Isaiah 61:6–7, 9 God says, "But ye shall be named the Priests of the Lord: men shall call you the Ministers of our God: ye shall eat [consume] the riches of the [wicked] Gentiles, and in their glory [Hebrew, "splendid, desirable, and glorious things"] shall ye boast [Hebrew, "exchange, change places with and boast"] yourselves.... And their seed shall be known among the Gentiles ["wicked Gentile world"], and their offspring among the people [of the world]: all that see them shall acknowledge them, that they are the seed which the Lord hath blessed."

Isaiah 62:1–3, 6, 10–12 outlines my assignment from God. He has instructed me to dedicate myself to it until He speaks otherwise to me. It says, "For Zion's sake will I not hold my peace...And the Gentiles shall see thy righteousness, and all kings thy glory: and thou shalt be called by a new name, which the mouth of the Lord shall name. Thou shalt also be a crown of glory in the hand of the Lord, and a royal diadem in the hand of thy God. Thou shalt no more be termed Forsaken; neither...any more be termed Desolate....I have set watchmen upon thy walls...which shall never hold their peace day nor night: ye that make mention of the Lord, keep not silence....Go through, go through the gates; prepare ye the way of the people; cast up, cast up the highway; gather out the stones; lift up a standard for the people. Behold, the Lord hath proclaimed unto the end [Hebrew, "border, brink, edge, outmost part"] of the world [a pre-Rapture phenomenon planned for the end of this age], Say ye to the daughter of Zion, Behold, thy salvation cometh; behold, his reward is with him, and his work before him. And they shall call them, The holy people, The redeemed of the Lord: and thou shalt be called, Sought out."

You might say, but are you sure God is speaking of the church, of the body of Christ? Are you certain He is talking about us? To answer that, let's read on to Isaiah 63:16: "Doubtless thou art our father, though Abraham be ignorant of us, and Israel acknowledge us not: thou, O Lord, art our father, our redeemer; thy name is from everlasting." It is obvious that this can not be Israel! He is prophesying about us!

Chapter Four

ALMIGHTY GOD:
THE GOD OF MATERIAL THINGS

Two thousand years ago the devil showed up on the Mount of Temptation and showed Jesus all the kingdoms of the world in a moment of time. Satan said to him, "All this power [Greek, *exousia*: 'authority, right, or jurisdiction'] will I give thee, and the glory of them: for that is delivered unto me; and to whomsoever I will I give it" (Luke 4:6).

Somehow the church got it into their minds that because Satan used the glory of the world to tempt Jesus, this made the glory of the world an evil thing. The gold, silver, and riches, along with the resulting influence it carries in the world is definitely what Satan used to tempt Jesus in the wilderness. But that does not make the glorious or desirable things of this world inherently evil! Jesus said, "Either make the tree good, and his fruit good; or else make the tree corrupt, and his fruit corrupt....A good man out of the good treasure of the heart bringeth forth good things: and an evil man out of the evil treasure bringeth forth evil things" (Matt. 12:33, 35). If you put "things" into the hands of a good man, because his heart is good toward God he will use it for good things. If you put "things" into the hands of an evil man, because his heart is not toward God he will use it for evil things! So, why would not God put the best, most durable, most desirable things into the hands of a good man? You will see that God knows and is planning to use the "good tree" principle in determining His judgment to redistribute the world's wealth to use for this great last-day harvest of souls.

I think that we can all agree that (hypothetically speaking) the glorious things of this world could be used for good things. I think we can further agree that God's people and the ministry of the church could use the mass of these things to further God's righteous cause in the earth, to buy the best the world has to offer for the support needed to get the gospel out to the whole earth and to spread abroad His kingdom. In fact, this is prophesied, as we will discuss later in greater depth. This type of anointing is detailed in Isaiah 23:18 (THE MESSAGE): "But everything she gets, all the money she takes in, will be turned over to God. It will not be put in banks. Her profits will be put to the use of God-Aware, God-Serving-People, providing plenty of food and the best of clothing."

The Bible is clear that God has not prevented, up until this period of time, the wicked from amassing great wealth and reaping its benefits using ungodly methods. Yet, some Christians will say, "Well, I just don't know if God would allow me to have it. I might abuse it!" It is abundantly clear that up until this time God has not disallowed the wicked to have it, even though they greatly misuse it and often abuse others with it.

Let me illustrate this point like this: Imagine that you have more than one family automobile, and your teenage son wants to drive the extra family car. Your neighbor down the street also has a teenage son ready to start driving. Now imagine yourself sitting down with your teen and explaining that he can not drive the family car because he might either wreck it or hurt someone else with it. Imagine your teen's bewilderment when you attempt to explain to him that you are going to allow the neighbor's teen to drive it. Now, let's go one step further. Imagine that as the neighbor's kid drives your family's car, he repeatedly wrecks it and harms others with it. But you continue not to allow your son to drive it.

You say, "No one would do that!" You're right! It would make no sense! But that is the kind of judgment that prevails among many Christians today. You see, if God had refused to put gold and silver and desirable treasures in the earth, requiring us all to wait until we get to heaven to enjoy them, explaining to us that we mortals might abuse it, then that would be one thing.

But God did put it in the earth! "The silver is mine, and the gold is mine, saith the LORD of Hosts [Jehovah Tsaba]" (Hag. 2:8). God did declare to us in our prior scripture that it belongs to the family ("the wealth of the sinner [finds its way eventually] into the hands of the righteous, for whom it was laid up" (Prov. 13:22, AMP), and He is not making rules, preventing us from enjoying it while allowing the wicked Gentile world to have the pleasure of using it! Ecclesiastes 2:24, 26 declares, "There is nothing better for a man, than that he should eat and drink, and that he should make his soul enjoy good in his labour. This also I saw, that it was from the hand of God.... but to the sinner he giveth travail, to gather and to heap up, that he may give to him that is good before God." This reflects God's attitude about the matter! We, the church, need to get a new attitude about it!

ABOUT WHO HAS AUTHORITY OVER THE GLORY OF THE KINGDOMS OF THE EARTH— TWO DIAMETRICALLY OPPOSING VOICES!

Mankind (Adam) bowed his knee to Satan and eventually turned his heart over to him. Satan used man's spiritual blindness, along with the lustful, selfish practices of men to his own purpose. We'll show you that the wicked Gentile nations of the world have actually been illegally possessing the glory of the earth's wealth! Almighty God, Jehovah, is actually the God of material things! The world's glory (its material wealth) is God's glory, divinely expressed in His creation!

I want to take you to two passages of Scripture to help you understand how Satan has taken advantage of man's dilemma with God and brought into his stronghold the created glory that belongs to God and His family in the earth. These two passages are found in Luke 4 and in Daniel 4:

First, we have Luke's depiction.

> And the devil, taking him up into an high mountain, shewed unto him all the kingdoms of the world in a moment of time. And the devil said unto him, All this power [Greek, *exousia*: "authority, right, jurisdiction"] will I give thee, and the glory of them: for that is delivered unto me; and to whomsoever I will I give it. If thou therefore wilt worship me, all shall be thine.
>
> —LUKE 4:5–7

Second, we have the depiction from the Book of Daniel.

> This matter is by the decree of the watchers, and the demand by the word of the holy ones [angelic messengers]: to the intent that the living may know that the most High ruleth in the kingdom of men, and giveth it to whomsoever he will.
>
> —DANIEL 4:17

We have two identical claims from two very divergent sources! Let's look at this in greater detail:

Nebuchadnezzar the king, unto all people, nations, and languages, that dwell in all the earth; Peace be multiplied unto you. I thought it good to shew the signs and wonders that the high God hath wrought toward me. How great are his signs! and how mighty are his wonders! his kingdom is an everlasting kingdom, and his dominion is from generation to generation. I Nebuchadnezzar was at rest in mine house, and flourishing in my palace: I saw a dream which made me afraid....I saw in the visions of my head upon my bed, and, behold, a watcher and an holy one came down from heaven; He cried aloud, and said thus, Hew down the tree, and cut off his branches, shake off his leaves, and scatter his fruit: let the beasts get away from under it, and the fowls from his branches: Nevertheless leave the stump of his roots in the earth...and let it be wet with the dew of heaven, and let his portion be with the beasts in the grass of the earth: Let his heart be changed from man's, and let a beast's heart be given unto him; and let seven times [years] pass over him. This matter is by the decree of the watchers, and the demand by the word of the holy ones [angelic messengers]: to the intent that the living may know that the most High ruleth in the kingdom of men, and giveth it to whomsoever he will, and setteth up over it the basest of men...Then Daniel, whose name was Belteshazzar...answered and said, My lord, the dream be to them that hate thee, and the interpretation thereof to thine enemies....This is the interpretation, O king, and this is the decree of the most High, which is come upon my lord the king: That they shall drive thee from men, and thy dwelling shall be with the beasts of the field, and they shall make thee to eat grass as oxen, and they shall wet thee with the dew of heaven, and seven times shall pass over thee, till thou know that the most High ruleth in the kingdom of men, and giveth it to whomsoever he will. And whereas they commanded to leave the stump of the tree roots; thy kingdom shall be sure unto thee, after that thou shalt have known that the heavens do rule. Wherefore, O king, let my counsel be acceptable unto thee, and break off thy sins by righteousness, and thine iniquities by shewing mercy to the poor;

if it may be a lengthening of thy tranquillity. All this came upon the king Nebuchadnezzar. At the end of twelve months he walked in the palace of the kingdom of Babylon. The king spake, and said, Is not this great Babylon, that I have built for the house of the kingdom by the might of my power, and for the honour of my majesty? While the word was in the king's mouth, there fell a voice from heaven, saying, O king Nebuchadnezzar, to thee it is spoken; The kingdom is departed from thee...until thou know that the most High ruleth in the kingdom of men, and giveth it to whomsoever he will. The same hour was the thing fulfilled upon Nebuchadnezzar...And at the end of the days I Nebuchadnezzar lifted up mine eyes unto heaven, and mine understanding returned unto me, and I blessed the most High, and I praised and honoured him that liveth for ever, whose dominion is an everlasting dominion, and his kingdom is from generation to generation...At the same time my reason returned unto me; and for the glory of my kingdom, mine honour and brightness returned unto me; and my counsellors and my lords sought unto me; and I was established in my kingdom, and excellent majesty was added unto me. Now I Nebuchadnezzar praise and extol and honour the King of heaven, all whose works are truth, and his ways judgment: and those that walk in pride he is able to abase.

—DANIEL 4:1–5, 13–17, 19, 24–34, 36–37

I hope you didn't skip over that somewhat long passage of Scripture. The revelation in these verses is vital in order to get your faith working accurately for what God is about to do in the earth where the wicked, rich Gentile world is concerned.

Did you notice the indistinguishable likeness of these two statements, made by two diametrically opposite forces? On the one hand, you have Satan—"because there is no truth in him. When he speaketh a lie, he speaketh of his own: for he is a liar, and the father of it" (John 8:44). On the other hand, you have the prophet Daniel bearing witness to an event. Jesus made reference to Daniel and declared him to be God's prophet in Matthew 24:15: "When ye therefore shall see the abomination of desolation, spoken of by Daniel the prophet."

So according to Daniel the prophet, there was first the dream of

Nebuchadnezzar, in which God said, "To the intent that the living may know that the most High ruleth in the kingdom of men, and giveth it to whomsoever he will" (Dan. 4:17). Second, there was Daniel's interpretation of the dream, through which God said, "Till thou know that the most High ruleth in the kingdom of men, and giveth it to whomsoever he will" (v. 25). Third, there was a voice from heaven that said, "Until thou know that the most High ruleth in the kingdom of men, and giveth it to whomsoever he will" (v. 32).

Then there is also a fourth witness of this event found in Daniel 5. Nebuchadnezzar died after many years, and his son, Belshazzar, reigned after him. Belshazzar was brought up by his father, who, following his ordeal, served and honored almighty God. Belshazzar went against the teachings of his father, and it resulted in God's judgment upon him. Then God sent Daniel to King Belshazzar. This is what he said:

> O thou king, the most high God gave Nebuchadnezzar thy father a kingdom, and majesty, and glory, and honour [Notice it doesn't say that Satan gave it to him, as he purported to be able to do for Jesus during the temptation]: And for the majesty that he gave him, all people, nations, and languages, trembled and feared before him: whom he would he slew; and whom he would he kept alive; and whom he would he set up; and whom he would he put down. But when his heart was lifted up, and his mind hardened in pride, he was deposed from his kingly throne, and they [the angelic messengers] took his glory [wealth, power and influence] from him...till he knew that the most high God ruled in the kingdom of men, and that he appointeth over it whomsoever he will. And thou his son, O Belshazzar, hast not humbled thine heart, though thou knewest all this.
>
> —Daniel 5:18–22

A Short Legal Brief on Authority

When God created the heavens and the earth, when He made man upon it, He delegated to him an authority to rule over it. There are several principles that you need to know to understand how authority works. I am going to list a few of the more important principles.

First, authority comes from privileges handed down through a legal right of domain. For example, the purpose of a title deed is to establish, at the highest possible level, where the authority begins. That is why the very first words in the Bible are "in the beginning God created the heaven and the earth" (Gen. 1:1). Then again in Psalm 24:1–2, God is staking His claim as the one who holds the right of imminent domain in the earth. He lets you know that He still holds the title deed: "The earth is the LORD's, and the fulness thereof; the world, and they that dwell therein. For he hath founded it upon the seas, and established it upon the floods."

Second, authority conferred is delegating rights, not giving them away. Unless you created and founded it, your authority comes from continuing to stay under delegated authority. The knowledge of the centurion in Matthew 8:9 impressed Jesus when he said, "For I am a man under authority, having soldiers under me."

Let me illustrate it like this: Let's say that a man owned a supermarket. He decided to go away on a journey for an extended period. He went to one of his employees and put him over the store while he was gone. Before he left on his journey the store owner called in his manager and said to him, "I give you the authority to run my store while I am gone. You will be in charge of personnel. You have the power to hire and dismiss employees whenever you feel it is necessary. You will open up and close the store each day. You will be responsible for what is stocked in the store. You have a stock list. See to it that it is maintained properly. Use your own judgment regarding running sale items. If it snows, be sure to get a plow to clear the parking area. Here are the keys to the store. There is one other thing. Do not open it up for business on Sunday! If you do, it will mean your dismissal. Do you understand? If you open it up on Sunday, and I have clearly said to you, 'Do not open it on Sunday,' then I will have to let you go! Is that clear? OK! That's great! Just to make certain that there is no misunderstanding, I have prepared an employment agreement stipulating your authority. I have actually itemized your authority in this document. Use it however you need to while I am gone to run my business."

His manager acknowledges his understanding of it, signs the document, and authority is delegated. The store owner has just delegated authority to the manager of his store. Now, keep this in mind: the store owner has not given up any rights; he has delegated his ongoing rights to someone. He is still the owner. He is still the boss. He still has the same power as before. The only change is with the store manager. He has rights only because he remains under authority! The store manager's new power and influence, flowing from that delegation of authority, requires him to be subject to that itemized list given him by the store owner! He has no inherent power, only delegated power. Inherent power, such as the kind God has as the creator and founder, is an independent ability, whereas delegated power, such as the kind Adam received from almighty God, is assigned or designated power. It only has force within the confines of the allocation of it.

The owner of the store in our story did not give, sell, or lease his store to the manager. The manager cannot sell the store. He cannot lease out the store. He cannot even move or change the store. His rights only consist of what was delegated to him by the owner. We do not have to wonder or use conjecture. It is not hard to interpret his ability. There is no mystery! We can go to the agreement and easily determine both the owner and the manager's rights.

Let's carry our story a little further. After the store owner leaves and some time passes, a friend of the store manager walks in. He says to the manager, "I'm curious. Why is it that you do not open on Sunday?" The store manager replies, "Because the owner gave me strict instructions that I am not to open it on Sunday. He said if I do, I'll be fired!" The friend replies, "He wouldn't fire you. In fact, if you opened on Sunday and he returned and saw that you were doing record business on that day, he would not fire you; he would give you a bonus and a raise!"

(This is like Satan saying to Eve and Adam, "Ye shall not surely die: For God doth know that in the day ye eat thereof, then your eyes shall be opened, and ye shall be as gods, knowing good and evil") (Gen. 3:4–5).

The store manager thought about it for a while and became convinced that his friend was right. So, he began opening the store on Sunday. (That is like Eve and Adam responding to the "suggestion" of Satan: "And when the woman saw that the tree was good for food, and that it was pleasant to the eyes, and a tree to be desired to make one wise, she took of the fruit thereof, and did eat, and gave also unto her husband with her; and he did eat") (Gen. 3:6).

One day the owner happened to be back in town briefly and went by the store. He noticed it was open on Sunday. The next morning, bright and early, he went to his store planning to confront the manager as soon as he arrived.

Much to his surprise, he found the door locked and that his key no longer fit! So, he was forced to wait until the manager arrived to get into his store.

(Now, that would be like God showing up to do something in the earth, just to find out that He was "locked out" of any power to do it! Note: You will never find God unable to do anything He wants to do in the earth, because He has never been "locked out"!)

When the manager arrived, he asked him, "Why did you have the lock changed? Was there a burglary or an employee fired?" "No," replied the manager. "My friend convinced me to open the store against your orders. He later explained to me that by disobeying your command and obeying his suggestion, I inadvertently gave away your rights over this store to him. You gave me the authority, and I gave it away to him. I am sorry, sir, but your rights have been compromised by my obeying my friend's suggestion."

What will the store owner now do? Will he allow himself to be made subject to either the manager or the manager's friend? Will he deal with the friend who made the suggestion? No! Will he allow himself to be subjected to this erroneous notion about the law? No! What will he do? He will dismiss that manager (and his influence) and continue operating as the owner of the store. He may hire another manager, he may sell the store and retire, he may do a hundred different things, but he will never be subject to his manager employee!

I am sure that in that context, you would say, "That whole scenario is absurd!" I agree with you. But this is the picture that some have had regarding the legal situation in the earth since Adam listened to and obeyed the suggestion of Satan in the Garden of Eden! They say, "Adam gave away his authority to Satan!"

This brings up a third principle. Authority conferred binds the principle. "Only within the limits" of the authority conferred, is an act by an agent in effect an act of the principle. When one is operating under authority, that person is always subject to the higher authority that conferred it upon them. Their legal rights are always controlled and limited. In order to establish legal rights, you always have to go back to the authority. For example, if a lease is given, you go to the lease agreement. If it is sold, you go to the rights conferred through a title deed. Both the terms *lease* and *title deed* have often been used to express Adam's authority over the earth. But we will show you that God neither gave, sold, nor leased the earth to Adam. He merely delegated limited authority to him!

If I sold you my house last year, I could not declare ownership this year, could I? So we know that Adam was not given "title deed" to the earth, because God does not say, "The earth *was* the Lord's." He still holds it in Psalm 24:1: "The earth is the LORD's, and the fulness thereof; the world, and all they that dwell therein, For he hath founded it."

What about a "lease"? While a lessee is still limited with regard to rights and privileges, it does also place more detailed restrictions on the lessor as well. In other words, the lessor gives up some power to the lessee within the confines of their agreement.

I never make apologies for being "one of those Word of Faith folks." I am one! We Word of Faith folks are real sticklers for words! We know that power is released through them. So we can go back to the document itself to see if Adam was given a "title deed," a "lease," or merely responsibilities (and a measure of authority) to carry out the instructions for the owner and possessor of the earth, much like the store manager in our story). The late Buddy Harrison, Kenneth E. Hagin's son-in-law, once said, "Beware of the person who talks all the time about authority more than they do about responsibilities, because the purpose of delegated authority is to carry out responsibility." As you study this out with me, you will find that Adam (mankind) had authority delegated to him in order to carry out specific responsibilities. You will agree with me, I believe, that there is a vast difference between an employment contract and a "title deed" or a "lease." It shouldn't take a high-level legal mind (thank God!) to sort out what God gave to Adam in the garden. Let's examine the document:

> And God said, Let us make man in our image, after our likeness: and let them have dominion [Heb., *radah*: "to crumble off; make to have dominion, rule over"] over the fish of the sea, and over the fowl of the air, and over the cattle, and over all the earth [Heb., *erets*: "to be firm; field, ground"], and over every creeping thing that creepeth upon the earth.
>
> —GENESIS 1:26

Hence, God delegated, or conferred, authority to Adam. Notice that it is a limited measure of authority. It is not anything close to what Jesus was given, and what He delegated to us in the authority of the believer "hath quickened us together with Christ…and hath raised us up together, and made us sit together in heavenly places in Christ Jesus….when he raised him from the dead, and set him at his own right hand in the heavenly places. Far above all principality, and power, and might, and dominion, and every name that is named, not only in this world, but also in that which is to come" (Eph. 2:5–6; 1:20–21).

Compared to our authority in the new creation, Adam's authority was very limited: "Let them have dominion [rule] over [1] the fish of the sea, and [2] over the fowl of the air, and [3] over the cattle, and [4] over all the earth [dry land, including, I believe, all the mining and farming privileges of whatever was produced or taken out of it], and [5] over every creeping thing that creepeth upon the earth" (Gen. 1:26).

Now, if we are going to take seriously the authority of man in the earth, we must by necessity take seriously the document giving that authority to him. And I've just read it to you from the legal document conferring that authority!

Many have suggested that when Adam obeyed Satan, God became restricted in His rights in the earth, just like the store owner in our story. According to some, no longer could God give orders without checking with man; God had somehow subjugated Himself to Adam (and Satan) and would have to use mankind as a medium to get His way in the earth. There have also been other variances of that same hypothesis.

Imagine delegating authority to a babysitter for an entire evening. You tell her that she must not leave the premises or take the children from the home, that you will return at 11:00 p.m. but that she is in charge of them until then. You arrive home early, at 8:00 p.m., just to find that her boyfriend came by and talked her into taking the kids to the skating rink against your instructions. Now you learn that you no longer have any authority over your kids because the babysitter gave your authority over your kids to her boyfriend when she obeyed his suggestion! Really? I don't think so!

Let's look closer. We really do need to get this straight for what God is going to do in the earth between now and the Rapture of the church! We know that Adam sinned. You see, if Satan was telling Jesus the truth during the temptation in the wilderness, then Satan, not God, has the ability to decide and give the kingdoms and glory of this world "to whomsoever he will." That would leave God powerless, in this prophetically planned event, to shake His hand upon the nations to give their glory (riches and glorious things) to the body of Christ, the church. Likewise, if Adam (mankind) gave dominion over this earth to Satan when he obeyed Satan's suggestion, and if that authority somehow belongs to Satan until the end of some kind of "lease period," then God would, again, be unable to affect a plan to take it from the world and give it to His people. Yes, he committed treason against God by disobeying Him. But he did not sell out the store or its goods (or give the kids away). When the sinful deed was done, was Satan then somehow moved upward in his legal rights (authority) in the earth? Was Satan now in a position of authority just because Adam obeyed his suggestion? No! Let's go back to the document:

> And the LORD God said unto the serpent, Because thou hast done this, thou art [promoted and increased in authority over all the things Adam had control of, such as, the cattle, the beasts, and so forth No! God forbid. No!] cursed [Heb., *arar*: "bitterly cursed"] above all cattle, and above every beast of the field; upon thy belly shalt thou go, and dust shalt thou eat all the days of thy life.
>
> —GENESIS 3:14

Notice that God insisted on illustrating how low Satan was after Adam's fall. To prove this, the serpent would have to crawl on his belly (the lowest position of any creature; Gen. 3:14, Rev. 12:9). Satan was not in a higher position but in a worse position after the terrible deed was done!

Did God still have the ability to do as He pleased in the earth without checking with anybody? Just look at these scriptures in Genesis 3 for the answer. Who came on the scene after Adam sinned? God did! Who took command when He came upon the scene? God did!

> And the LORD God said unto the woman...And the LORD God said unto the serpent...Unto the woman he said...And unto Adam he said...Unto Adam also and to his wife did the LORD God make coats of skins, and clothed them...Therefore the Lord God sent him forth from the garden of Eden...So he drove out the man; and he placed

at the east of the garden of Eden Cherubims [angelic keepers], and a flaming sword...to keep the way of the tree of life."

—GENESIS 3:13–14, 17, 21, 23

Did God have to check out any of this with Adam or Satan before He acted? Of course not! God was and has always been in complete and total rule over the earth. There has never been and never will be any other legal sovereign over the earth's domain!

In the past some have declared that when Adam sinned, he gave his authority away to Satan. Of course, we found out that you don't give your authority away when you delegate it to a subordinate. Adam did not have a title deed to grant a change in ownership. Others declare that there was a transference of legal rights to Satan and that this state of things remained until Jesus came and got them back for us. But legal rights are not transferred in this manner, merely by delegating authority.

Let's test that theory out by going back again to the document and seeing who has clear legal control of things in the earth. Let's look at things where Noah and God are concerned after the Flood. Genesis 8:21 says, "And the LORD [not Satan] smelled a sweet savour; and the LORD [not Satan] said in his heart, I will not again curse the ground any more [or any longer] for man's sake." Do you recall that when Adam sinned, God spoke then and said, "Cursed is the ground for thy sake; in sorrow shalt thou eat of it all the days of thy life" (Gen. 3:17)? Now, if we can somehow get past an erroneous doctrine that slipped in—you know how we tell religious folks that we hate teaching for doctrine the manmade traditions—then it will prove to be a breakthrough for this end-time revelation. God, as Jehovah Tsaba (Lord of Hosts), is sending His angel to the wicked Gentile world. God's great angelic army, under His direction, will take back the glory held until now in a stronghold of the world. This great army of angels will shake the nations. They will shake loose their glory and give it to us to finance, and to take the glory of God to the lost.

All of my life I have heard preachers tell us about the curse that came upon the ground when Adam sinned. They have told us we must "labor by the sweat of our brow and struggle to get anything out of it." Well, that just is not true. Did you catch what God did when Noah offered up his offering to the Lord? He removed the curse that He had put on Adam in the garden concerning his working the ground: "I will not again anymore curse the ground for man's sake" (Gen. 8:21). Notice that Satan did not show up on legal grounds before the Judge of all the earth. You do not find him saying to God, "God, sorry, but you can't do that! You gave away your authority in the earth to Adam. Adam gave it to me. Now I have it and can legally give it to whomsoever I please! I'm not allowing the curse to be lifted!" No! Humankind does not know the truth yet. The church has never proclaimed this portion of the good news. God's curse is no longer on the ground. As far as God is concerned, the earth may freely bring forth fruit. It now contains a blessing that was simultaneously given by God at the time He lifted the curse on the ground.

> God smelled the sweet fragrance and thought to himself, "I'll never again curse the ground because of people....For as long as Earth lasts, planting and harvest, cold and heat, Summer and winter, day and night will never stop.
> —Genesis 8:21–22, The Message

Satan has to hang around in darkness and pick on blind, spiritually dead, or deceived people. Satan knows most folks are still spiritually blind. He can deceive them, and they will fall for almost anything. They will usually perceive his suggestions as reasonable. This allows him to continue to abuse them.

Have you got your shoutin' clothes on again? What comes next will settle whether Satan bettered himself and whether "Poor ol' God" got Himself into a fix through what Adam did. Of course, I am speaking facetiously! There is nothing "poor" or "ol'" about almighty God. He is and always will be the Most High, the Sovereign, the Possessor of heaven and earth!

Now back to the document: "And God blessed Noah and his sons, and said unto them, Be fruitful, and multiply, and replenish the earth" (Gen. 9:1). Where have we heard that before? Let's go back this time to Genesis 1:28: "And God blessed them, and God said unto them, Be fruitful, and multiply, and replenish the earth."

Does it look to you like God has recognized any change in His agreement with mankind? What about His ability to continue delegating authority as the Head over all the earth? Let's go on with what God said to Adam:

"God blessed them, and God said unto them, Be fruitful, and multiply, and replenish the earth, and subdue it: and have dominion over the fish of the sea, and over the fowl of the air, and over every living thing that moveth upon the earth" (Gen. 1:28).

Now go back to Noah in Genesis 8:1–2, "Be fruitful and multiply, and replenish the earth. And the fear of you and the dread of you shall be upon every beast of the earth, and upon every fowl of the air, upon all that moveth upon the earth, and upon all the fishes of the sea; into your hand [Hebrew, *yad*: "power, means, or direction"] are they delivered."

We need to recall what Satan said to Jesus on the Mount of Temptation: "It is delivered unto me; and to whomsoever I will I give it" (Luke 4:6). Many times I have heard ministers say, "Adam delivered it to Satan in the garden." But God said He delivered it to Noah in Genesis 8:1–2! He delegated the authority to Noah! So, God still had the legal right to delegate authority in Noah's day (to give it to whomsoever He would). More than that, under God's delegation of authority Noah had it in Noah's day!

God also proved His rights over the earth in Abraham's day. Can you imagine God showing up to make a covenant with Abraham? He says to Abraham, "If you will walk perfect before Me, I will bless you. Walk the length and breadth of the land. I will give it to you." But then imagine Satan comes to Abraham and says, "Sorry Abraham, but I have legal rights here, and God gave the earth's authority away to Adam; Adam sold it out to me, so until Jesus comes, it belongs to me. I say you can't have that land God promised you." So Abraham goes back to God and says, "God, I had a visit from Satan, and he informed me that neither You nor I can claim any rights to this land without first checking with him. And He says no." So, as a furrow forms in God's brow, He responds to Abraham, "Abraham, I am sorry. But Satan is right! I should have gone to him first and made a deal with him before attempting to give you any rights over the earth. Yes, Abraham, it is true. I gave it to Adam, and Adam sold it out to the devil." Praise God that is not the way it went down. God is the legal owner and possessor of heaven and earth. The heavens still rule!

Try this one: David hears Goliath roaring his threats against the armies of Israel. David goes up against the giant. Goliath is claiming rights to the land occupied by Israel. In effect, Goliath is saying to Israel, "This was our land before your ancestors came out of Egypt, and we want it back." David defies him and says, "But I come against you in the name of the Lord of Hosts [Jehovah Tsaba]." Suddenly, Satan shows up in the midst of their argument and says, "David, son of Jesse, I am calling the Most High to record. He gave the authority over this and all lands of the earth to Adam, and Adam committed high treason and sold it all out to me. Someday Jesus will come and fight to get it back from me. Until then, if you or the Most High, in whose name you claim to come, wants possession of this or any other land, you will have to deal on legal grounds with me! And I say no to you. Adam delivered it unto me, and I can give it to whomsoever I will. I gave it into Goliath's hands, and there it must remain." Now, if it happened that way (of course, it did not), David would have no power to defeat the Philistines in the name of Jehovah Tsaba (Lord of Hosts). He would be forced to whip Goliath with his own power or else back down (or get permission from Satan)! Praise God! Again, we see who really had the power and authority in the earth.

GOD OF THIS WORLD

"But Pastor, doesn't the Bible say Satan is the god of this world?" Perhaps we need to deal with a verse from the apostle Paul to eliminate any confusion. In 2 Corinthians 4:3–4, we read, "But if our gospel be hid, it is hid to them that are lost: In whom the god of the world hath blinded the minds of them which believe not, lest the light of the glorious gospel of Christ, who is the image of God, should shine unto them."

Some have attempted to use the scripture to confer some type of legal title upon the devil stemming from his dealings with Adam. Please understand something about Satan. He is a defeated, evil prisoner on death row. Like any bully, he uses darkness, ignorance, and fear to push around people who will fall for his subtleties and pressure. The fact that the Scriptures refer to something called "the god of this world," especially in light of what we have learned in previous Bible passages, does not acknowledge or infer some legal position of Satan over the earth, the world, or the glory of it.

In Philippians 3:18–19, we also read, "For many walk, of whom I have told you often, and now tell you even weeping, that they are the enemies of the cross of Christ: Whose end is destruction, whose God is their belly, and whose glory is in their shame, who mind [serve] earthly things." Recall with me also what the apostle Paul said in 1 Corinthians 8:4, "As concerning therefore the eating of those things that are offered in sacrifice unto idols, we know that an idol is nothing in the world, and that there is none other God but one." So then, if Satan holds no legal title, or if one's belly is really no god of any legal standing, then what of these two references using the term *God*?

The answer is found in Romans 16:18 and 6:16, respectively: "For they that are such serve not our Lord Jesus Christ, but their own belly....Know ye not, that to whom ye yield yourselves servants to obey, his servants ye are to whom ye obey?"

The world may serve the devil. They may make him their god by serving his individual suggestions. But he does not now, nor will he ever hold a legal position of authority over the earth. Almighty God is the God of material things and all of the kingdoms of the world!

The Scriptures tell us that Satan was arrested: "I beheld Satan as lightning fall from heaven" (Luke 10:18); "And his tail drew the third part of the stars of heaven, and did cast them to the earth" (Rev. 12:4). He was convicted: "Now is the judgment of the world: now shall the prince of this world be cast out" (John 12:31); "Of judgment, because the prince of this world is judged" (John 16:11); "And there was war in heaven: Michael and his angels fought against the dragon; and the dragon fought and his angels, And prevailed not; neither was their place found any more in heaven. And the great dragon was cast out, that old serpent, called the Devil, and Satan, which deceiveth the whole world: he was cast out into the earth, and his angels were cast out with him. And I heard a loud voice saying in heaven, Now is come salvation, and strength, and the kingdom of our God, and the power of his Christ: for the accuser of our brethren is cast down, which accused them before our God day and night" (Rev. 12:7–10). And Satan is now awaiting his sentencing, which will be carried out at the very Last Judgment immediately after the one-thousand-year reign of Christ here on the earth.

> And when the thousand years are expired, Satan shall be loosed out of his prison, And shall go out to deceive the nations which are in the four quarters of the earth...to gather them together to battle...and fire came down from God out of heaven, and devoured them. And

the devil that deceived them was cast into the lake of fire and brim-stone…and shall be tormented day and night for ever and ever.

—REVELATION 20:7–10

So what do we do about our scripture in 2 Corinthians 4:4, where Paul speaks of the "god of this world"? The answer lies in the context of that verse. Notice that this "god" uses "darkness." This is the key to Satan's power: blindness and the resulting darkness upon humanity. Legal methods do not need the cover of darkness!

God made humankind to rule. He made us rulers in the earth with del-egated authority to have dominion in the earth. Satan perverted God's Word and led humanity into spiritual blindness and darkness.

Satan knew enough to twist God's plan. In Genesis 3:5 Satan declared, "For God doth know that in the day ye eat thereof, then your eyes shall be opened, and ye shall be as gods, knowing good and evil." Now, if that had been the truth, then after they sinned they would have had perfect knowledge of good and evil. The tree of the knowledge of good and evil was not a tree to make one able to know good and evil. You need to get this next point straight! It was a tree to make one responsible to know between good and evil, to be accountable! Notice the Scriptures say, "And the Lord God said, Behold, the man is become as one of us, [accountable] to know good and evil" (Gen. 3:22). Notice it does not say "knowing," but "to know"! So, Adam left the garden with a new responsibility. He left the garden in spiritual blindness when he became accountable for good and evil! He was walking in darkness.

Had Adam's delegated authority been lifted or shifted in any way? No! He was just as responsible over the earth as ever, but now he was a blind ruler. Satan has always found his ability to operate in the earth through the spiritual blindness and ignorance of humanity. If he can find those with legal rights to dominate the earth's resources, gain their control using fear and deception, and get them to obey his veiled suggestions, then he can use them to operate his underworld kingdom of darkness in the earth. Satan's kingdom mirrors the way the Mafia rules in the natural world. Notice how these words reflect this idea: "And this is the condemnation, that light is come into the world, and men loved darkness rather than light, because their deeds were evil. For every one that doeth evil hateth the light, neither cometh to the light" (John 3:19–20).

The apostle Paul recognized Satan's real power when he wrote, "This I say therefore...that ye henceforth walk not as other Gentiles walk, in the vanity of their mind, Having the understanding darkened, being alienated from the life of God through the ignorance that is in them, because of the blindness of their heart" (Eph. 4:17–18).

Paul speaks of the answer to this predicament in Colossians 1:13: "Who hath delivered us from the power of darkness [not the legal authority of Satan, but his ability to rule the spiritually blind], and hath translated us into the kingdom of his dear Son." Again he says in 2 Corinthians 4:6, "For God, who commanded the light to shine out of darkness, hath shined in our hearts, to give the light of the knowledge of the glory of God." And again we read in 1 John 1:5 and 2:8, "This then is the message which we have heard of him, and declare unto you, that God is light, and in him is no darkness at all...I write unto you, which thing is true in him and in you: because the darkness is past, and the true light now shineth."

When you were born again, you became a new creature. The life of God in you brought you out of the darkness and into the light. Satan, being illegal, must always remain in the darkness, operating through fear and ignorance, which are the foundations of doubt and unbelief.

When God taught the apostle Paul about the new creation, He revealed to him the authority given to the believer in Christ Jesus. Now, keep in mind, humanity had authority in this earth, an authority that he was unable to exercise because of his blind and darkened condition. Satan took constant advantage of that blindness. Paul's revelation in Ephesians 1:21 reflects the fact that man's authority was already in existence over this earth: "Far above all principality, and power, and might, and dominion, and every name that is named, not only in this world [the acknowledgment of the limitations of the Adamic authority], but also in that which is to come: And hath put all things under his feet."

So remember this: God has never relinquished even the slightest amount of His power and rule over the earth. He has never in the least subjugated His rights nor been put in a position of inferiority over His heavens and earth!

The Sevenfold Nature of Almighty God

> For I am the Lord, I do not change; that is why you, O sons of Jacob, are not consumed.
>
> —Malachi 3:6, amp

I will show you that God is a God of love, power, wisdom, righteousness, mercy, justice, and judgment. Every time God does something, each and every part of His nature is in play. His character, how He responds to our human behavior, and His subsequent actions, are the product of this sevenfold nature.

Please understand, every single one of these factors of His sevenfold nature is engaged with everything God does. He is not sometimes a God of love and other times a God of judgment. He is, at all times, the God of love, power, wisdom, righteousness, mercy, justice, and judgment. Yes, all of the time!

Interestingly, one must begin with God's love as the starting point of understanding His nature and end with His judgment. To take these two elements and turn them around confuses who He is. First John 4:8 (amp) says, "He who does not love has not become acquainted with God [does not and never did know Him], for God is love." This means that He can never be separated from this attribute of His nature. Everything He does emanates from His heart of love.

For example, when God brought the flood of Noah upon the earth, all seven of these aspects of His divine nature were seen. Since there has been no harsher judgment upon the earth than Noah's flood, it makes for a perfect event to study God's nature. As we will see, God's sevenfold nature is readily seen. Let's identify each characteristic.

Love

Many centuries before the Flood, there was a man named Enoch. Enoch stands out in Scripture because Enoch escaped death only seven generations from Adam, after Adam had brought sin and death upon mankind. The Scriptures declare that he "walked with God...and God took him" (Gen. 5:24). Hebrews 11:5 relates that "by faith Enoch was translated that he should not see death." During Enoch's lifetime here on earth he had a son, whom he called Methuselah.

Biblical names often differ from our current "common names" in that the Hebrew name is selected to represent a statement about the individual. In modern culture, oftentimes the cutest-sounding, most popular name, or someone's favorite, is used. The way the name sounds in our ears is the primary criterion. But in ancient times a person's name was designed to make a statement. Jabez is an excellent example of ancient name selection. His mother, when she was giving birth, had much sorrow and pain, so she named him Jabez, meaning "sorrowful sort." He gave her sorrow, so she named him Sorrowful Sort. Can you just imagine coming in the room and someone saying, "Hey, there goes little Sorry Sort out to play"? That could create quite a complex for a child. Of course, Jabez called on God and was delivered from the curse placed upon him at birth, and God greatly blessed him.

God apparently revealed to Enoch the judgment of the Flood. According to Strong's Hebrew and Greek Dictionary, Methuselah's name, as referenced in the genealogy of Jesus in Luke 3:37, means "he dies and it [the Flood] is sent." Strong's, in defining this name, goes on to say, "According to Hebrew chronology, [Methuselah] was 969 years old when he died. He died in the year of the Flood and was the oldest man who ever lived."

Can you see God's love in this prelude story concerning the Flood? God revealed that Enoch would live until it was time for the Flood: "He dies, and the Flood is sent!" The fact that he is the oldest man on record to ever live in the earth—God knowing in His plan that this man was to bear witness of God's long-suffering nature with humanity, not wanting judgment to be brought upon them—stands out as a monument to the love of God. First Corinthians 13:7 declares that love is extremely long-suffering, willing to bear up under anything, and endures with steadfast hope. That is a picture of the love of God, and Methuselah's extremely long age is a testament of the love of God preceding Noah's flood.

Power and Wisdom

We will combine these two of the seven aspects of God's nature in looking at Noah's flood. The word *power* represents the "raw energy," or physical ability, of God. Wisdom is the ability to fit unrefined pieces of knowledge together in a manner that creatively works to produce a wanted action. In the Flood, we certainly have evidence of the operation of these two ingredients of God's nature.

I want you to think of the attributes of God's nature linearly, as if, beginning with love, He passes through each of these attributes but inevitably arrives at the end in judgment. Deuteronomy 32:4 reveals, "He is the Rock, his work is perfect: for all his ways are judgment: a God of truth and without iniquity, just and right is he."

Here we have, in one verse, many of God's sevenfold attributes. Notice, however, that ultimately we come to God's judgment, "for all his ways are judgment." The sum total of all of His ways, His divine nature, is judgment. In the Hebrew, the word for *judgment* means "a verdict." When all is said and done, we arrive at judgment. Keep in mind, judgment is not always against us. The verdict, for example, for a believer in Christ, is "not guilty, righteous and blameless in the sight of God through the shed blood of Jesus." God's ways stem from a heart filled with love, but as He engages all of His attributes during the process, the final judgment may be punishment or vengeance, especially for the wicked.

Let's carry our journey across the linear path of His nature to see how He arrives at judgment. So, in the Flood we saw His love through His refusal to allow Methuselah's death, extending his life over and over again, desiring not to have to see him die, thus bringing the great judgment against humanity. We also saw His power and wisdom as He directed Noah in how to build the ark, prepare the animals for species preservation, and sent the mighty torrents of water that actually flooded the earth.

Righteousness

This deals, in God's nature, with His accountability to Himself. Just and right is He. He is, Himself, the righteousness of God. It is this attribute of His nature that prompted Him to place His word of promise above all His name. Psalm 138:2 (AMP) says, "I will worship toward Your holy temple and praise Your name for Your loving-kindness and for Your truth and faithfulness; for You have exalted above all else Your name and Your word and You have magnified Your word above all Your name!"

God found Noah. He found a man walking in his integrity. Abraham, later, in trying to intercede for Sodom, cried out, "Shall not the Judge of all the earth do right?" (Gen. 18:25). Of course He will. But, although God did not rush to judgment, the linear pathway, passing through all the other attributes of His nature nevertheless, led Him to destroy the cities of Sodom and Gomorrah. Thus, God spared Noah and his family.

Mercy

In the flood, we arrive at mercy. God spared Noah and his family, along with two of all of the species of animals. Mercy. It is that attribute of God's sevenfold nature that is so vital to who He is. The psalmist David, more than any other biblical writer, understood the importance of God's mercy. We read in Psalm 69:13 (AMP), "But as for me, my prayer is to You, O Lord. At an acceptable and opportune time, O God, in the multitude of Your mercy and the abundance of Your loving-kindness hear me, and in the truth and faithfulness of Your salvation answer me."

You see, David understood the linear importance of God's nature. He knew that God is always a God of mercy, that His nature is consistent, and He never fails to demonstrate that attribute within His divine nature. He also understood from His experience with God's judgment both after numbering Israel and after his affair with Bathsheba and the resulting murder of her husband that if one scorns the time of God's mercy, ultimately facing His last two attributes is inevitable: justice and judgment. In the time of judgment, one can never accuse God of not allowing a time of mercy to enable the offender to repent.

Justice

You will recall in Deuteronomy 32:4 the final words of our prior reference to it: "Just and right is he." You can know for certain that when you are seeing the judgment of God in the earth, you are seeing the results of a God of love, as He has linearly passed through His wonderful, loving, divine nature, arriving only after exhausting all other remedies at His divine judgment.

Judgment

Remember, judgment is not always a negative thing, thanks to the perfection of God's divine nature and His faithfulness to remain absolutely the same all of the time. You might rush to judgment in a moment of anger. God, too, has anger, but never experiences a rush to judgment without all of the other aspects of His nature in play.

In the Book of James we have a vital principle revealed that helps to assure us of this. James 2:13 says, "For he shall have judgment without mercy, that hath shewed no mercy; and mercy rejoiceth against judgment." The Amplified Bible renders that last part "mercy...exults victoriously over judgment." Praise God!

We have already seen God's goodness in the fact that He will always provide an acceptable and opportune time during which He extends His mercies. When humanity responds in repentance during this period, they do not receive "justice." Instead, they receive mercy, which rejoices over justice and judgment, and they bring an outcome representing God's divine nature of love.

I heard one minister interviewed by one of the secular news media outlets during a great time of national tragedy. He was asked, "How could a God of love allow this kind of suffering and difficulty?" I watched in amazement as the minister stressfully stammered and squirmed, and finally, intimidated by the question, proved unable to give an accurate accounting. I also heard as still another minister was asked, "How can a loving God send a person to hell?" The minister quickly removed God from the position of Judge, proclaiming, "Oh, God never sends anyone to hell. That is a product of that person's own decision!" Wrong! Hell is the product of God's judgment.

Still, that does not discount His great love and mercy. Jesus was the manifestation of "an acceptable and opportune time." He is God's own remedy for His own wrath. What a profoundness that is! God had to judge the sin of Adam. But, to be true to His own sevenfold divine nature, He also had to provide an opportunity for His mercy to be extended. He did this through Christ Jesus. Jesus was not about wrath or judgment; He was about love and mercy. But for those who spurn that opportunity offered through Christ, judgment and the wrath of God is certain.

I have a great appreciation for the evangelist Billy Graham. To me, the most outstanding thing about his ministry is that he preaches the whole gospel—all of the sevenfold nature of God. He preaches both the wrath of God upon humanity because of Adam's sin and God's own mercy through Christ Jesus, extended to them because of His great love for them. He preaches that God had to be righteous as the Judge of all the earth, but He offered a remedy of mercy for mankind to escape a guilty sentence and find eternal life through His Son.

For God so greatly loved and dearly prized the world that He [even] gave up His only begotten (unique) Son, so that whoever believes in (trusts in, clings to, relies on) Him shall not perish (come to destruction, be lost) but have eternal (everlasting) life. For God did not send the Son into the world in order to judge (to reject, to condemn, to pass sentence on) the world, but that the world might find salvation and be made safe and sound through Him. He who believes in Him [who clings to, trusts in, relies on Him] is not judged [he who trusts in Him never comes up for judgment; for him there is no rejection, no condemnation—he incurs no damnation]; but he who does not believe (cleave to, rely on, trust in Him) is judged already [he has already been convicted and has already received his sentence] because he has not believed in and trusted in the name of the only begotten Son of God. [He is condemned for refusing to let his trust rest in Christ's name.]

—JOHN 3:16–18, AMP

As we see the "vengeance to comfort," come to pass, heralded from Isaiah 61:2–6, we see God's sevenfold nature exhibited. Also, as shown previously, His authority rules the earth. We have cleared the air of any uncertainty of His right to do as He wishes in the affairs of mankind. Now, with an understanding of His sevenfold nature, you will be able to rest assured that everything that takes place—the plunder of the wicked rich, the bringing down of the haughty and proud, and the conversion of the world's wealth into the hands of the righteous—all fits into that which is just and right in God's eyes.

Chapter Five

MAMMON: THE WORSHIP OF MATERIAL THINGS

SOME TIME AGO, I was the Sunday morning guest minister at New Life Fellowship in Memphis, Tennessee. While in my hotel room getting ready for the service, I flipped on the television to see if any of my favorite national ministries were on. While turning the channels I came across a program in which a local minister was speaking to her congregation: "Don't you listen to those preachers who are following the god of material things!" Since I had just completed an extensive teaching series titled "Almighty God: The God of Material Things," her statement really got my attention. As I listened, I realized that this church fellowship had become confused concerning who is the God of material things.

I want you to know right now, I am going to follow the God of Material Things, Creator of all things. His name is Jehovah! He is the almighty God (El Shaddai) who is more than enough! This pastor, I feel certain, was sincerely trying to guard over her flock. She was confused about the matter, however. If she would have said, "Don't follow those who are caught up in serving and worshiping material things," then she would have been correct. That is why we need more teaching on godly prosperity.

In Matthew 6:24, Jesus said, "No man can serve two masters: for either he will hate the one, and love the other; or else he will hold to the one, and despise the other. Ye cannot serve God and mammon."

Let me help you with this. If you are a believer, you can agree that God created all things: "The earth is the LORD's, and the fulness thereof; the world, and they that dwell therein. For he hath founded it upon the seas, and established it upon the floods " (Ps. 24:1–2). God is the God of material things!

73

Psalm 50:10–12 states, "For every beast of the forest is mine, and the cattle upon a thousand hills. I know all the fowls of the mountains: and the wild beasts of the field are mine. If I were hungry, I would not tell thee: for the world is mine, and the fulness thereof." In Haggai 2:8 we read, "The silver is mine, and the gold is mine, saith the LORD of hosts."

Mammon, on the other hand, is a religion of the worship of material things in the place of almighty God! Mammon is making material things your god! In mammon they serve and worship money and other material things. They give their lives over completely, or at least primarily, to the quest of making money. In Christianity we recognize that money and material things are here to serve us and God's righteous purposes! God gives us richly all things to enjoy. (See 1 Timothy 6:17.) Everything we in the church stand for diametrically opposes the religion of mammon.

Romans 1:25 explains, "Who changed the truth of God into a lie, and worshipped and served the creature [created things] more than the Creator, who is blessed forever. Amen." Notice it says that they "changed the truth of God into a lie." Since the writer of Romans went on to say that they "worshipped and served the [created things] more than the Creator," then it stands that if you reverse what they changed, you would have the truth. Let's reverse it back and see: "They worshipped and served the Creator more than the [created things]." All we had to do to get it right was to reverse back what they changed to make the truth into a lie! We made the lie back into a truth!

It is a fact that we all worship things. God has no problem with that in the simple context of the word. While *worship* may be expanded to mean "religious reverential behavior," in its simplest context it is, in the Greek text, *sebazomai*, "to stand in awe; to adore." When you stood at the rim of the Grand Canyon and went, "Oooh! Ahhh! Wow," you were worshiping God's creation. Guess what? God had no problem with you worshiping His glorious handiwork. When you bought your new car and stood there going, "Nice. Very, very nice," you were again worshiping. What God would have a problem with, according to our prior scripture, is you worshiping the creation more than the Creator. Mammon changes the order of the adoration. It sets worship of the creation (e.g., gold, silver, glorious goods, etc.) above almighty God, the Creator.

You could also illustrate this out of a few words quoted in the next paragraph found in 1 Timothy 6:5. It says, "Destitute of the truth, supposing that gain is godliness." Again you can see that the philosophies of mammon turn the truth around backward and turn it into a lie. We'll test out our method by checking this out the same way. If we take the lie that "gain is godliness" and turn it around backward, it would read, "godliness is gain." Now to see if that is true we'll read 1 Timothy 4:7–8, which says, "But refuse profane and old wives' fables, and exercise thyself unto godliness. For bodily exercise profiteth little: but godliness is profitable unto all things, having promise of the life that now is, and of that which is to come. This is a faithful saying and worthy of all acceptation." So while "gain always produces godliness" is a lie, it is truth that "godliness always produces gain." You could say it like this: "Gain never produces godliness, but godliness always produces gain!"

Let me quote an entire passage found in 1 Timothy 6:3–5, 9–10, 17 to further describe the mammon philosophy:

> If any man teach otherwise, and consent not to wholesome words, even the words of our Lord Jesus Christ, and to the doctrine which is according to godliness; He is proud, knowing nothing, but doting about questions and strifes of words, whereof cometh envy, strife, railings, evil surmisings, Perverse disputings of men of corrupt minds, and destitute of the truth, supposing that gain is godliness: from such withdraw thyself.... But they that will be rich fall into temptation and a snare [fall into the trap of running after, setting their heart upon, and coming under the servitude of its evil influences], and into many foolish and hurtful lusts, which drown men in destruction and perdition. For the love of money is the root of all evil [money itself is not the evil]: which while some coveted after, they have erred from the faith, and pierced themselves through with many sorrows.... Charge them that are rich in this world, that they be not highminded, nor trust in uncertain riches, but in the living God, who giveth us richly all things to enjoy.

There is a great and very important truth for us to understand here. We must not set the center focus of our heart upon riches or anything of this world. We are to keep our primary focus set upon God. Jesus is the Lord of our lives. Everything we do or aspire to must be centered upon His will for our lives. A believer who is following after the spiritual things of God will use his faith instead of using the world's system of selfishness, greed, and covetous practices for his needs and desires. God does not expect you to have all of your focus on Him. This is important to keep you from feeling guilty as you put your concentration on "things." God does not demand that you focus only on Him. You would have to leave the world to do that. You have personal needs, goals, and desires you wish to fulfill. God understands that. He really only asks that you keep Him in the middle of it all, the center focus of all you are doing. He wants to be present in your daily life. He does not have to dominate it. He is not jealous of the things, provided you allow Him to be present by keeping Him in the center of your focus.

Spiritually speaking, only a fool would believe that mere gain of this world's goods is a sign of godliness. But there is a more sinister plot of Satan that often snares people, even Christian believers. He tempts them to go after riches, leaving God aside. They get caught up in making money. Then he tempts them to begin to put their trust in the world's system of gathering their riches. They may obsess over climbing the socially acceptable ladder of success. To keep up with society many leave their children to themselves as they busy themselves with their new home, fashionable autos, soccer, dance lessons, and the like. God somehow gets pushed out of the picture. They may become slaves to a career in order to continue climbing up to the corporate top. There is not time to play or bond with family members, and God's presence in their lives becomes less and less a part of the focus of life. Family devotions and spiritual instruction of the children go by the wayside. Eventually they may turn away from trusting God and living by principles of faith.

The result is that their intense desire and love for wealth may turn to covetousness and greed. They wake up one day and realize that they have no love (or time) for God and are no longer following His will for their lives. Their time in the Word of God, diminished by the time they must spend in their quest to keep up financially, goes by the wayside. Paul said to Timothy, they "pierce themselves through with many sorrows" (1 Tim. 6:10).

While God is stirring Himself up to get vast resources into the hands of His people, we must always guard our hearts. It is possible to get drunk on money and the influence it brings. It is also possible to get caught up in projecting a front of prosperity while going from bill to bill, payday to payday, with nothing left over for God's work. God gives us riches to serve us for our personal comfort and to be a blessing for Him and those in need. Abraham's blessing could be summed up as, "I will bless you, and you will be a blessing to many." The apostle Paul encouraged us to make faith the avenue of our blessings and our trust in God and His Word the foundation for our prosperity.

A SPECIAL WORD FOR PASTORS

I often hear church leaders who feel some overwhelming urge to constantly speak in terms that scare their people away from great riches. I heard one pastor, for example, say, "I'm afraid for some Christians who hear the prosperity message. They run with it, and its riches are very dangerous!" (This is spoken with a negative connotation on the word *run*!) You would think that if it is a promise of God found throughout the Word they would want someone in the congregation to get hold of it and "run." This pastor didn't realize it, but in continual subtleties (and some not so subtle), he actually put fear into the hearts of the people regarding great riches. One of the great needs of the church at this time is an abundance of finances in order to use modern means to spread the gospel to the whole earth.

When a believer receives the baptism of the Holy Spirit and begins speaking with tongues, we who are charismatic Christians don't gang up on him, telling him not to pray "too much" in tongues. When someone gets healed, we don't tell her not to spend too much time in healing scriptures. So why do that with God's great blessing of wealth?

The answer lies in many misunderstandings about scriptures that appear to deal with this subject. I heard one pastor preach a message along the following lines. He used 1 John 2:15–17 as his text: "Love not the world, neither the things that are in the world. If any man love the world, the love of the Father is not in him. For all that is in the world, the lust of the flesh, and the lust of the eyes, and the pride of life, is not of the Father, but is of the world. And the world passeth away, and the lust thereof: but he that doeth the will of God abideth for ever."

The pastor in reference used this scripture to say to the people, "This is speaking of the danger of riches." He went on to say, "You have to keep a balance when it comes to money!" I thought as he said that, "Well, the church certainly isn't balanced right now. We are way overbalanced on the lack and want, on the barely getting along, on the not enough or just enough side of riches!" The people in his congregation, for the most part, are having to work from morning to night and live in a very small circle in order to be in position to do that each day. They are so tired that it's hard for them to come to church because of the slavery of their lifestyle, and this pastor was "feeling led" to encourage them, "It's dangerous for you to get money and riches out of balance!" As I heard it, I thought of that Texas saying I've heard Kenneth E. Hagin say many times: "That's ignorance gone to seed!"

As I go about my daily activities, I pass many things of the world. I don't partake of them, even though they are there. I don't even know where the nightclubs, saloons, or other drinking joints are located. As I pass by them, it is not important spiritually whether I pass them in a beautiful new expensive car or in an old junker! What is important is that I develop a lifestyle that is holy and separated from the world's lusts.

The word *world* used in this context of Scripture denotes the order of things in the mind and affairs of the world's system. It is the lust and the pride that is evil. It is not the glorious things put here by God that are the problem. It is what the world is doing with those things. They operate out of the lusts and passions of their heart. It is the evil, covetous, greedy, lustful, selfish practices that God is warning us against. It is not gold and silver and money that are the problem. Rather, it is what the world is doing with it that displeases God.

As pastors looking out over our congregations, we are looking at those who are, at the very least, searching for God. We need to let them know that God wants to raise them up to be the head and not the tail, to have great ability in every area of life! God tells us in 2 Peter 1:3–4 that He has provided for us everything that pertains to life and godliness and that by using His exceeding great and precious promises to obtain these wonderful provisions, we escape the corruption that is in the world through lust.

Pastors, I encourage you never to tell your people that riches and wealth are dangerous. Tell them sin is dangerous no matter whether it is done in a Cadillac or in a broken-down old Chevy! Encourage them to use their faith, to stand strong on God's Word for the things of this life. They need someone pulling for them, someone to help them get their heart opened up and enlarged to be able to feel the liberty and freedom to obtain God's promise of wealth.

This is no different than the way some denominational churches close their people's hearts to the gifts of the Holy Ghost. They put down anyone who really is inspired about speaking in tongues or prophecy. The almighty order of the service might get interrupted! The result is that the hearts of the people don't open up to the moving of the Holy Spirit. God needs to move with financial revivals in our churches also. As pastors we have a great role to play in preparing the hearts of the congregation to receive it!

One pastor told his people, "Too much money and emphasis on wealth will drive you away from your love for God." He went on to explain that the desire to have riches is carnal. He then quoted Romans 8:6, "For to be carnally minded is death." According to him, the meaning of 3 John 2 would then be interpreted, "Beloved, I wish above all things that thou mightest prosper [become carnal and die]." He must render 2 Corinthians 9:11, "Being enriched [carnal and depraved] in every thing to all bountifulness [exceptionally carnal and depraved]." No, that is not what these scriptures mean, but that is the subtle suggestion held in many exhortations to watch out for too much money.

In actuality, I have found that there are also many, many temptations to sin when you have too little money. Whatever balance we are looking for, it need not exclude an abundance of wealth! Wealth is ability in the earth to do things. Righteous men and women need the ability, power, and influence to accomplish righteous purposes.

PASTORS WILL HAVE TO LEARN HOW TO LEAD A WEALTHY CONGREGATION!

Some pastors, especially those of smaller congregations, are afraid to let their people prosper. They don't trust them with a lot of money because they may not be able to control them as well. Some pastors have a habit of keeping a really tight rein on their people. They should be at every service, even if they have no particular responsibility to serve at that service. If they aren't there, the pastor is on the phone telling them that they are displeasing to God. Sometimes, a young convert may need a helping hand to get started with the discipline of attending church, but some pastors are out there calling folks in the congregation who have been faithfully attending for years: "Where were you last night? Don't you know that you need to be here in the service?" Many times it is not so much the welfare of the person as it is the welfare of the church service that is motivating those calls.

When someone begins prospering and we learn that they were absent last week at service because they were in New York City shopping and enjoying a time of entertainment, we immediately judge. "Oh no! They are getting worldly!" No, they are not getting worldly just because they were out of town enjoying New York City. They have just broken out of that little cycle holding most folks captive. You know, the cycle of getting up at 7:00 a.m. and being home by 6:00 p.m., then up the next day at 7:00 a.m. and home by 6:00 p.m. When people live with just enough to get by, they live in a very small circle—to work, to Walmart, to church, to work, to Walmart, to church, and so on. That is where most of our congregation members have lived. We have become accustomed to them always being available to attend every service and extra activity of the church.

We, as pastors, will have to break out of the old mold and develop a new attitude with regard to our "exceedingly wealthy flock" and the lifestyle that will come with that great ability. Our people may become globetrotters, frequenting Europe or the Far East, where the wicked rich have become accustomed to doing their shopping. There are just some things you can't find down at Walmart, things possibly not found except in some exotic place in the world.

As long as they humbly bring their tithe to their pastor and the main passion of their lives is helping get the gospel out to the world, then we'll have to learn to respond differently to their luxurious lifestyle. God is not going to bless them with great abundance to get the gospel out but refuse to let them enjoy the fruits of it in their own personal lives. Just pastor them! Help them keep Jesus as the central focus of their lives. If we resist their lifestyle we will drive them from our churches!

Here is the balance God wants you to keep in your message to believers: "And it shall be, when the LORD thy God shall have brought thee...houses full of good things...wells digged...vineyards and olive trees....A land wherein thou shalt eat bread without scarceness, thou shalt not lack any thing...a land whose stones are iron, and out of whose hills thou mayest dig brass. When thou hast eaten and are full, then thou shalt bless the LORD thy God for the good which he hath given thee....When thou...hast built goodly houses...And when thy herds and thy flocks multiply, and thy silver and gold is multiplied, and all that thou hast is multiplied...thou shalt remember the LORD thy God: for it is he that giveth thee power to get wealth, that he may establish his covenant which he sware unto thy fathers, as it is this day" (Deut. 6:10–11, 8:9–10, 12–13, 18).

GOD'S PLAN IS NOW UNFOLDING

You are going to see that God, who is the all-conquering and all-victorious One who never fails at anything and who refuses to accept anything but victory, is going to set things right in the earth before He wraps up this dispensation. Prophetic promises currently unfulfilled in the area of prosperity will come to pass.

It all started out in the right hands. In Genesis 2:10–12, we read, "And a river went out of Eden to water the garden; and from thence it was parted, and became into four heads. The name of the first is Pison: that is it which compasseth the whole land of Havilah, where there is gold. And the gold of that land is good." God created it "good"! Gold is not evil unless something has happened to it since almighty God put it there! We know that something did happen in the Garden of Eden. We know that Adam sinned, and the wickedness of mankind's heart increased. Wicked men seized upon the gold (most of the world's vast wealth), took possession of it, and made a stronghold to keep it in their control. All of this was Satan's plan to keep it out of the hands of the rightful owners of it, God's people who will favor His righteous cause!

Religion helped to forward Satan's plan. This is something that you might have overlooked, but it is a fact that we will explore. Whether you know it or not, Satan and his demonic forces go to church. One thing he does is assign demons (we call them "religious spirits") to come into a body of Christian believers. If he can't get you to leave the church and go out into the world, he'll try to get you to accept a religious philosophy designed to get you out of the truth of God's Word. He'll get some well-intentioned church leader to make you believe that God does not want you to prosper. Satan will do anything to get the rich material things of the earth into the hands of the wicked Gentile world. He knows that God intended it for the righteous and that it will eventually come to us. Satan knows that if we get our hands on it we will use it for God's righteous purposes! But when God swears to something, He sees to it that it is done. And He declared in Proverbs 13:22, "The wealth of the sinner is laid up for the just."

God Uses Gold for Adornment

I had to be gone from our pulpit one week, so I asked Peggy Clements of our congregation, who has been a part of our ministry for over thirty years, to minister in my absence. I am going to give you a synopsis of what she taught in my absence. If you think about it carefully, you may find it as profound as I did.

God likes gold! Don't ever forget this truth. Gold is not needed in heaven for currency. Money has no place in heaven, because they operate with a different, non-commercial system there. There is only one reason why there is gold in heaven: *God likes gold*! God uses wealth in heaven strictly for adornment.

There are crowns of gold (Rev. 4:4); the walls of God's heavenly city are of jasper, and the whole city is made of gold (Rev. 21:18); the foundations of the city walls are garnished with every precious gem imaginable: the first foundation is jasper, the second is sapphire, the third is agate, the fourth is emerald, the fifth is onyx, the sixth is carnelian, the seventh is chrysolite, the eighth is beryl, the ninth is topaz, the tenth is chrysoprase, the eleventh is jacinth, and the twelfth is amethyst (Rev. 21:19–20); and finally, the twelve gates are twelve pearls, each gate a single pearl, and the main street of the city is pure gold, translucent as glass (Rev. 21:21).

Now get this: *God likes gold so much, He won't live with any other surroundings except gold*!

The next section of scripture verses is quite lengthy, but also quite necessary. Let me explain why. You see, there are many skeptics who resist this type of teaching from the Bible. If we do not put this into the record, they may dispute its veracity or say we are taking something out of context. Usually when quoting the teachings of the prosperity preachers, critics will quote statements made in passing, and unfortunately the minister is not there to prove it in a contextual setting. I encourage you to read through each of the following verses of Scripture, paying close attention.

God spoke to Moses: "Tell the Israelites that they are to set aside offerings for me. Receive the offerings from everyone who is willing to give. These are the offerings I want you to receive from them: gold, silver, bronze; blue, purple, and scarlet material; fine linen; goats' hair; tanned rams' skins; dolphin skins; acacia wood; lamp oil; spices for anointing oils and for fragrant incense; onyx stones and other stones for setting in the Ephod and the Breastpiece. Let them construct a Sanctuary for me so that I can live among them. You are to construct it following the plans I've given you, the design for The Dwelling and the design for all its furnishings. First let them make a Chest using acacia wood: make it three and three-quarters feet long and two and one-quarter feet wide and deep. Cover it with a veneer of pure gold inside and out and make a molding of gold all around it. Cast four gold rings and attach them to its four feet, two rings on one side and two rings on the other. Make poles from acacia wood and cover them with a veneer of gold and insert them into the rings on the sides of the Chest for carrying the Chest. The poles are to stay in the rings; they must not be removed. Place The Testimony that I give you in the Chest. Now make a lid of pure gold for the Chest, an Atonement-Cover, three and three-quarters feet long and two and one-quarter feet wide. Sculpt two winged angels out of hammered gold for either end of the Atonement-Cover, one angel at one end, one angel at the other. Make them of one piece with the Atonement-Cover. Make the angels with their wings spread, hovering over the Atonement-Cover, facing one another but looking down on it. Set the Atonement-Cover as a lid over the Chest and place in the Chest The Testimony that I will give you. I will meet you there at set times and speak with you from above the Atonement-Cover and from between the angel-figures that are on it, speaking the commands that I have for the Israelites. Next make a Table from acacia wood. Make it three feet long, one and one-half feet wide and two and one-quarter feet high. Cover it with a veneer of pure gold. Make a molding all around it of gold. Make the border a handbreadth wide all around it and a rim of gold for the border. Make four rings of gold and attach the rings to the four legs parallel to the tabletop. They will serve as holders for the poles used to carry the Table. Make the poles of acacia wood and cover them with a veneer of gold. They will be used to carry the Table. Make plates, bowls, jars, and jugs for pouring out offerings. Make them of pure gold. Always keep fresh Bread of the Presence on the Table before me. Make a Lampstand of pure hammered gold. Make its stem and branches, cups, calyxes, and petals all of one piece. Give it six branches, three from one side and three from the other; put three cups shaped like almond blossoms, each with calyx and petals, on one branch, three on the next, and so on—the same for all six branches. On the main stem of the Lampstand, make four cups shaped like almonds, with calyx and petals, a calyx extending from under each pair of the six branches, the entire Lampstand fashioned from one piece of hammered pure gold. Make seven of these lamps for the Table. Arrange the lamps so they throw their light out in front. Make the candle snuffers and trays out of pure gold. Use a seventy-five-pound brick of pure gold to make the Lampstand and its accessories. Study the design you were given on the mountain and make everything accordingly.

—Exodus 25:8–40, The Message

I hope you did as I suggested and carefully read the preceding scripture. If so, you may have noticed that it was not enough for the items to be a golden color. It wasn't enough to just look like gold. No gold-painted wood was allowed. No costume jewels here! God made sure the people understood that the items in the temple were to be made of the real stuff. His preference had nothing to do with "investment value." That would have to do with commerce and economy. God owns everything in heaven and in earth. He needs no accounting for economic purposes. Think about it carefully! There is only one single, solitary reason why God insists on gold for His physical presence—because He loves gold for adornment!

The next time you are tempted to feel guilty standing in the jewelry shop looking at the finest, most beautiful gold and silver jewels, I want you to remember why God favors gold and the finest jewels—because He loves it for adornment!

Unless God is stingy, greedy, and put gold in the earth only for His own personal use; unless He, as a Father, resents His children enjoying the same qualities that He enjoys; then we should conclude that God likes for gold and silver to be in the hands of His own children in the earth—to enjoy! It is their portion.

The church is a reflection of the glory of God's people in the earth.

Furthermore David the king said unto all the congregation...the work is great: for the palace is not for man, but for the LORD God. Now I have prepared with all my might for the house of my God the gold for things to be made of gold, and the silver for things of silver, and the brass for things of brass, the iron for things of iron, and wood for things of wood; onyx stones, and stones to be set, glistering stones, and of divers colours, and all manner of precious stones, and marble stones in abundance. Moreover, because I have set my affection to the house of my God, I have of mine own proper good, of gold and silver, which I have given to the house of my God, over and above all that I have prepared for the holy house. Even three thousand talents of gold, of the gold of Ophir, and seven thousand talents of refined silver, to overlay the walls of the houses withal: The gold for things of gold, and the silver for things of silver, and for all manner of work to be made by the hands of artificers. And who then is willing to consecrate his service this day unto the LORD? Then the chief of the fathers and princes of the tribes of Israel and the captains of thousands and of hundreds, with the rulers of the king's work, offered willingly, And gave for the service of the house of God of gold five thousand talents and ten thousand drams, and of silver ten thousand talents, and of brass eighteen thousand talents, and one hundred thousand talents of iron. And they with whom precious stones were found gave them to the treasure of the house of the LORD, by the hand of Jehiel the Gershonite. Then the people rejoiced, for that they offered willingly, because with perfect heart they offered willingly to the LORD: and David the king also rejoiced with great joy. Wherefore David blessed the LORD before all the congregation: and David said...Thine, O LORD is the greatness, and the power, and the glory, and the victory, and the majesty: for all that is in the heaven and in the earth is thine; thine is the kingdom, O LORD, and thou art exalted as head above all. Both riches and honour come of thee, and thou reignest over all; and in thine hand is power and might; and in thine hand it is to make great, and to give strength unto all. Now therefore, our God, we thank thee, and praise thy glorious name. But who am I, and what is my people, that we should be able to offer so willingly after this sort? for all things come of thee, and of thine own have we given thee....O LORD our God, all this store that we have prepared to build thee an house for thine holy name cometh of thine hand, and is all thine own.

—I CHRONICLES 29:1–14, 16

The world is supposed to see the brightness of our glory in the earth. When God starts talking about His glory coming upon us in Isaiah 60:1–2—"Arise, shine, for thy light is come, and the glory of the LORD is risen upon thee...the LORD shall arise upon thee, and his glory shall be seen upon thee"—He also notes that the world (the rich, wicked Gentile world) will come to your light and see the "brightness of your rising" (Isa. 60:3). He goes on to say that the wealth of the world will be "converted unto thee, and the forces [Heb., *chayil*: 'wealth, riches, goods, means, substance, resources'] of the Gentiles shall come unto thee" (Isa. 60:5). Then again in Isaiah 61:6 we learn that the church would consume the riches of the Gentiles and change places with those who are now enjoying the wealth and are at ease: "But ye shall be named the Priests of the LORD: men shall call you the Ministers of our God; ye shall eat [consume] the riches of the Gentiles, and in their glory shall ye boast [Heb., *yamar*: 'to exchange, change places with and boast'] yourselves."

Again, it is very important to take time to read the entire passage of Scripture that follows. Later we will use this to show you how to release wealth and influence into your own life.

And when the queen of Sheba heard of the fame of Solomon concerning the name of the LORD, she came to prove him with hard questions. And she came to Jerusalem with a very great train, with camels that bare spices, and very much gold, and precious stones....And when the queen of Sheba had seen all Solomon's wisdom, and the house that he had built, And the meat of his table, and the sitting of his servants, and the attendance of his ministers, and their apparel, and his cup-bearers, and his ascent by which he went up unto the house of the LORD; there was no more spirit in her. And she said to the king...I believed not the words, until I came, and mine eyes had seen it: and, behold, the half was not told me...Happy are thy men, happy are these thy servants...Blessed be the LORD thy God, which delighted in thee.... Now the weight of gold that came to Solomon in one year was six hundred threescore and six talents of gold, Beside that he had of the merchantmen, and of the traffick of the spice merchants, and of all the kings of Arabia, and of the governors of the country.... Moreover the king made a great throne of ivory, and overlaid it with the best gold.... there was not the like made in any kingdom. And all king Solomon's drinking vessels were of gold, and all the vessels of the house of the forest of Lebanon [his palace in the country] were of pure gold; none were of silver: it was nothing accounted of in the days of Solomon. For the king had at sea a navy of Tharshish with the navy of Hiram: once in three years came the navy of Tharshish, bringing gold, and silver, ivory, and apes, and peacocks.... And all the earth sought to Solomon, to hear his wisdom, which God had put in his heart. And they brought every man his present, vessels of silver, and vessels of gold, and garments, and armour, and spices, horses, and mules, a rate year by year. And Solomon gathered together chariots and horsemen: and he had a thousand and four hundred chariots [a fourteen hundred car garage!], and twelve thousand horsemen [twelve thousand chauffeurs]...And the king made silver to be in Jerusalem as stones, and cedars made he to be as the sycomore trees that are in the vale, for abundance. And Solomon had horses brought out of Egypt, and linen yarn: the king's merchants received the linen yarn at a price. And a chariot came up and went out of Egypt for six hundred shekels of silver, and an horse for an hundred and fifty...for all the kings of the Hittites, and for the kings of Syria, did they bring them out by their means.

—1 Kings 10:1–2, 4–9, 14–15, 18, 20–22, 24–29

Imagine, if you can, a lifestyle supporting a fourteen-hundred-car garage with twelve thousand chauffeurs! Imagine doing that while furthering God's righteous cause!

Can you use your faith for this to happen?

I want to teach you how to prophesy this upon your family. If you are a minister I want you to prophesy it upon your church and the body of Christ. It is important that you shout it and boldly proclaim it with specific declarations over your household! David referred to it as a "shouting anointing"!

Let them shout for joy, and be glad, that favour my righteous cause: yea, let them say continually, Let the LORD be magnified, which hath pleasure in the prosperity of his servant.

—PSALM 35:27

WHAT IS THE MYSTERY BEHIND SOLOMON'S PROSPERITY PHENOMENON?

There is a wonderful revelation found in Psalm 72 indicating that what happened to Solomon had its root in the faith of his father, King David. For those learning how to walk by faith and patience, it reveals a deep truth. It shows God's divine ability to bring your words of faith to pass. It shows how powerful the tongue is as words are released. I have taught that words are like heat-seeking missiles that continue until they hit their intended mark. This psalm also reveals that we can use our faith for specific measures of wealth to occur in the earth for God's people. You can literally prophesy this kind of wealth upon your family, upon your church, and upon the ministries taking the gospel to the world! Go with me now into this important psalm.

David is soon to leave the scene through death. He begins to release his faith for his son after him. It was David's faith the apostle Paul was referring to in 2 Corinthians 4:13: "We having the same spirit of faith, according as it is written [see Psalm 116:10], I believed, and therefore have I spoken; we also believe, and therefore speak." David knew it was God's will for Solomon to prosper, so he released faith into the earth. You can do the same! Remember the words in this psalm were written before they occurred to Solomon (coming to pass even after David was dead).

Give the king thy judgments, O God, and thy righteousness unto the king's son. He shall judge thy people with righteousness, and thy poor with judgment.... In his days shall the righteous flourish [Remember that they threw the silver outside the city gates because of the abundance of gold.]; and abundance of peace... He shall have dominion also from sea to sea, and from the river unto the ends of the earth.... The kings of Tarshish and the Isles shall bring presents: the kings of Sheba and Seba shall offer gifts. Yea, all kings shall fall down before him: all nations shall serve him.... And he shall live, and to him shall be given of the gold of Sheba.

—PSALM 72:1–2, 7–8, 10–11, 15

Glory to God! It did not just happen to Solomon through chance. No! It was a product of the words of faith spoken by his father, David, long before it happened! I believe this is why God has given me this revelation of Jehovah Tsaba to give to you.

BUT DIDN'T GOD GIVE SOLOMON WEALTH BECAUSE HE ASKED FOR WISDOM INSTEAD OF RICHES?

All my life, I heard this: "God gave Solomon wealth because he sought for wisdom instead of riches." Perhaps you heard this, too. So which was it? Did his riches come as a result of the prophetic prayer of David, his father (as illustrated above), or was it a reward from God for Solomon's seeking of wisdom instead of wealth?

I certainly believe that of the two, wisdom is the greater blessing, as one primary message of the Book of Proverbs plainly reveals. Also, I am not suggesting that you do not seek for God's wisdom in your life. Just the opposite. Proverbs 4:7 (MSG) teaches us, "Above all and before all, do this: Get Wisdom! Write this at the top of your list: Get Understanding!"

Notwithstanding, and with that being said, Solomon's wealth was not given to him by God as a bonus for his asking for wisdom instead of riches. The following scripture will prove this important point:

That night, there in Gibeon, God appeared to Solomon in a dream: God said, "What can I give you? Ask." Solomon said, "You were extravagantly generous in love with David my father, and he lived faithfully in your presence, his relationships were just and his heart right. And you have persisted in this great and generous love by giving him--and this very day!--a son to sit on his throne. "And now here I am: God, my God, you have made me, your servant, ruler of the kingdom in place of David my father. I'm too young for this, a mere child! I don't know the ropes, hardly know the 'ins' and 'outs' of this job. And here I am, set down in the middle of the people you've chosen, a great people—far too many to ever count. "Here's what I want: Give me a God-listening heart so I can lead your people well, discerning the difference between good and evil. For who on their own is capable of leading your glorious people?" God, the Master, was delighted with Solomon's response. And God said to him, "Because you have asked for this and haven't grasped after a long life, or riches, or the doom of your enemies, but you have asked for the ability to lead and govern well, I'll give you what you've asked for—I'm giving you a wise and mature heart. There's never been one like you before; and there'll be no one after. As a bonus, I'm giving you both the wealth and glory you didn't ask for—there's not a king anywhere who will come up to your mark. And if you stay on course, keeping your eye on the life-map and the God-signs as your father David did, I'll also give you a long life." Solomon woke up—what a dream!"

—1 Kings 3:5–15, MSG

Did you read that carefully? *It was all a dream!* Solomon merely lay down for a night's sleep, and dreamed a dream. It all happened to him—not by him! How can you be rewarded for something that happened to you in a dream, an event you had no control over, of which you did not yourself author? Solomon didn't ask God for wisdom. *He dreamed he asked God for wisdom!* Can you see the significance of this fact? It was a prophetic dream. Yes, the dream was illustrative, and no doubt taught Solomon an important truth about wisdom, that with wisdom comes wealth and honor. But, in all actuality, it was a prophetic dream stemming from the faith of David, his father who asked God to give his son wisdom to rule His people. Psalm 72:1 says (MSG), "A Solomon psalm. Give the gift of wise rule to the king, O God, the gift of just rule to the crown prince." According to the last verse of this Psalm, it was a prayer by David for his son. Psalm 72:20 reads, (AMP) "The prayers of David son of Jesse are ended."

This is God's will for you and your family. Why not use your faith, like David? Say out loud right now: "My family will be known among the Gentiles, and my offspring among the people." Say it aloud with me now! "All that see them shall acknowledge them, that they are the seed which the LORD hath blessed" (Isa. 61:9)! Amen!

Chapter Six

JEHOVAH TSABA

JEHOVAH TSABA, THE LORD OF HOSTS, IS ON THE MOVE!

The earth is the LORD's, and the fulness thereof; the world, and they that dwell therein. For He hath founded it upon the seas, and established it upon the floods.... Who is this King of glory? The LORD of hosts [Jehovah Tsaba], he is the King of glory.

—PSALM 24:1–2, 10

Prosperity angels

HERE IS AN important revelation that up until now has held secret an obscure Jehovah name: Jehovah Tsaba (Lord of hosts)! While most believers know that "Lord of Hosts" is in the Bible, they do not know Him as Jehovah Tsaba. This end-time prosperity phenomenon requires an engagement of the ministry of the angels of God. In the Bible when God refers to the "Lord of Hosts," He is referring to the ministry of His great angelic hosts. They are His army of heavenly ministers, messengers, and warriors. While some refer to the body of Christ as "God's army," the truth is we are "His family," while the angelic order make up "His army"! I will evidence this with much Scripture.

The word *host* comes from the Hebrew *tsaba* (pronounced "tsaba, tsaw-baw") and means "a mass of persons (or fig. things), messengers espec. reg. organized for war (an army)." God's army of angels are His hosts. We will see in this study that God often manifests Himself through his name, Jehovah Tsaba (the Lord of Hosts).

While these angelic hosts answer to God and thus serve Him, they are primarily used at this time to minister (or serve) for the benefit of all born-again believers. We see this in Hebrews 1:7, 13–14: "And of the angels he saith,

Who maketh his angels spirits, and his ministers a flame of fire.…But to which of the angels said he at any time, Sit on my right hand, until I make thine enemies thy footstool? Are they not all ministering spirits, sent forth to minister for them who shall be heirs of salvation?"

There is an important connective foundational scripture in Psalm 103:20–21: "Bless the Lord, ye his angels, that excel in strength, that do his commandments, hearkening unto the voice of his word. Bless ye the Lord, all ye his hosts; ye ministers of his, that do his pleasure."

Jacob acknowledged the Lord's host in Genesis 32:1–2, "And Jacob went on his way, and the angels of God met him. And when Jacob saw them, he said, This is God's host: and he called the name of that place Mahanaim."

Therefore, the hosts referred to in the context of these scriptures are angels (or, more specifically, the ministry of God's angelic army to believers) and clearly speak of a Jehovah covenant name of God is Jehovah Tsaba, the Lord of Hosts.

Again, the primary purpose for writing this book is to bring an important revelation to light regarding supernatural prosperity happening at this moment of the church! I like connective Scripture, so let's connect another verse to Psalm 103:21. It is found in Psalm 35:27: "Let them shout for joy, and be glad, that favour my righteous cause: yea, let them say continually, Let the Lord be magnified, which hath pleasure in the prosperity of his servants." Now we'll put them together to form a particular context of Scripture. (Remember that Isaiah 28:10 declares, "For precept must be upon precept, precept upon precept; line upon line, line upon line; here a little, and there a little.") By placing these two referenced scriptures in Psalm together we get this truth: "God has pleasure in the prosperity of those who favor his righteous cause. Bless the Lord, ye his angels, all ye his hosts that do his pleasure." Angels "do his pleasure." God has pleasure in the prosperity of those who favor His righteous cause, so we can expect God to use His angelic hosts to bring prosperity to those who favor His righteous cause. Later we will detail God's righteous cause for this time. If you are going to get in on God's plan to bring you into such a wealthy place that the world will stand in awe, you are going to need, during this period, to get to know God as Jehovah Tsaba (Lord of Hosts).

You are greatly blessed to have this revelation. I believe this is why God has led you to this book at this time.

I am going to show you a clear prophetic picture of God as He releases an end-time event, a phenomenon, before the Rapture of the church. It is an inversion of wealth—a transfer of the wealth of the world into the hands of the righteous—resulting from a plunder of those who currently possess it!

Tyre–Epithet of an Ancient Economic System

Zechariah 9:3–5 states, "And Tyrus did build herself a strong hold, and heaped up silver as the dust, and fine gold as the mire of the streets. Behold, the LORD will cast her out, and he will smite her power in the sea; and she shall be devoured with fire. Ashkelon shall see it, and fear; Gaza also shall see it, and be very sorrowful, and Ekron; for her expectation shall be ashamed."

Tyrus (Tyre), known for its ability to attract money, represents an economic system of greed and dishonesty resulting in enormous but wicked monetary gains. Verse 4 lets us know that it will be overthrown. Ashkelon (which means "market" or "mart") represents our modern Wall Street stock markets. The markets will see the end of the current economic strength, and they will become fearful. Fear always has a very crippling effect on Wall Street. Ancient Gaza was a monetary stronghold and therefore represents our Federal Reserve Bank. According to Zechariah's prophecy, the Federal Reserve leader will see this great economic upheaval and "whirl and writhe in pain" and "be disappointed and confounded" (the original Hebrew uses the word "sorrowful"). Ekron, which represents "pride or haughtiness," lets us know that the world's expectation will be "disappointed, delayed, and confounded" (the original Hebrew uses the word "ashamed").

God warned the wicked of this in James 5:1–3, "Go to now, ye rich men, weep and howl for your miseries that shall come upon you. Your riches are corrupted, and your garments are motheaten. Your gold and silver is cankered; and the rust of them shall be a witness against you, and shall eat your flesh as it were fire. Ye have heaped treasure together for the last days" (the Greek, *eschatos*, is used only in scriptural reference for "the very end of the age," and never as the end of the span of a man's life). This speaks of an end-time, pre-Rapture event! God also speaks prophetically about a transfer of wealth in Job 27:13–17: "This is the portion of a wicked man with God, and the heritage of oppressors, which they shall receive of the Almighty. If his children be multiplied, it is for the sword: and his offspring shall not be satisfied with bread. Those that remain of him shall be buried in death: and his widows shall not weep. Though he heap up silver as the dust, and prepare raiment as the clay; He may prepare it, but the just shall put it on, and the innocent shall divide the silver." Psalm 146:9 also speaks of this inversion of the wealth of the world's wicked systems: "The LORD preserveth the strangers; he relieveth the fatherless and widow: but the way of the wicked he turneth upside down."

To further understand the part angels play in all of this, let's go back and hook up with our James 5:1–3 scripture and go on into verse 4: "Behold, the hire of the labourers who have reaped down your fields, which is of you kept back by fraud crieth: and the cries of them which have reaped are entered into the ears of the Lord of sabaoth." The title "Lord of Sabaoth" is the Greek transliteration of the Hebrew title "Jehovah Tsaba, Lord of Hosts."

James tells us that Jehovah Tsaba is on the move in these last days. (Remember, God does not use His name "Jehovah Tsaba" after Old Testament times until His prophetic mention of it here.) In verses 5–6 we continue reading of God's vengeance and inversion of the world's finances: "Ye have lived in pleasure on the earth, and been wanton; ye have nourished your hearts, as in a day of slaughter. Ye have condemned and killed the just; and he doth not resist you."

An Amazing Revelation! We Have Re-opened the Book of Isaiah Where Jesus Closed It in the Synagogue!

An interesting observation of Luke 4, in which Jesus stood up in the synagogue and turned to the book of the prophet Isaiah, reveals something about a "vengeance" of God in the last days of this age. It is particularly important to note that when He stood up in the synagogue He found Isaiah 61:1–2 and read from it. He read all of verse 1 but only the first half of verse 2! Verse two declares, "To proclaim the acceptable year of the LORD, and the day of the vengeance of our God; to comfort all that mourn (in Zion)."

What makes this passage so important is that in Luke 4, Jesus only read the first to proclaim the acceptable year of the Lord. He replaced the conjunction *and* with a period, just prior to Isaiah's "and the day of the vengeance of our God." Luke 4:2021 reads, "And he closed the book, and he gave it again to the minister, and sat down...And he began to say unto them, This day is this scripture fulfilled in your ears."

He could not read the last half of the verse and still proclaim it fulfilled at that time! In other words, the last half of the verse was to be fulfilled at a later time. "The day of the vengeance of our God" and the special "comfort to all that mourn in Zion" was not yet to be. We see from a careful study of the scripture that it is to be completed in a great pre-Rapture event at the very end of this age. I believe it is for *today*! It is a special blessing to "comfort all that mourn in Zion." It is to give them "beauty for ashes, the oil of joy for mourning, the garment of praise for the spirit of heaviness" (Isa. 61:3). As the "priests of the LORD...Ministers of our God," we shall consume the riches of the Gentiles, and in their glory shall we boast ourselves (Isa. 61:6).

There is a further explanation in Zechariah 1–2. You will see that God's vengeance in this case involves Him (as Jehovah Tsaba) "raising up out of his holy habitation" (Zech. 2:13). We immediately become aware of the very intense use of God's angelic hosts to set aright a terrible injustice in the earth, namely that the worldly wicked are "at ease" and "prospering" while "Zion" (God's church and its people) are downtrodden and suffering.

> And the LORD answered the angel that talked with me with good words and comfortable words. So the angel that communed with me said unto me, Cry thou, saying, Thus saith the LORD of hosts [Jehovah Tsaba]; I am jealous for Jerusalem and for Zion with a great jealousy. And I am very sore displeased with the heathen that are at ease: for I was but a little displeased, and they helped forward the affliction...Cry yet, saying, Thus saith the LORD of hosts [Jehovah Tsaba]; My cities through prosperity shall yet be spread abroad; and the LORD shall yet comfort Zion, and shall yet choose Jerusalem.
> —ZECHARIAH 1:13–15, 17

At this point, let's connect this scripture with Jesus's prophetic statement in Matthew 24:14: "And this gospel of the kingdom shall be preached in all the world for a witness unto all nations; and then shall the end come." Notice that at the very end of this age, Jesus describes a pre-Rapture event. In the prior paragraph we found that this will occur through prosperity: "Through prosperity shall [my cities, kingdom] be spread abroad; and the LORD shall yet comfort Zion."

In Zechariah 2:3, 8–11 we continue:

> And, behold, the angel that talked with me went forth, and another angel went out to meet him.... For thus saith the LORD of hosts [Jehovah Tsaba]; After the glory hath he sent me unto the nations which spoiled you: for he that toucheth you toucheth the apple of his eye. For, behold, I will shake mine hand upon them, and they shall be a spoil to their servants: and ye shall know that the LORD of hosts [Jehovah Tsaba] hath sent me. Sing and rejoice, O daughter of Zion: for, lo, I come, and I will dwell in the midst of thee, saith the LORD. And many nations shall be joined to the LORD in that day, and shall be my people: and I will dwell in the midst of thee, and thou shalt know that the LORD of hosts [Jehovah Tsaba] hath sent me unto thee.

We see here that God (as Jehovah Tsaba) sent the angel unto the nations "after the glory"! Hebrews 1:14 declares of the angels, "Are they not all ministering spirits, sent forth to minister for them who shall be heirs of salvation?" What was God's purpose in sending an angel unto the nations? He sent him after the glory, the glory of the nations!

In these scriptures you can see Jehovah Tsaba raising Himself up to manifest a special blessing for Zion, the church. He will give us the "treasures of darkness, and hidden riches in secret places" (Isa. 45:3). He will take the wealth of sinners and bring it into our possession. (See Proverbs 13:22.) Get ready now for an increase in God's anointing to take you to a greater level of prosperity, to be rich beyond anything the world could ever offer you! Your ability to serve God in the earth without limitations of any lack and want will become a reality. You will be "enriched in every thing to all bountifulness" (2 Cor. 9:11) and be able to abound to every good work. You will come into the fulness of God's will for your prosperity.

Chapter Seven

THE SECRET OF THE GLORY

Arise, shine; for thy light is come, and the glory of the LORD is risen upon thee. For, behold, the darkness shall cover the earth, and gross darkness the people: but the LORD shall arise upon thee, and his glory shall be seen upon thee.

—ISAIAH 60:1–2

LET'S REVIEW SOME scripture found in Zechariah 2:8–9: "For thus saith the LORD of hosts [Jehovah Tsaba]; After [in pursuit of] the glory hath he sent me unto the nations which spoiled [plundered] you...For, behold, I will shake mine hand upon them, and they shall be a spoil...and ye shall know that the LORD of hosts [Jehovah Tsaba] hath sent me."

In this section we are going to unfold a most wonderful revelation of prophetic truth! Psalm 24:8, 10 asks and answers a vital question for our study: "Who is this King of glory? The Lord strong and mighty, the LORD mighty in battle....Who is this King of glory? The LORD of hosts [Jehovah Tsaba], he is the King of glory."

Isaiah 6:3 depicts a scene from a vision shown to Isaiah at the throne of God. He saw the angels of God as they worshiped around the throne: "And one cried unto another, and said, Holy, holy, holy, is the LORD of hosts [Jehovah Tsaba]: the whole earth is full of his glory."

Psalm 104:24 states, "O LORD...the earth is full of thy riches." Who would you say is right now in possession of it? Who has possession of God's glory (the riches) in the earth? The invisible, international power brokers, those who control the world's wealth.

The solution to this dilemma lies with two passages in the Bible: portions of Psalm 73:3–5, 7 and Isaiah 2:7. The former states, "When I saw the prosperity of the wicked... their strength is firm... They are not in any trouble as other men... they have more than their heart could wish," the latter concluding, "Their land also is full of silver and gold, neither is their any end of their treasures."

Jehovah Tsaba is the King of Glory (Ps. 24:8–10). Until now, however, His glory has been held captive by the wicked, rich Gentile world!

Notice that God is sending angelic hosts unto the nations to "shake [His] hand upon them." For what purpose is He sending them? To shake loose the glory of the nations! That is what the whole world is watching take place at this precise moment in time. Everything that can be shaken is being shaken!

Remember that the glory shown to come on us in Isaiah 60:1–2 is designed to produce a conversion of the world's wealth to the body of Christ. Thus, Isaiah 60:2, 5, and 11 reveal, "the LORD shall arise upon thee, and his glory shall be seen upon thee... because the abundance of the sea [Moffatt: rich sea trade and wealth of nations] shall be converted unto thee.... Therefore, thy gates shall be open continually; they shall not be shut day nor night; that men may bring unto thee the forces (riches, wealth, goods, substance, means, men and other resources) of the Gentiles." Keep in mind that is the same glory that Satan illegally offered to Jesus when He tempted him in the wilderness. You will revel in the fact, as it unfolds to you, that God is shaking loose the glory and wealth of the nations of this world to give it to the church. The body of Christ will enjoy a season of tremendous prosperity to spread the gospel to the world, proceeds of which will greatly bless hurting humanity. God is going to give us the glory of the kingdoms of the world, along with all of the influence and majesty originally intended to reflect His own glory.

Created things (the things of this world) are a reflection of the glory of God. Romans 1:19–21, 23, 25 states, "Because that which may be known of God is manifest in them; for God hath shown it unto them. For the invisible things of Him from the creation of the world are clearly seen, being understood by the things that are made, even his eternal power and Godhead... they are without excuse: Because that, when they knew God, they glorified him not as God.... And they changed the glory of... God.... changed the truth of God into a lie, and worshipped and served the creature more than the Creator."

God has always had an anointing in the earth to allow His people to take back the earth's glory—its gold, silver, and desirable things.

We read about this in Haggai 2:4–5: "Yet now be strong... saith the LORD of hosts [Jehovah Tsaba]. According to the word that I covenanted with you when ye came out of Egypt, so my spirit remaineth among you: fear ye not." This refers to the anointing that came upon Israel just before leaving Egypt. God promised Abraham that his seed would come out of Egypt "with great substance." Notice what it says in Genesis 15:13–14: "And he said unto Abram, Know of a surety that thy seed shall be a stranger in a land that is not theirs, and shall serve them; and they shall afflict them four hundred years; And also that nation, whom they shall serve, will I judge: and afterward shall they come out with great substance." Israel spoiled the Egyptians of the gold, the silver, and the jewels just before their departure into the wilderness. God says that the residue of that same anointing remains and is present among us now! Why has He allowed that same anointing to remain? I believe it is because we are going to lay spoil to the world just prior to leaving in the Rapture in like manner as Israel did in Egypt.

Say aloud right now, "The same anointing that came upon Israel when it spoiled Egypt of its gold and desirable things remains here among us now!" Now just reach up into the air and signify that you are taking back that anointing for yourself right now!

Let's pick up Haggai again, beginning with verse 6 and ending with verse 11: "For thus saith the LORD of hosts [Jehovah Tsaba]; Yet once [once more], it is a little while [a later time set by God], and I will shake the heavens, and the earth, and the sea, and the dry land; And I will shake all nations, and the desire [desirable things] of all nations shall come: and I will fill this house with glory, saith the LORD of hosts [Jehovah Tsaba]. The silver is mine, and the gold is mine, saith the LORD of hosts [Jehovah Tsaba]. The glory of this latter house [in the Hebrew, *house* is used in the most varied sense, e.g., the house of Israel, house of David, house of the Jews, house of God, etc., as a family] shall be greater than of the former, saith the LORD of hosts [Jehovah Tsaba]: and in this place [it speaks here of a place in time during which this prophecy would be fulfilled] will I give peace, saith the LORD of hosts [Jehovah Tsaba]." The New Testament scripture of Hebrews 12:26 refers to this prophecy happening at the end of this age.

There are some blessings for this life that you will never receive if you do not engage the ministry of the angels of God. In the Bible, when God refers to the Lord of Hosts, He is referring to the ministry of His great angelic host. They are His armies of heavenly ministers, messengers, and warriors. Remember, the word *host* [Hebrew, *tsaba*] means "a mass of persons (or fig. things), messengers especially regularly organized for war (an army)." God's army of angels are His hosts. God often manifests Himself through His name Jehovah Tsaba, the Lord of Hosts.

While these hosts answer to God and thus serve Him, they are primarily used at this time to minister (or serve) for the benefit of all born-again believers. We see this in Hebrews 1:7, 13–14: "And of the angels he saith, Who maketh his angels spirits, and his ministers a flame of fire.... But to which of the angels said he at any time, Sit on my right hand, until I make thine enemies thy footstool? Are they not all ministering spirits, sent forth to minister for them who shall be heirs of salvation?"

We've already shared an important connective foundational scripture found in Psalm 103:20–21: "Bless the LORD, ye his angels, that excel in strength, that do his commandments, hearkening unto the voice of his word. Bless ye the LORD, all ye his hosts; ye ministers of his, that do his pleasure."

Remember these two very important foundational points: (1) the hosts referred to in the context of these scriptures are speaking of angels (or more specifically, the ministry of angels to believers), and (2) one of the covenant names of Jehovah is the Lord of Hosts.

Now let me go again to God's primary purpose for leading me to write this book: it is to bring a revelation regarding supernatural prosperity! There is presently underway a great prosperity revival taking place in the body of Christ. If you are going to get in on God's plan to bring you into a wealthy place at the end of this age, you are going to need to get to know Him as Jehovah Tsaba.

I believe God has led you to me at this time. You see, I am walking in the manifestation of what I am writing. You, too, were made to walk in this revelation when you received Jesus Christ as Lord. God's plan is for you to be very rich during this end-time period, to abundantly bless God's kingdom, and to greatly influence nations of the earth.

BREAKING THE MARGINS OF THE PAST
FREE TO OPERATE WITHOUT LIMITATIONS

Loosed from the chain

Many years ago, when I was still in my twenties, I worked for a company that required me to make calls occasionally at people's homes to collect past-due debts. In a particular succession of attempts to negotiate a payment I called on the home of a certain man.

Walking up the sidewalk approaching the front entrance of this man's house, I suddenly noticed over to my right a ferocious Doberman pinscher charging me. He came around the corner of the house! His face was all twisted as he snarled and growled angrily. His eyes had a red glow, indicating his invisible need to defend against my encroachment.

I reacted by lunging backward. About the same time the dog's charge came to an abrupt halt as he literally flipped backward. He had come to the end of his chain! He whimpered, ran around in circles for a few moments still snarling, and then took off back around the house. I recovered myself and continued to the entrance of the house.

No one was home, so I returned the next day. As I walked up the sidewalk again I saw the dog coming! With some caution I looked for and spotted the chain. With more boldness now, I smiled, waved, and made some cute remark at what I knew was the harmless animal. When he reached the end of his chain he very suddenly again flipped over backward and retreated.

I had this experience with the dog two or three more times as I continued trying to catch the owner at home. He would charge at me, just to come to the same end, as at previous times.

Then one day I made what was to be my final attempt to contact the owner of the house. On that day I went as previously described. As the Doberman came around the corner of the house, I fearlessly greeted him. I said something like, "Hello, doggy." About that time I realized a horrifying fact. The dog had passed the point where he normally flipped backward. That is when I saw that he had been "loosed from the chain!" He no longer had the prior limitations attached to him. I turned and ran back toward my car, which was sitting at the street curb. I flew over the hood of my car, slid across, and landed on the far side. I scrambled as if my life depended upon it. I opened the car door and made it inside just as the dog came around the car. It ended with him lunging at my car window! I never returned to that house ever again!

I have often recalled this event, but God especially brought it to my mind as He began teaching me about this great pre-Rapture event described as a "Prosperity Phenomenon." God said, "I have loosed you from the chain. There is no more 'end of your rope'!" He said, "In the past you have seen these prosperity truths. You would lunge out (just like that Doberman) as you began charging toward an expected end of greater success. Until now, you have had challenges that proved to limit how far you could financially go forward. You would go so far and then flip backward, just like the dog that was charging you." Again He repeated, "But now I have loosed you from the rope!" The devil was obviously in for a very big surprise the next time I started taking steps of faith in the area of finances! I was loosed!

Chapter Eight

THE LAND OF
MORE THAN ENOUGH

JEHOVAH TSABA HAS an angel to bring you in!

"Who is this King of glory; The Lord of Hosts [Jehovah Tsaba], he is the King of glory."

—PSALM 24:10

Faith in God's Word is the most powerful force in the world. Those of us who have developed our faith to work in the area of finances have experienced a wonderful measure of success. But there is so much more to come for all of us!

You will see unveiled in these pages a divine plan to prosper you. This plan is of God and is right on schedule. God's design is threefold. It is to bring you personal comfort as a believer. It is to financially sponsor the cost of spreading the gospel of the kingdom throughout the earth. It is also to bring a measure of vengeance upon the wickedness of the world as He causes their wealth to tumble into your hands!

So the angel that communed with me said unto me, Cry thou, saying, Thus saith the Lord of hosts [Jehovah Tsaba], I am jealous for Jerusalem and for Zion [the church triumphant] with a great jealousy. And I am very sore displeased with the heathen [Gentiles] that are at ease: for I was but a little displeased, and they helped forward the affliction...Cry yet saying, Thus saith the Lord of hosts [Jehovah Tsaba]; My cities [kingdom] through prosperity shall be spread abroad; and the Lord shall yet comfort Zion.

The Earth Is Full of His Riches

You can not imagine how vast are the riches of this earth. Psalm 104:24 declares, "O Lord, how manifold are thy works! In wisdom hast thou made them all: the earth is full of thy riches."

Likewise, Isaiah 6:3 says, "And one cried unto another, and said, Holy, holy, holy is the Lord of hosts [Jehovah Tsaba]: the whole earth is full of his glory."

Speaking of the rich, wicked Gentile world, Psalm 73:7 says, "Their eyes stand out with fatness: they have more than heart could wish."

Nahum 2:9 reveals a remarkable glimpse into the hoarded-up riches of the world, "Take ye the plunder of silver, take the spoil of gold: for there is none end of the store and glory out of all the pleasant furniture." The Amplified Bible renders that verse, "Take the spoil of silver, take the spoil of gold! For there is no end of the treasure, the glory and wealth of all the precious furnishings." Beck's translation says, "No limit to what is stored up." The Berkeley translation explains, "The plunder is endless." The Jerusalem Bible says, "No end to the treasure." Again Beck translates another part of the verse, "The rich abundance of delightful things," and the Berkeley version says, "All kinds of precious things, untold amounts."

Speaking of the commerce of the world, Nahum 3:16 says, "Thou hast multiplied thy merchants above the stars of heaven." Beck translates it, "Produced more businessmen than stars in the sky." The Jerusalem Bible states it, "Your commercial agents outnumber the stars." Moffatt's translation reads, "Your traders be more than the stars."

God is going to use this prophetic event to get His gospel to the ends of the earth. It will not be done through the endless, menial finances of a body of Christ who are sacrificing as they struggle to pay the bills. Gone will be the days of evangelistic telethons! Gone will be the days when churches and ministries will struggle to move forward in their visions! This will be a great time of rejoicing. If you say yes to this call, you will laugh and cry all at the same time as you rejoice along with multitudes of other believers who are favoring God's righteous cause.

A picture is painted in Isaiah 23:18: "And her merchandise [profits of trade], and her hire [wages] shall be holiness to the Lord: it shall not be treasured [laid in store] nor laid up [hoarded up]; for her merchandise [profits of trade] shall be for them that dwell before the LORD, to eat sufficiently, and for durable clothing." If you are reading this in one of the fivefold ministry offices, you really should be shouting!

The Amplified Bible states, "But her gain and her hire [the profits of Tyre's new prosperity] will be dedicated to the Lord [eventually]; it will not be treasured or stored up, for her gain will be used for those who dwell in the presence of the Lord [the ministers], that they may eat sufficiently and have durable and stately clothing [suitable for those who minister at God's altar]."

The Living Bible renders its paraphrase, "But in the end her profits will be given to the Lord. Her wealth will not be hoarded but will provide good food and fine clothing for the Lord's priests."

In Zechariah 2:3, 8–9, 11 we read, "And, behold, the angel that talked with me went forth, and another angel went out to meet him.... [And he said] For thus saith the LORD of hosts; After the glory hath he sent me unto the nations which spoiled you: for he that toucheth you toucheth the apple of his eye. For, behold, I will shake mine hand upon them, and they shall be a spoil to their servants: and ye shall know that the LORD of hosts hath sent me.... And many nations shall be joined to the LORD in that day, and shall be my people: and I will dwell in the midst of thee, and thou shalt know that the LORD of hosts [Jehovah Tsaba] hath sent me unto thee."

You can see that this prophecy is for the body of Christ during this church-age period. It is for a day when not just the Jewish people but "many nations shall be joined to the Lord." Praise God, it is for today!

God declares that He is going to send angels (His hosts) unto the nations of the world to seize their glory and bring it to us to enjoy and use to fulfill His will during these End Times.

"THE GOSPEL MUST BE PREACHED"

In Matthew 24:14 Jesus said, "And this gospel of the kingdom shall be preached in all the world for a witness unto all nations; and then shall the end come."

As Zechariah begins to prophesy, there is a divine connection between the prosperity of believers at this time and a need to propagate this gospel to the ends of the earth. Added to that is God's personal desire to bless His children with the wealth of the world. You saw this previously in Zechariah 1:14–15,

17: "So the angel that communed with me said unto me, Cry thou, saying, Thus saith the LORD of hosts [Jehovah Tsaba]; I am jealous for Jerusalem and for Zion with a great jealousy. And I am very sore displeased with the heathen that are at ease: for I was but a little displeased, and they helped forward the affliction.... Cry yet, saying, Thus saith the LORD of hosts [Jehovah Tsaba]; My cities [in ancient times ruling over two or more cities made up "a kingdom"] through prosperity shall yet be spread abroad; and the LORD shall yet comfort Zion, and shall yet choose Jerusalem."

The fact that God "shall yet choose Jerusalem" is added to speak to us of a time after the church age is completed and the church (as Zion) has been delivered up in the Rapture, when God will again return to Israel. He will deal graciously with the Jewish people and will again inhabit Jerusalem.

You will need to remember that God often mirrors certain promises in prophecy for both the Jewish nation and the church of God. That is why God mentions both Jerusalem and Zion in this prophetic word. He is describing His plans for both the Jews (Jerusalem) and Zion (the church). He says that He is very sorely displeased with the way His people (both the Jews and the church) have been treated in the earth. He is very jealous to correct this injustice. Then in verse 17, He proclaims that prosperity is what will make the real difference in the spreading of the growth of His kingdom throughout the earth.

Chapter Nine

THE PROPHECY OF THE FIFTH CHAPTER OF JAMES

W E HAVE COME a long way in our revelation of the Day of Jehovah Tsaba, that is, from a scriptural standpoint. But what about the reality of the current world condition with regard to this event? It there really a cause? Is there a vital connection to the reality of your life, of mine, and of the rest of the body of Christ?

You are about to be taken into the recesses of the evil, wicked Gentile world for a look at what we are facing. We will spend a bit of time looking at the James prophecy itself, then we will unveil a most remarkable discovery.

In James 5, God breaks a New Testament precedent. He reveals Himself directly using one of His Jehovah names, our newly revealed name, Jehovah Tsaba! The New Testament is largely silent about the Jehovah names of God. Once Jesus came, He was God in the flesh: "In him dwelleth all of the fullness of the godhead bodily. And [we] are complete in him, which is the head of all principality and power" (Col. 2:9–10).

When Peter saw the man at the Gate Beautiful in Acts 3, he did not say, "In the name of Jehovah Rapha, rise up and walk." He said, "In the name of Jesus." In Philippians 4:19 it does not say, "My God shall supply all of your need according to his riches in glory by Jehovah Jireh." Rather, it says, "...by Christ Jesus."

Now in James 5:4 God says a startling thing: "Behold, the hire of the labourers who have reaped down your fields, which is of you kept back by fraud, crieth: and the cries of them which have reaped are entered into the ears of the Lord of sabaoth [Jehovah Tsaba]." *Lord of Sabaoth* is the Greek transliteration for the Hebrew *Jehovah Tsaba.*

What is the significance of this discovery? It is that God, in this cleverly placed prophecy, is declaring that He is raising Himself up (one more time) at the very end of this age to fulfill a promise made in the Old Testament as Jehovah Tsaba, Lord of Hosts! Through James's prophecy, we have a connection, a connective scripture, a line upon a line, here a little, there a little, as spoken of in Isaiah 28:10: "For precept must be upon precept, precept upon precept; line upon line, line upon line; here a little, and there a little."

Remember, the promise is found in Haggai and again in Zechariah regarding a prosperity phenomenon in which the wealth of the evil, wicked Gentile world will be converted out of their hands and into the hands of the body of Christ. It was Jehovah Tsaba who made the promise in Haggai 2:7–8: "And I will shake all nations [Gentile world], and the desire of all nations shall come: and I will fill this house with glory, saith the LORD of hosts [Jehovah Tsaba]. The silver is mine, and the gold is mine, saith the LORD of hosts [Jehovah Tsaba]."

Again it was God as Jehovah Tsaba who echoed the same prophetic word through Zechariah 2:8–9, "For thus saith the LORD of hosts [Jehovah Tsaba]; After the glory hath he sent me unto the nations which spoiled you: for he that toucheth you toucheth the apple of his eye. For, behold, I will shake mine hand upon them, and they shall be a spoil to their servants: and ye shall know that the LORD of hosts [Jehovah Tsaba] hath sent me."

THE JAMES 5:1-6 ANOMALY

Now we will deal with the issue of this prophetic event directly from the New Testament. James, a younger brother of Jesus, was the pastor of the early period of the church at Jerusalem.

While some religious groups wish to make Mary a virgin throughout her lifetime, the Scriptures do not agree. Matthew 12:46 (AMP) tells us, "Jesus was still speaking to the people when behold, His mother and brothers stood outside, seeking to speak to Him." Again we read of Jesus in Mark 6:3 (AMP), "Is not this the Carpenter, the son of Mary and the brother of James and Joses and Judas and Simon? And are not His sisters here among us? And they took offense at Him and were hurt [that is, they disapproved of Him, and it hindered them from acknowledging His authority] and they were caused to stumble and fall." It is clear from these scriptures that Mary was the mother of a number of children.

Writing about "James, the brother of Jesus," as he became known according to custom after the death of Jesus, authors Hershel Shanks and Ben Witherington III, state in their book *The Brother of Jesus*, "James became one of the most important leaders of the emerging Christian community following the crucifixion of Jesus and the dispersion of the Twelve. Although James does not seem to have been a follower of Jesus during Jesus' lifetime, it is recorded in the New Testament that the resurrected Jesus nevertheless appeared to James (1 Corinthians 15:6). Furthermore, three years after his conversion on the road to Damascus, Paul traveled to Jerusalem, where, he tells us, he 'saw none of the apostles except James, the Lord's brother' (Galatians 1:19)."

According to the authors of *The Brother of Jesus*, quoting the second-century Hegesippus, "James was the first bishop of Jerusalem." So, James became a pastor, the head of the Jerusalem church. As you read the Book of James, you get the sense of his pastoral heart. In the first four chapters he exhorts, encourages, and teaches the Jewish-born Christians. Typical of the pastor's heart, faith, patience, love, and Christian service are all part of his ministry.

However, James 5:1–6 quickly stands out as an anomaly. The words of this gentle soul suddenly and erratically leap off of the page like the words of an Old Testament prophet, filled with fire and judgment. Then, just as quickly, beginning with the seventh verse, James returns to his gentle and pastoral nature for the remainder of the book. Those first six verses of chapter 5, clearly not written for believers but to the wicked rich, sit totally out of sync with the rest of the Book of James like some prophetic glitch.

Did James just have a momentary lapse of focus in his pastoral message? Or is it possible that the Holy Spirit moved upon him to insert, like the lost piece of an ancient prophetic puzzle, a connective piece of revelation about a pre-Rapture event spoken of by various Old Testament prophets? I believe that as we study this out together you will see James 5:1–6 as a vital connective scripture unveiling, by name, what we now have come to know as the Day of Jehovah Tsaba.

> Go to now, ye rich men, weep and howl for your miseries that shall come
> upon you. Your riches are corrupted, and your garments are motheaten.

Your gold and silver is cankered; and the rust of them shall be a witness against you, and shall eat your flesh as it were fire. Ye have heaped treasure together for the last days. Behold, the hire of the labourers who have reaped down your fields, which is of you kept back by fraud, crieth: and the cries of them which have reaped are entered into the ears of the Lord of sabaoth. Ye have lived in pleasure on the earth, and been wanton; ye have nourished your hearts, as in a day of slaughter.

—James 5:1–5

Notice that he is not speaking of a rich man, per se, but rather of an organized financial cartel. This is evidenced by the words of James 5:3: "Ye have heaped treasure together for the last days." In the Greek, the word is θησαυρι?ζωthe?saurizo? thay-sow-rid'-zo, which means "to amass or reserve (literally or figuratively), lay up (treasure), (keep) in store, (heap) treasure (together, up)." This comes from the Greek θησαυρο?ςthe?sauros thay-sow-ros', meaning "a deposit, that is, wealth (literally or figuratively), treasure." This is also from; θε?ω theo?, which is used only as an alternate in certain tenses to mean "to place (in the widest application, literally and figuratively) properly in a passive or horizontal posture."

Using the Greek word definition for the James 5:3 phrase, we understand this to be, in our language of today, a worldwide financial cartel. (If not worldwide, it could not have universal significance to the church.) Our definition speaks of "amassing financial reserves" and "keeping in store" "a deposit of wealth" in a "passive or horizontal position."

For the Last Days

One of the most pertinent portions of our verse is at the very end of the James 5:3 phrase: "Ye have heaped treasure together for the last days." This term *last days* is unique in New Testament writing in that it is only used to express the end of an era or dispensation of time. The Jamieson, Fausset, and Brown commentary renders it, "Ye have heaped together…against the last days, namely, the coming judgment of the Lord." The same Greek word is used for other expressions in New Testament Scripture speaking of the end of this dispensation. It is not used as the end of the span of a man's life but rather the end of the age of mankind as a whole, namely the end of the dispensation of time. Thayer's New Testament Greek Lexicon states concerning this phrase that it is "used substantively in phrases, of the time immediately preceding Christ's return from heaven and the consummation of the divine kingdom."

The super-rich powers spoken of who are heaping up treasures for themselves were actually hoarding them with God's eye upon them to be used to reconcile their abuse through a distribution to His church at the very end of this age. Its purpose is revealed in James 5:7–8:

> Be patient therefore, brethren, unto the coming of the Lord. Behold, the husbandman waiteth for the precious fruit of the earth, and hath long patience for it, until he receive the early and latter rain. Be ye also patient; stablish your hearts: for the coming of the Lord draweth nigh.

It would be restored to be used to usher in the great final harvest of souls into the kingdom of God at the time period immediately prior to the coming of the Lord, as suggested by the Greek word used in James's "in the last days" phrase.

THE CRY OF THE WAGES OF THE LABORERS–FRAUD!

James 5:4 says, "Behold, the hire of the labourers who have reaped down your fields, which is of you kept back by fraud, crieth." The wages of the laborers cry, "Fraud!" Notice how the rich, wicked organized cartel managed to isolate the wealth of the world into their hoards. They "kept back" true wealth from the laborers by paying them in fraudulent wages.

As we go deeply in this chapter into the current worldwide reality of this matter, you will see this scripture literally unfold before your very eyes. You will be amazed that society, including nations and their governments, has allowed such a thing to occur.

Blood, money, and greed

In his book, *Blood, Money, and Greed*, Cliff Ford, former host and coanchor of the widely acclaimed *International Intelligence Briefing* television program sponsored by Trinity Broadcasting Network, unveiled what he termed a "money trust conspiracy." In fascinating detail we are taken into the history of how the collective gold, silver, and natural resources of the world were siphoned from every echelon of the world's labor force, from blue-collar workers to the top executives of the Fortune 500 companies, and brought under the complete control and possession of a financial cartel. A few super-wealthy families now control all of the nations of the world, holding them in their economic and financial claws. While not making the connection himself, a few excerpts from Cliff Ford's book are capable of identifying in current times what James prophesied in the first six verses of the fifth chapter of James.

Cliff Ford writes:

> One would assume that once money was invented, the concept of banking evolved as a method of handling that money. In reality, banking came first. Money was an invention of banking! The invention of banking preceded that of coinage, or money. Banking originated in Ancient Mesopatamia where the royal palaces and temples provided secure places for the safe-keeping of grain and other commodities. Receipts came to be used for transfers not only to the original depositors but also to third parties. Eventually, private houses also got involved in these banking operations and laws regulating them were included in the code of Hammurabi. Those receipts were the first paper money. Paper money has always been representative of something of value, a token completely devoid of any intrinsic value of its own. A person would exchange a receipt for grain on deposit in exchange for goods or services. Historically, it was a barter system. The receipt could be "cashed in"—and that is what gave it value…Banks served as guarantors; they attested to the fact the monetary unit was in fact a representation of real wealth stored by them on deposit. Therefore, any person holding a receipt for a measure of wealth could have confidence that receipt would be exchanged on demand for the wealth it represented.

Now remember, James's prophetic outburst in those six verses of chapter 5 is accusing a rich cartel of paying the laborers with fraudulent wages. It stands that the rich cartel would have to be, by necessity, a banking cartel, since money is their invention. They control the money supply. James does not suggest that the laborers are not being paid; rather, they are being paid with fraudulent wages. It is not the laborers who are crying out. It is the wages of the laborers in James's prophecy crying out, "Fraud!" The wages are being paid in money that is in all actuality a certificate designed to represent something of real value stored away in a vault someplace.

Mr. Ford continues:

> In medieval societies, the receiver of deposits of wealth was usually the local goldsmith. By virtue of his trade, he was in the best position to guard the wealth of the community. Gold and silver were locked away in his vault, and a warehouse receipt was issued. The goldsmith would charge a small fee for storing the wealth which was deducted before the receipt was issued. The receipt was redeemable at its face value on demand. The community's confidence in the value of the receipt was directly related to their confidence in the integrity of the issuer. As deposits grew, greater numbers of transactions were completed by the exchange of these warehouse receipts. They became "as good as gold." The keepers of the gold noticed that the gold in storage remained more or less constant. As long as confidence in the receipts remained high, there was always more gold in the vault than there were receipts presented for payment. The goldsmith could safely issue more receipts for gold than the amount on deposit—in effect, creating money out of nothing. The effect was that each fraudulent receipt (emphasis not included in Mr. Ford's writing) reduced the value of the gold on deposit by the amount of the bogus receipt issued. But as long as there wasn't a "run on the bank"—that is, as long as everybody didn't show up at the same time, the thefts would remain undiscovered."

Notice that as you read Mr. Ford's historical account, you get the feeling of a white-collar crime being perpetrated. Step-by-step the methods are created to deceive and defraud those using the goldsmith's vaults who trust in the true value of their receipts. As this history lesson continues, the ability to get away with it becomes so apparent, as the goldsmiths found still another way to increase their debauchery.

Mr. Ford goes on to say:

> Our goldsmiths branched out into the loan business, following the same principle. They would lend gold, in the form of paper receipts, at interest, and take title to real property as collateral. The gold they

lent was not theirs, it was the property of the depositors. Provided there was enough gold to cover any receipts presented for payment, there was no problem. This laid the foundation of a fractional reserve monetary system, and our goldsmiths became bankers. Bankers created money out of nothing in the form of loans against which victims pledged real property. If the loan was repaid, the banker reaped a profit from money that did not exist in the form of interest. If the loan went into default, the banker took possession of real wealth by writing off as a loss money that didn't exist in the first place!...

Here's an illustration of the flaw inherent in fractional reserve banking. Our goldsmith is holding $50 worth of gold for two citizens, Fred and Bill. So the two receipts form the total number of "dollars" in circulation. Suppose Fred wanted to buy a piece of land from Bill. Bill wants $100 for it. Fred only has $50. Fred returns to the goldsmith for a $100 loan. Fred agrees to repay it at 10 percent interest in equal installments over 30 years. That works out to...$316.81. Like all mortgages, by the time Fred pays it off, the land cost him three times what it was worth. But notice something else. The total dollars in circulation is $200. But Fred is obligated to pay back $316.81. If Fred fails to repay the loan, the goldsmith then takes possession of Fred's land, writing off the "bad debt" in the process. Multiply this transaction many times, and you have just invented banking.

As Cliff Ford shows us, banking is a process of creating money out of nothing in the banker's pocket, using others who have entrusted their wealth to the bank. But it is the goldsmith who got all of the profits from the loans repaid, as well as the ability to take over the real wealth—the possession of real property, should the loan be in default. The banker is taking no risk of his own, but rather he is risking the wealth of others who have placed money on deposit. By loaning out the money on deposit by others, he is actually placing them at risk. This has been proven in the past when a run on a bank occurred, and the depositors found that their wealth wasn't actually there for them to withdraw.

In the 1980s we saw the banking and savings-and-loan scandals as the taxpayers had to bail out billions of dollars in failed institutions, yet we saw no organized outcry from the taxpayers, who to this day feel helplessly caught in the financial system that eats up a large portion of their earned income in increasingly more taxes. In fact, most people fall for the idea that the FDIC insures their deposit, guaranteeing them the safe return of their money if the bank or savings and loan failed. The problem with that reasoning is that the FDIC is a debt against your future taxes, so the bank in reality either risked your deposited money or is risking your having to fork up more taxes from your hard-earned income, should they get caught with more money loaned out than you and the other depositors collectively had left on deposit with their bank.

"Go to now, ye rich men"

As James begins his prophetic proclamation, he declares in James 5:1, "Go to now, ye rich men, weep and howl for your miseries that shall come upon you."

We cannot therefore deal with this prophecy without specifically addressing the cartel, the conglomeration of rich men, who have this prophetic woe pronounced upon them. To address them we obviously have to first find them and identify them. That is the main purpose of this chapter.

Perhaps you have heard of the Rothschild international banking family of Europe. It is interesting that they enter the picture predominately at the same time that our nation, the United States of America, was being founded. They are thought of as a family, but in reality they are a banking cartel. The head of the Rothschild family created a banking cartel when his name was yet Bauer. His goldsmith/banking business used a red shield as its logo. In German, it is Rothschild. Mr. Bauer formed his banking cartel under the name Rothschild, or "Red Shield." He then changed the family name from Bauer to Rothschild; however, Rothschild, in relation to its immense worldwide financial influence, consists not of the Rothschilds as a family but rather as a huge banking cartel. It has since become the richest and most powerful group in the world, so rich, so far above any other person or entity, that they are left out of accounting for their riches. They never make the list of the wealthiest people or business entities. They are so far above those making the popular lists that they have basically become invisible. Today, as we will see, they control the financial powers of every civilized nation on the face of the earth.

No money circulates without the Rothschilds receiving a royalty payment from it. All of the central banks of the world, including the Federal Reserve of the United States, are owned and controlled by them. When the United States Treasury wants to issue more currency into our system it must borrow its own currency from them, money that costs the Rothschild-controlled Federal Reserve Central Bank nothing to print, as they have the power to demand our government printing presses to print the money, from which they pay for the currency that is being created by them. Then they ask our government to issue them bonds backed by the personal estates of the United States taxpayers, which they may hold on demand for the currency they created and loaned to our Treasury Department.

It really gets confusing, doesn't it? Believe me when I say that they count on it being so confusing that no one will want even to show interest in the process. They count on ignorance of the masses to continue milking the workers and wage-earners of all nations out of the real wealth created by their labor. I believe that God is saying to the body of Christ, "It's time to wake up!" I believe it is time to arise, shine, for the light is come! It is time for the wealth of the wicked, evil Gentile world to come to the righteous who favor God's righteous cause.

An ancient cartoon of 1848 published throughout Europe depicted the world leaders all prostrate before a wicked, sinister Rothschild, who as illustrated here, had wielded complete control of the central banking systems of all of Europe. It also shows the near revolution unrest of the common citizens in the background.

ANON., ANBETUNG DER KÖNIGE (1848)

Cliff Ford explains further:

Two hundred and twenty plus years ago, the British Crown made a power grab, hoping to take control of the largest emerging free market in the world at that time. The original thirteen colonies founded by English settlers had grown beyond the wildest dreams of even the most optimistic investors in the New World. The potential wealth was enormous, but the settlers wanted to control that wealth themselves.

England was prepared to be accommodating, until Benjamin Franklin announced the colonists' plan to create their own central bank of issue. The American War for Independence began, therefore, not so much over political self-determination, as over who would control that wealth.

Ford clues us in further:

The British Crown arranged through Mayer Amshel Bauer to purchase an army of mercenary soldiers, the Hessians, to fight on the British side. The Americans won, the British lost, but Mayer Amshel Bauer learned an important lesson. It doesn't matter who wins or loses. Wars cost money, and there are big profits to be made. Mayer Amshel Bauer changed his last name to "Rothschild" after the red shield on the door of the [goldsmith/banking] house he shared with the Schiff family in Frankfurt, Germany. By 1812, Rothschild was worth one billion francs. His five sons founded banks in Paris, London, Austria, and Germany. The third son, Nathan, was soon the most powerful banker in England. By 1812, he was the undisputed head of the Bank of England. To England, the outcome of the Napoleonic War was critical both politically and economically. Nobody recognized that more clearly than Nathan Rothschild. If Napoleon won, England's economic woes would be just beginning. England had borrowed huge sums of money for the prosecution of that war. England's international prestige was on the line, as well as its bank balance. Her defeat would also mean she would be unable to pay off her huge debts, most of which were held by the Rothschild interests. If there was something big happening in the world of high finance, Nathan knew it first. And everybody knew it. It was therefore not surprising that all eyes were on Rothschild on June 20, 1815. News had already reached England that Napoleon's armies had begun massing for battle outside Waterloo two days before. But the outcome was still in question. In the early hours of June 20, 1815, an exhausted Rothschild courier named Rothworth gave Nathan the news. Victory was England's, and, at that point, nobody else in England knew except Rothschild.

That morning, Lord Rothschild took up his usual place by the pillar at the Exchange and began to sell. The "smart" money interpreted his move as confirmation that Napoleon had won, and that their British securities would soon be worthless. Everybody began to sell, and prices plummeted. Eventually, prices collapsed altogether. Rothschild made his move, reversing his call, and cornered the entire market in government bonds. In a few hours, he had accumulated the bulk of England's entire debt for a tiny fraction of its value. All five sons recognized that big money came not from home equity loans but from loaning money to governments. Nathan's first big loan to the British government came in 1819, a loan worth $60 million. Over the next 12 years, he loaned the Crown another $105,400,000. All told, by 1836, the Crown was in hock to Nathan Meyer Rothschild to the tune of $700 million—an enormous sum at that time. All five Rothschild banks prospered as bankers to the crowned heads of Europe. The *New York Times* wrote: "The Rothschilds were the servants of money who undertook to reconstruct the world as an image of money and its functions. We no longer have nations, but economic provinces." The power such wealth could buy was so great that another New York paper was of the opinion that, "The Kaiser had to consult Rothschild to find out whether or not he could declare war."

After the American Revolution, the European Houses of Rothschild saw an opportunity to seize control of the emerging United States. As Nathan Rothschild observed at the time, "Give me control of a nation's currency, and I care not who makes its laws." There were a couple of problems, however. The U.S. Constitution put complete control of the nation's currency in the hands of Congress and made no provision for Congress to delegate that authority. It had been established a basic currency unit, the dollar. The Currency Act of 1792 (which has never been repealed) defines a dollar as 412.5 grains of 9/10s fine silver. Consequently, a Federal Reserve Note is not a dollar in lawful US money.

The Constitutional provisions were designed to keep the American money supply out of the hands of the banking industry. The Bank of England [Rothschild] made several attempts to usurp control of the U.S. money supply. The First Bank of the United States was charted by the Rothschild Bank of England in 1791 to finance the war debt of the Revolutionary War. It was abolished by Congress in

1811. Along came the War of 1812, followed by the Second Bank of the United States, also chartered by the Rothschild Bank of England to carry the American war debt. When its charter expired in 1836, President Andrew Jackson refused to renew it, saying a central bank concentrated too much power in the hand of unelected bankers. The Rothschild Bank of England immediately divested itself of all its American holdings. Rothschild instituted a two-stage plan. First, he issued an order to extend almost unlimited credit for good security, placing plenty of money into circulation. When just about everybody of any financial standing was mortgaged to the hilt, orders were issued to restrict credit, call in outstanding loans, and reduce the overall money supply. By refusing credit to American notes and stocks, the Bank of England caused a financial panic, known to history as the Panic of 1837. This depression enabled this small group of European owners of the Bank of the United States, a private corporation, to buy up depreciated stocks for just pennies on the dollar."

Connecting the dots of "ye rich men"

A few privileged banking families always seemed to have their holdings somewhere else when an ill wind was blowing their way. One of the most "fortunate" families was the House of Morgan.

Of this Cliff Ford writes:

The House of Morgan was actually founded by an American named George Peabody. In 1837, he made a trip to England to try to round up investors for the Chesapeake Ohio Canal project. He didn't receive a very warm welcome among most British investment houses. Soon after he arrived in London, Peabody was summoned to an audience with Baron Nathan Meyer Rothschild. Rothschild recognized he was not entirely popular with London's aristocracy and proposed that Peabody be established as his proxy to represent his interests. Rothschild backed Peabody financially in return for a promise that Peabody would serve as one of the House of Rothschild's most important agents.

Ford continues:

In 1850, George Peabody met Junius P. Morgan at a London dinner party. Morgan impressed Peabody immediately, and Peabody began to take an interest in young Morgan's background. The meeting resulted in a relationship that brought Morgan into the firm as a full partner in 1854, and the firm soon became known as Peabody, Morgan, and Company. Ten years later, Peabody retired, and the firm immediately began doing business as J.P. Morgan and Company. His son, John Pierpont Morgan, was educated in European schools of higher education to round out his background. John Pierpont Morgan excelled in his father's business, branching out the family firm, eventually setting up a New York branch in partnership with Anthony Drexel of Philadelphia. Drexel, Morgan, and Company did business from 1871 to 1895. When Drexel died in 1895, the firm of J.P. Morgan & Company of New York brought the House of Morgan full circle from London to New York—a thoroughly American banking firm.

During the Wall Street Panic of 1857, many U.S. buyers were unable to pay their bills, and Morgan was expected to make good on their guarantees. Peabody and Morgan didn't have the money, either, but they knew where they could get it. According to Stanley Jackson's biography of J.P. Morgan: "The clouds lifted dramatically when the Bank of England announced a loan to Peabody of 800,000 pounds, at very reasonable interest, with the promise of further funds up to a million sterling if and when required. It was a remarkable vote of confidence as Thomas Hankey, governor of the Bank of England, had already rejected similar appeals from various other American firms who did not measure up to his standards." Those "standards" included the direct support of the House of Rothschild, to whom such sums were mere pocket change.

This is representative of the manner in which the banking elite of the Federal Reserve owe their allegiances to the London banking establishment backed by the House of Rothschild. Brown Brothers (now Brown Brothers-Harriman) was also a creation of the Rothschild European interests in 1835. The Rothschild European banks financed many other American dynasties, becoming the real power behind the Rockefeller family and "Americanized"

European banking houses like Kuhn, Loeb Co., J.M. Schroeder, and Jacob Schiff.

It is important to remember that the U.S. was founded under a barter system similar to that of ancient times. A dollar was a weight of silver. Two dollars were twice that amount in weight. A twenty dollar gold coin weighed twice as much as a ten dollar gold coin. And inflation was impossible because you could not create money out of nothing. There was no substitute for gold and silver coin. Prices remained as constant as the money supply.

Mr. Ford writes:

> Bankers didn't care much for this system, so they began issuing their own scrip—receipts for gold on deposit, just like the goldsmiths of old. Bankers got rich under the credit system they created. The government did not, due to the honest nature of the barter system. The banking establishment made several attempts to create a central banking system in the United States, but the U.S. officially remained on a gold-backed barter economy for 137 years, until 1913, when the Federal Reserve was created.

THE CREATURE FROM JEKYLL ISLAND

The Fed is a privately owned banking system run for profit. It is not a government agency. Its officers are not government officials. The Federal Reserve Act replaced the American barter economy with that of a fractional reserve, the same system used by our goldsmith to create money out of nothing, using that "phantom" money to expropriate real property.

Federal Reserve Notes replaced "Certificates of Deposit" of gold and silver. Originally, the notes were IOU. A holder of a Federal Reserve Note could demand payment from the U.S. Treasury in "lawful money" of the United States, silver and gold coin. The crash of '29 changed all of that when the demand for redemption of the Federal Reserve Notes exceeded the supply of silver and gold. You will recall that the goldsmiths were safe so long as there was not a run on their supply with receipts being cashed in. It seems to me that the Banking Reform Act of 1933 was, in reality, a bankruptcy admission by the United States. The former Republic of the United States of America was replaced by "the Corporation of the United States."

The European-family-owned Federal Reserve demanded the U.S. surrender its gold. The government demanded all citizens turn over their gold coins in return for Federal Reserve Notes, and private ownership of gold became a crime punishable by ten years and a ten thousand dollar fine.

I believe the Secretary of the Treasury is not a government employee but an employee of the bankruptcy trustees, the privately owned Federal Reserve Banks. This is a matter of historical record; check it out for yourself.

Cliff Ford states:

> The United States, in order to stay in business, pledged its collateral— the property and income of its citizens—in exchange for loans to keep the country running. The National Debt is the accrued interest due on these loans.

Paul Warburg was the first and founding governor of the Federal Reserve. In 1910, working with Senator Nelson Aldrich (maternal grandfather of the Rockefeller family), he began writing the Federal Reserve Act. The Act was put before the House on December 23, 1913—when most opposing members of Congress were home for Christmas—and it was signed into law immediately.

After the vote, Congressman Charles Lindbergh told Congress: "This act establishes the most gigantic trust on earth...When the President signs this act, the invisible government by the money power, proven to exist by the Money Trust Investigation of Congress, will be legalized...The new law will create inflation whenever the trusts want inflation."

President Woodrow Wilson signed the Federal Reserve Act into law. He was later to state:

> I am a most unhappy man. I have unwittingly ruined my country. A great industrial nation is controlled by its system of credit. Our system of credit is concentrated. The growth of the nation, therefore, and all our activities are in the hands of a few men. We have come to be one of the worst ruled, one of the most completely controlled and domi- nated Governments in the civilized world—no longer a Government by free opinion, no longer a Government by conviction and the vote of the majority, but a Government by the opinion and duress of a small group of dominant men.

A dollar was no longer a unit of measurement. Instead it became the thing it was supposed to measure, like trying to turn a quart into milk. The Federal Reserve System, a private banking system, belongs to its stockholders, who are not the American people. The only stockholders in the Fed are chartered, private banks. All the main stockholders in the current Fed are owned, dominated, and controlled by the banking families of Europe.

Cliff Ford continues:

> Paul Warburg, the first governor of the Fed became a naturalized US citizen. Now pay attention here—this is a matter of historical record, as incredible as it may sound! While Paul Warburg headed the US Federal Reserve, his brother Max headed the German Secret Service. During World War I, both sides were ably represented by members of the Warburg family. You might pause to consider that, with the Fed being in New York, perhaps this apparent conflict of interest would be picked up by the newspapers. After all, the *New York Times* built its reputation on investigative journalism. But they somehow missed the story! Perhaps it was due to the fact that the *New York Times*, during World War I, was owned by Warburg, Kuhn and Loeb! Conspiracy? You decide!
>
> To make the mix even more interesting, consider that another Warburg brother served as commercial attaché in Stockholm, a traditional listening post for warring nations. And Warburg partner Sir William Wiseman headed the British Secret Service during the same period that Max Warburg headed up the German Secret Service.
>
> Still not convinced of an international banking cartel conspiracy? Let's add this bit of information. The Schiff Brothers financed the German war effort. Another partner, Bernard Baruch, was chairman of the War Industries Board. Another key banking insider, Eugene Meyer, financed the war as chairman of the War Finance Corporation. When the war was over, they all met to sign the Treaty of Versailles. Baruch headed the War Reparations Board; Max Warburg represented German at the signing; and Paul Warburg served as advisor to President Wilson. "Cozy, isn't it?"

So how do we now connect the dots to find "ye rich men," as spoken of in James 5? Through a series of mergers and "acquisitions," the Warburgs, Schiffs, Morgans, et al., came to control giant stock investment banking firms. There are few people who have never heard of Morgan-Stanley or one of its affiliates. J.P. Morgan Bank only recently became J.P. Morgan Chase Bank, one of the largest banks in the United States. Warburg Bank (now SBC Warburg) announced in August 1997 its intention to expand its operations more deeply in the U.S., Japan, and Russia. A listing of the majority stock brokerage houses of the world read like a "family tree," with a dozen or so names broken up, all intertwined into various combinations. The same names appear as stockholders in the Federal Reserve, investment banking houses, the board of governors of the Central Banks of Europe, and so on. The roster of the new European Commission reads like a European Bankers' reunion.

Every year, the United States borrows its operating capital from the Federal Reserve at interest. Like the goldsmiths of old, for many years the Fed created that money out of nothing by issuing fraudulent receipts (Federal Reserve Notes) for gold it claimed to have in reserve. Except the gold disappeared. Most of it ended up in the hands of European banking houses that own the American banks. They are the principal stockholders in the Federal Reserve.

Again, Cliff Ford explains:

The principal stockholders in the twelve Federal Reserve Banks, either directly or through their various interlocking directorates, are:

Rothschild Bank of London
Warburg Bank of Hamburg
Rothschild Bank of Berlin
Lehman Brother of New York
Lazard Brothers of Paris
Kuhn Loeb Bank of New York
Israel Moses Seif Banks of Italy
Goldman, Sachs of New York
Warburg Bank of Amsterdam
Chase Manhattan Bank of New York (Rockefeller).

Resting on the bedrock of Manhattan Island, eighty feet below street level, is the world's largest known accumulation of gold. The gold vault of the Federal Reserve Bank of New York attracts thousands of visitors a year. The bank does not own the gold; it serves at its custodian. Almost all of the gold bars or bullion belong to foreign Central Banks and international monetary organizations controlled by the Rothschild dynasty and its various agent banks and investment houses.

It is well know that after the assassination of President Kennedy a new Federal Reserve Note was issued. President Kennedy ordered, by executive order, the abolition of debt-based fiat money. Immediately thereafter, he was assassinated. The inconsistencies surrounding his death remain unresolved almost a half-century later. Immediately following the assassination, President Johnson cancelled the order. Prior to Kennedy's death, all Federal Reserve Notes promised to "pay to the bearer on demand, in lawful United States money." After 1963, "lawful United States money" underwent a silent and illegal transformation.

The story is told that some years ago, a Mr. A. F. Davis mailed a ten-dollar Federal Reserve Note to the Treasury Department. In his letter, he called attention to the inscription on the bill, which said it was redeemable in "lawful money," and then requested that such money be sent to him. In reply, the Treasury merely sent him two five-dollar bills from a different printing series bearing a similar promise to pay. Lawful U.S. money is silver and gold coin. It was defined rather specifically, as we have already seen, by the currency Act of 1792. That promise disappeared in 1964. Our currency no longer contains a promise to pay; instead, it claims itself to be money. Today the legend reads, "This note is legal tender, for all debts, public and private." Remember, a "dollar" is a measure of a specific weight of silver (412.5 grains of nine-tenths fine silver). Take away the silver or its equivalent in gold, and a dollar is a measure of an unspecified weight of nothing! We will explain this in more detail in a later chapter titled "Vengeance to Comfort."

STILL CONNECTING THE DOTS

Who really is in control of the new Corporation of the United States, which replaced the original republic of the United States of America?

In 1933, President Roosevelt issued the following executive orders:

EO6073, EO6102 and EO6111. These executive orders were, in fact, an admission of bankruptcy of the original republic. Then, on April 5, 1933, President Roosevelt issued executive order EO6260. The executive order proclaimed:

> All persons are required to deliver, on or before May 1, 1933, all gold coins, gold bullion, and gold certificates now owned by them to a Federal Reserve Bank, branch or agency, or to any member bank of the Federal Reserve System.

This executive order established that any American citizen holding onto any gold would become an enemy of the new Corporation of the United States. Hard to believe, isn't it? The American citizens had no choice but to obey. To do otherwise would have required anarchy and rebellion against our government.

Most of us who know the history of Old Glory, think that we trace our national flag back to Betsy Ross. However, the new corporation even issued a new flag symbolizing its conquest by the international money cartel. In any courthouse or post office, that flag is on display. We see it in official photographs of our president. The gold fringe around that official flag is not decoration. It is the flag unique to the new corporation of the United States. "Old Glory" had no such fringe! No previous flag bore such a gold trim. The gold trim officially represents the country's new owners, the holders of the gold, the European Banking and Investment firms, all owned or directly controlled by the Rothschild dynasty.

Congress officially confirmed the bankruptcy of the Untied States of America under House Joint Resolution 192. It was passed during the first Session of the Seventy-Third Congress. In 1968, President Johnson issued another executive order (EO) that made the takeover complete and absolute. That EO removed all silver backing from our currency. Silver was removed from official U.S. coins, and a cheaper substitute metal took its place. Without silver, the dollar is valueless, and the United States of America became utterly insolvent, operating exclusively now as the Corporation of the United States.

To further understand who the new trustees of our republic are, it is necessary to complete our mission of "connecting of the dots." Have you ever noticed that the Fed chairman never comes to the Congress to ask them for anything? Rather, he comes to inform them of the decisions of the Federal Reserve Board. While he goes through the courtesy of appearing and "testifying" before Congress, they have no power to force him to do so, nor do they have any power over him. He shows up and, apart from any elected official, tells the government what the fiscal policy will be! Simply put, he represents an aristocracy that has the power to dictate policy to the elected officials of our government. Have you ever thought about that or wondered why he has that kind of power? I believe it is because his boss, the European-family-owned Federal Reserve Bank, now serves as the sole trustee of our nation.

Cliff Ford writes:

> As we've seen, the Federal Reserve is largely controlled by its principal stockholders. The largest stockholders in the Fed are the Rothschild Banks of London and Berlin. Nathan Meyer Rothschild began developing an American version of his European dynasty by recruiting, training and underwriting international bankers like Paul Warburg. Under Rothschild tutelage, the great banking houses of both Europe and America developed, thrived and intermarried into a kind of financial royalty. There were several branches of this "family" which has grown, as families do, by generation, until it is almost impossible to separate each from the other. The Rothschild Banks nurtured and promoted the J. Henry Schroeder Bank family. Over the generations, J. Henry Schroeder and Sons began Paul Warburg, Kuhn, Loeb and Company, who through a series of strategic intermarriages within the "royal family" saw the creation of some of the largest banking fortunes in America. The European parent banks have grown in power and influence in this country while still remaining well in the shadows. This particular branch of the "family" today controls the voting stock in Fed shareholders such as the National Bank of commerce of New York, Hanover National Bank and Chase Manhattan Bank, among others. J. Henry Schroeder Trust Company, New York's influence in American politics, includes seeing two of its former directors, John Foster Dulles and Allen Dulles, respectively, occupy the seats of US Secretary of State and Director of the CIA. Schroeders Banking family was instrumental in bringing along a young, globetrotting financier, Herbert Hoover. Hoover, who lived abroad for most of his life, was

tapped by the Rothschild dynasty as a candidate for President of the United States at a time when his only American address was the office of J.M. Schroeder Bank of New York. The home office branch of J.M Schroeder Bank served as Hitler's personal bankers during the years up to and including all of World War II.

Follow the dots carefully

Ford details some of the facts:

In early 1933, Schroeder Bank was represented by two American lawyers in a meeting with Adolf Hitler. Hitler needed money to finance his army of Brownshirts, and the bank wanted to see the power of labor unions diminished. A deal was cut, the financing was arranged, and the two American lawyers obtained the necessary contracts. Those two American lawyers were John Foster Dulles and his brother, Allen Dulles.

Continuing as Ford makes the connection of the dots:

Other familiar names in the banking and investment industry whose earliest incarnations were born under the Rothschild wing include Brown Brothers Harriman, J.P. Morgan, Morgan-Stanley, Guaranty Trust, Drexel Burnham Lambert, M.M. Warburg and Lehman Brothers. Together, they control the Federal Reserve Bank of New York, National City Bank and Hanover National Bank. Former Chairman of J. Henry Schroeder Bank, Sir Gordon Richardson was appointed in 1973 as governor of the Bank of England, an unabashed Rothschild property for over 200 years. Through this series of interlocking directorates, the corporate and banking influence of the European house of banking under the Rothschild dynasty is complete and almost unbelievable. As we have already discussed, this influence is so pervasive that most people will find it stretches the limits of credulity. And that, remember, is their greatest strength.

Let's connect one more dot

John D. Rockefeller was the patriarch of this most influential of families. John D. made his fortune drilling for oil, founded Standard Oil, and dedicated the rest of his life to acquiring everything else he could make a deal for. But early in his career, he came to the attention of the Rothschild group in London.

Cliff Ford goes on to say:

> He received his early financing for his empire from the National City Bank of Cleveland. NCB Cleveland was identified by Congressional investigators as one of three principal Rothschild banks operating in the United States at that time. Using his "seed money" from NCB Cleveland, Rockefeller set out to earn his title as the country's "robber baron." Old John D. crushed anything, or anyone who got in his way, including competitors, labor unions and attempts at regulatory legislation. Today, The Rockefeller Oil Trust, in its various guises, forms the backbone of the so-called "military industrial complex." The Rockefeller Medical Monopoly has afforded virtual control of the health care industry, while the Rockefeller Foundation has a stranglehold on the religious and educational facets of this nation, through its endowments of Public Broadcasting and specific "nondenominational" religious programming. The contributions made directly by the various Rockefeller companies, provided Hitler with all the money and material he needed to plunge the world into war. That war made huge sums of money for the "military industrial complex" of both sides. When the war was over, and the dust had cleared, there were plenty of national IOU's. There were also plenty of people who owed favors to the Rockefeller family.
>
> Chief among them was David Rockefeller. John D. founded the CFR. Later David founded the Trilateral Commission. Together the CFR and the Trilateral Commission was instrumental in the establishment of the United Nations. The land and money for the building of the UN was donated by the Rockefeller Foundation.
>
> Today, the Rothschild Bank of England holds the largest amount of US debt. But the same names that we have seen as the owners of the Federal Reserve and the Central Banks of Europe also are posted as the chief controllers of the World Bank and the IMF, which now also hold control of Japan through its loans in the 1990s to bail the banking industry of that nation out of economic chaos. In exchange

for IMF loans, the World Bank required the Central Bank of Japan, and more recently several other nations, to give it complete control of their local banking establishments within the country. Now, in almost every major civilized country, the Rothschild dynasty stands as the major controlling financial influence over the world banking community, putting them in control of the currencies of the world. No wonder Nathan Meyer Rothschild is quoted as saying, "Give me control of the currency of a nation, and I care not who makes its laws."

I think we have found the purpose of the James 5:1–6 anomaly: "Go to now, ye rich men, weep and howl for your miseries that shall come upon you" (v. 1). God, in the Book of James, is exhorting (not prophesying). Suddenly, in chapter 5, He begins a prophetic word, "Go to now, ye rich men, weep and howl for your miseries that shall come upon you. Your riches are corrupted, and your garments are motheaten. Your gold and silver [notice the mention of these items, just as Jehovah Tsaba did in Haggai] is cankered; and the rust of them shall be a witness against you, and shall eat your flesh as it were fire. Ye have heaped treasure together [notice these words taken from Old Testament statements, such as the Job 27:13–17 passage, 'This is the portion of a wicked man with God...Though he heap up silver as the dust, and prepare raiment as the clay; He may prepare it, but the just shall put it on, and the innocent shall divide the silver.'] for the last days" (James 5:1–3).

Let's rehearse again, the two significant things about the last part of James 5:3. The word *together* is important. It signifies that this is not a rich man singled out for his bad behavior, but rather God is calling to record a conglomerate of evil, wicked rich men: "Ye have heaped treasure together." Then there are the very last words of the verse, "For the last days." The Greek word *eschatos*, according to scholars, was used exclusively in Scripture to mean the end of the age. This is in reference not to their final days on earth but rather to the end of the age. This is proven by the specific form of the Greek word used in this context. It is used as an adjective. Used in the New Testament, John's Gospel identifies the "last day" as the day of the resurrection (John 6:39–40, 44, 54; 11:24). Peter understood it as the time of ultimate salvation (1 Pet. 1:5). But it will be the day of judgment for those rejecting Jesus and His Word (John 12:48). In Acts, Luke speaks of dispensation as the Last Days instituted at Pentecost (Acts 2:17). It is also used to speak of the very end of this age in 2 Timothy 3:1, 2 Peter 3:3, 1 John 2:18, and Jude 18, declaring that the "last days" will be perilous times.

The evil, wicked, rich Gentile world has heaped up its treasures for these last days. Why has God allowed it? To understand why, we must divide up James 5:1–11 into two parts: verses 1–6, written to the Gentile world, and verses 7–11, written to the body of Christ. You will recall our study of Isaiah 61:2 (the last half of the verse), which stated that God would bring "vengeance . . . to comfort all that mourn in Zion." On the one part, you have vengeance. On the other, you have comfort. Notice it is in some way the act of vengeance that is producing the comfort. The act of judgment is taking it away from the sinner and placing it into the hands of the righteous ones. It is the vengeance of taking from these evil rich men and the act of giving it to God's people who have struggled that will produce the comfort spoken of in Isaiah.

THE KEY WORD *THEREFORE*

For the first six verses of James 5, God pours out His vengeance upon the wicked rich Gentiles, declaring that they have actually been hoarding up their treasures together for the Last Days. Then in verse four, God addresses the reason for the vengeance: "Behold, the hire of the labourers who have reaped down your fields, which is of you kept back by fraud, crieth: and the cries of them which have reaped are entered into the ears of [Jehovah Tsaba] the Lord of sabaoth." (Remember, the title given here in the Book of James for God, "Lord of sabaoth," is the Greek transliterated term for the Old Testament Hebrew "Jehovah Tsaba.") This makes this verse one of the most startling scriptures in the New Testament, as God makes a unique and singular reference to one of His Jehovah names after the Old Testament.

In verse 7, at our dividing point in this scripture, we notice that as suddenly as He began addressing the evil, rich Gentile world with, "Ye rich men, weep and howl," in verse one, God now turns just as abruptly to the righteous ones, the saints of God: "Be patient therefore, brethren, unto the coming of the Lord. Behold, the husbandman waiteth for the precious fruit of the earth, and hath long patience for it, until he receive the early and latter rain. Be ye also patient; stablish your hearts: for the coming of the Lord draweth nigh" (James 5:7–8).

Why do I get excited over the word *therefore*, found in verse 7? It is because of how it ties each of us to the fallout of what is happening to the wicked rich men of the world. The word *therefore* is defined in Merriam-Webster Online Dictionary as "for that reason, consequently; because of that; on that ground; to that end." So what preceded verses 7 and 8? Verses 1–6! He is saying that His exhortation to be patient "unto the coming of the Lord" or when "the coming of the Lord draweth nigh" is connected to what He is going to do to the wicked rich of the earth. He also speaks of waiting for the early and latter rain, in which He will gather "the precious fruit of the earth."

All of the prophecies we have seen in the Old Testament of a day when He would gather the wealth of the sinner and lay it at the feet of the righteous is echoed at the very end of time in this passage in the Book of James! An Old Testament prophecy speaks of it as the Day of Jehovah Tsaba! It does not say "a day" but "the day"! He declares it as an event which I believe is looking down through the ages to the end of time—just before the coming of the Lord revealed in James 5. Let's go back to the Old Testament passage that speaks of this prophetic event. But first, remember that we covered information in Isaiah 61:1–2 and found the last half of verse two yet unfulfilled. You will recall that it spoke of "the day of the vengeance of our God...to comfort all that mourn...in Zion." That comfort is described as we read the succeeding verses. Isaiah 61:6 reads, "but ye shall named the Priests of the Lord: men shall call you the Ministers of our God: ye shall eat [consume] the riches of the Gentiles, and in their glory shall ye boast yourselves [exchange, change places with]." Revelation 1:6 states, "And hath made us [the Church] Kings and priests unto God." First Peter 2:9 also says, "but ye are a chosen generation, a royal priesthood." Second Corinthians 5:18.20 reveals, "Who hath reconciled us to himself by Jesus Christ, and hath given to us the ministry of reconciliation." Furthermore, in 2 Corinthians 3:6 we read, "Who also hath made us able ministers of the new testament.") Clearly, reference to the church is being made as the "Priests of the Lord," and "the Ministers of our God. Thus we conclude the Church to be also the same "ye" as the verse continues explaining that "ye" will consume the riches of the Gentiles, and in their glory boast ourselves. This is also undoubtedly referencing the previous chapter's rendering of Isaiah 60:5, "The abundance of the sea [Moffatt: rich sea trade and the wealth of nations] be converted [Hebrew: turn about or over, overturn, overthrow, cause to tumble, turn back again] unto thee."

You can see from these verses that God's purpose in visiting an economic vengeance upon the Gentile world is necessary for the economic comfort that is to come upon the Christian believers. This is what Isaiah was speaking of in the last half of Isaiah 61:2, which Jesus did not include in His prophetic use of that scripture in Luke 4:17–21. Isaiah was speaking of an event that we have covered from many different prophetic scriptures. He was speaking of "the Isaiah 2:12 event." He was speaking of "the Isaiah 14:24–27 event." He was speaking of "the Isaiah 23:9 event." He was speaking of the "Haggai 2:5–9 event." He was speaking of "the Zechariah 2:8–11 event." He was speaking of "the Malachi 3:16–18 event," and finally, praise God, He was speaking of the "James 5 event"! All of these events are one and the same event, which God made reference to in Hebrews 12:26–27, "But now he hath promised, saying, Yet once more I shake not the earth only, but also heaven. And this word, Yet once more, signifieth the removing of those things that are shaken, as of things that are made, that those things which cannot be shaken may remain."

With this information fresh in our minds, let's go back to the Old Testament prophecy that speaks specifically of the Day of Jehovah Tsaba. In Isaiah 2:10–12 God says, "Enter into the rock, and hide thee in the dust, for fear of the LORD, and for the glory of his majesty. The lofty looks of man shall be humbled, and the haughtiness of men shall be bowed down, and the LORD alone shall be exalted in that day. [I believe this is in reference to the day of vengeance against the wicked rich of James 5:4, "The cries…are entered into the ears of the Lord of sabaoth (Jehovah Tsaba)."] For the day of [Jehovah Tsaba] the LORD of hosts shall be upon every one that is proud and lofty, and upon every one that is lifted up; and he shall be brought low." Continuing to speak of the event, the prophet says in Isaiah 14:24, "The LORD of hosts [Jehovah Tsaba] hath sworn, saying, Surely as I have thought, so shall it come to pass; and as I have purposed, so shall it stand."

God then proceeds to focus the next verse specifically upon a local event to be for that current period against the Assyrians. While verse 25 only addresses God's local vengeance upon the Assyrians, in the next two verses (verses 26–27) He speaks of a more distant event in which the whole earth would be affected: "This is the purpose that is purposed upon the whole earth:

and this is the hand that is stretched out upon all the nations. For the LORD of hosts hath purposed, and who shall disannul it? and his hand is stretched out, and who shall turn it back?"

So, in one breath God speaks of two separate events producing the same judgement, except one is local and the other is to come upon the whole earth. God has always hidden His prophetic words for the church in this manner. You might say that He chose a local situation to demonstrate what He would later do on a vastly larger scale. It is this larger scale portion of the prophecy that He refers to as the Day of Jehovah Tsaba. The Day of Jehovah Tsaba is pointing to what James 5 reveals as "the cries...have entered into the ears of the Lord of sabaoth."

Let's pick up some other important connective scriptures to this prophetic word. Isaiah 23:9 says, "The LORD of hosts [Jehovah Tsaba] hath purposed it, to stain the pride of all glory, and to bring into contempt all the honorable of the earth."

Notice a similarity between these Old Testament prophesies and James 5. In Isaiah 23:1, speaking of the local event of this word, He says, "Howl, ye ships of Tarshish." Later, in Isaiah 23:14, God says again, "Howl, ye ships of Tarshish: for your [economic] strength is laid waste." To the local event He prophesies, "Howl!"

Now look at the common threads that run between that prophecy and the one in James 5! The James passage begins, "Go to now, ye rich men, weep and howl for your miseries that shall come upon you....Behold, the hire of the labourers who have reaped down your fields, which is of you kept back by fraud, crieth: and the cries of they which have reaped are entered into the ears of the Lord of sabaoth" (vv. 1, 4).

You can see the threads that tie these prophecies together. In Isaiah God speaks of the Day of Jehovah Tsaba and says, "Howl!" In James, He says, "Weep and howl," as the cries enter into the ears of Lord of Sabaoth [Jehovah Tsaba]! Isaiah, Haggai, Zechariah, and Malachi all point to a similar event out in the distant future at the end of this age!

All down through time God allowed the collective stronghold of wealth to accumulate for His own purpose. Jesus made the first one and one-half verses of Isaiah 61 unique to the particular period while He was here on earth.

Halfway through verse 2 He closed the book, but in James 5 God is reopening the book!

Now, by the Spirit of God, as I write this book and bring this message to you, I am opening it where Jesus left off. Beginning there I am declaring a new day—*today*! I am declaring to you, "This day is this scripture fulfilled in your ears" (Luke 4:21)! The multitude of burden-bearing labor to bring goods (such as eighteen-wheelers) will overwhelm you. (See Isaiah 60:6.) Your gates will be open continually; they will not be shut day nor night, that men may bring unto you the forces ("riches, wealth, substance, goods, means, men, and other resources") of the Gentiles, the wicked rich spoken of in the fifth chapter of James. (See Isaiah 60:11.) We who are called the priests of the Lord, the ministers of our God, the body of Christ, the church of the living God (Rev. 1:6), shall eat (consume) the riches of the Gentiles, and in their glory shall we boast (the word *boast* in the Hebrew means "to exchange, change places with, to boast one's self"] ourselves in it! (See Isaiah 61:6–7.) Collectively, the rich of the earth will weep and howl for the miseries that shall come upon them!

Also, concurrently, the righteous ones of the earth crying out to God in their struggles who have been trodden down by the fraud and abuse of this conglomerate of wealthy individuals in society will be heard by Jehovah Tsaba, the Lord of Hosts (the Lord of angelic armies)! God will send His angelic army out to the nations that plundered us. He will find the sinners that have heaped up their silver, their gold, and their fine raiment, and He will cause it to be converted unto us! *At this moment, daily headlines are filled with news of confounding global disastrous conditions destabilizing the world, with governments paralyzed in the clutches. The angel of Zechariah 2, destined to shake all nations, has gone out after the glory!*

Collectively, we as the body of Christ will rise up to send the gospel into all of the earth. We will saturate the earth with a great latter-rain period to bring in God's precious fruit of the earth. Then the end will come! The Rapture of the church will take place, signaling the end of this age!

I want to share another scripture with you from the Old Testament that I believe bears witness to this event found in James. It is taken from Isaiah 2. Isaiah 2:2 begins, "And it shall come to pass in the last days [Remember our study on the meaning of those words, *the last days*. It is the same as Peter quoted on the Day of Pentecost from the prophet Joel, which also begins in

Joel 2:28, "And it shall come to pass afterward."] that the mountain of the LORD's house shall be established in the top of the mountains." It is interesting in my study of the Hebrew language that the writers not only used this word *mountain* in a literal sense. They also used it as an idiom, and when used in this sense, figuratively, the word means "promotion."

Now what would happen if we took that verse and used it not as a literal mountain but in terms of promotion? Additionally, the word *house* is intended in the widest sense as "a family" instead of the way we normally think of it, as a building. Also, there is the word *top* that I find equally interesting. In the Hebrew it means, "chief, high place, head, far above." Let's venture to quote that same verse, using the figurative meanings: "It shall come to pass in the last days that the [promotion] of the Lord's [family] shall be established in the [chief or highest places] of [promotion]."

Using that same context of thought, let's go on with the remainder of the passage there in Isaiah 2:2–3, again making substitutions in order to read it in a figurative setting: "All nations [Gentiles] shall flow unto it. And many people shall go and say, Come ye, and let us go up ["Arise, shine; for thy light is come," Isaiah 60:1] to the [promotion] of the LORD...and he will teach us his ways, and we will walk in his paths." Could it be that Isaiah 2 was looking not only through certain events to come but also to the very end of the age?

I want to conclude our study of James with one other observation. The prophetic portion of this scripture ends as abruptly as it began. In verse eleven, James declares, "Behold, we count them happy which endure. Ye have heard of the patience of Job, and have seen the end of the Lord; that the Lord is very pitiful [compassionate], and of tender mercy."

God concludes this prophecy of James with a great clue regarding its timing: the end of the Lord is very, very good!

Chapter Ten

A VENGEANCE TO COMFORT

PROPHETICALLY UNDERSTANDING 9/11: THE WORLD TRADE CENTER DISASTER

IS IT POSSIBLE that Scripture details this historic event? I do not consider myself to be in the office of a prophet, however, in the offices of both teacher and pastor, I believe God spoke prophetically to me regarding 9/11 from the Scriptures.

This chapter may occasionally seem redundant. You will find that we repeat some of the information already covered in previous chapters. However, you may consider it to be a refresher of all that we have already shown you. Please bear with that, because you will also find this chapter to be unique in that it will speak directly to the 9/11 incident, in which an attack was made upon United States soil on September 11, 2001, and also of the economic global shaking that is occurring at this very time.

What is happening to our nation and the world at this moment? Is it the devil or God? In this chapter we make the connection of the exact moment when Jehovah Tsaba declared war, not on the United States of America but on the rich, haughty, global economic powers of this world's kingdom.

GOD'S NAME JEHOVAH TSABA

We have shown you this prophetic event concerning a Jehovah name that has been obscured in the church. The name is Jehovah Tsaba, clearly identified as a name of God in both the Old and New Testament writings.

You will recall the name is derived from two Hebrew words in the Old Testament Scriptures. It is translated in the King James Version as "the Lord of Hosts."

- Lord (הוהההוהי): the Self-existent or eternal; transliterated as Jehovah, the Jewish national name of God, the Lord

- Hosts (אבצצבא): a mass of persons (or figurative things), especially regularly organized for war (an army); by implication a campaign, literally or figuratively (specifically hardship, worship), appointed time, army, battle, company, host, service, soldiers, waiting upon, war (-fare)

Psalm 24:8–10 clearly defines a title, character, and Jehovah name of God:

Who is this King of glory? [Here we have a title.] The Lord [Jehovah] strong and mighty, the Lord mighty in battle. [Here we have a character description.] Lift up your heads, O ye gates; even lift them up, ye everlasting doors; and the King of glory shall come in. Who is this King of glory? [Again He is referenced by title.] The Lord of hosts [Jehovah Tsaba; here we have His Jehovah name], he is the King of glory. Selah.

It is a little-known fact that the Scriptures declare an event called the Day of Jehovah Tsaba. By declaring it a day, the Scriptures identify it as "an appointment, an appointed time" (to the Hebrew mind, a *moed*). This means that Jehovah Tsaba has an appointment set to fulfill His purpose. I will share more about the Day of Jehovah Tsaba later in this writing. But first, let's learn more about this powerful name.

Isaiah 47:4 speaks concerning this Jehovah name: "As for our redeemer, the Lord of hosts [Jehovah Tsaba] is his name, the Holy One of Israel." The church has not known Jehovah Tsaba. We have known our Father God as Jehovah Shalom, our Peace. We have known Him as Jehovah Jireh, our Provider, and as Jehovah Rapha, our Healer. We have also been introduced to God as Jehovah Tsidkenu, our Righteousness; Jehovah Shammah, the Lord is Present; and Jehovah Elohim, the Creator; and other character-identifying names, all foreshadowing our current rights and privileges now in Christ Jesus. But up to this point we have not known Him as Jehovah Tsaba, the Lord strong and mighty in battle, the King of glory! What little is known has been mostly misunderstood.

Who is Jehovah Tsaba? What is He like, and what attributes identify

His character? The body of Christ and the world are about to learn, in no uncertain terms, the answers to these questions.

Relevance of Jehovah Tsaba

From Psalm 24:8, we learn that He is "the LORD [Jehovah] strong and mighty, the LORD mighty in battle." In Psalm 24:10 we find, "The LORD of hosts [Jehovah Tsaba], he is the King of glory."

We also find specifically that Jehovah Tsaba is in reality our Redeemer. Isaiah 47:4 tells us, "As for our redeemer, the LORD of hosts [Jehovah Tsaba] is his name, the Holy One of Israel."

We get acquainted with Him in David's battle against Goliath.

> Then said David to the Philistine, Thou comest to me with a sword, and with a spear, and with a shield: but I come to thee in the name of the LORD of hosts [Jehovah Tsaba], the God of the armies of Israel, whom thou hast defied. And all this assembly shall know that the LORD saveth not with sword and spear: for the battle is the LORD 's, and he will give you into our hands.
>
> —I SAMUEL 17:45, 47

So David, in ancient Israel, knew Jehovah Tsaba as the Lord, strong, mighty in battle.

Let's review Isaiah 60:1–3, 5–6, 11:

> Arise, shine; for thy light is come, and the glory of the LORD [Jehovah] is risen upon thee. For, behold, the darkness shall cover the earth, and gross darkness the people: but the LORD shall arise upon thee, and his glory shall be seen upon thee. And the Gentiles shall come to thy light, and kings to the brightness of thy rising.... because the abundance of the sea [MOFFATT: "the rich sea trade and the wealth of nations"] shall be converted unto thee, the forces [Hebrew, "riches, wealth, goods, substance, means, men and other resources"] of the Gentiles shall come unto thee. The multitude of camels [Hebrew, *gamal*, "burden bearing labor to bring goods"] shall cover [Hebrew, "overwhelm"] thee.... Therefore thy gates shall be open continually;

> they shall not be shut day nor night; that men may bring unto thee
> the forces of the Gentiles, and that their kings may be brought.

I believe this will be the most exciting period in the history of the church age. The wealth of the wicked Gentile world, the individual wealth of the nations, is coming into the hands of the righteous. The lifestyle of believers during this last great end-time period will stagger the imagination of the world in their ability to live richly and to take the gospel of the kingdom of God to this lost generation.

Manifesting a great excellence, Christian believers will show love, joy, peace, and humility with a material opulence that previously has primarily been associated with pride, deceit, covetousness, and greed. The glorious lifestyles of King David and his son, King Solomon, along with that of Israel as a nation during their respective reigns, are displayed by God in the Scriptures as a part of His will for His people.

A global revival will be the result of the unselfishness and generosity of a group that is revealed in Scripture as "the rich and righteous." Psalm 112:3 declares, "Wealth and riches shall be in his house: and his righteousness endureth for ever."

As we will further scripturally demonstrate in the pages of this book, the church institutions will become the wealthiest in the world as the judgment of God brings the world's economy to a plunder, bringing about a transfer of wealth into the hands of the body of Christ. In the past they have stretched their pennies and nickels to care for humanity, but during this time they will be empowered to do so with great abundance.

Masses of believers will experience a no-budget anointing, foreshadowed by Joseph in Genesis 41:49: "And Joseph gathered corn as the sand of the sea, very much, until he left numbering; for it was without number." Peterson's *The Message* translation renders the verse, "Joseph collected so much grain—it was like the sand of the ocean!—that he finally quit keeping track."

THE BOOK IS BEING REOPENED

> And when he had opened the book, he found the place where it was
> written, The Spirit of the Lord is upon me, because he hath anointed
> me to preach the gospel to the poor; he hath sent me to heal the bro-
> kenhearted, to preach deliverance to the captives, and recovering of

sight to the blind, to set at liberty them that are bruised, To preach the acceptable year of the Lord. And he closed the book, and he gave it again to the minister, and sat down...And he began to say unto them, This day is this scripture fulfilled in your ears.

—LUKE 4:17–21

You will notice that Jesus opened the book, He read to them, and then He closed the book and declared, "This day is this scripture fulfilled in your ears."

As briefly mentioned at the end of chapter 6 in Luke's Gospel, there is clearly a period at the end of the nineteenth verse. So, going back to Isaiah, where He was reading from, you would expect to also find a period at the end of those words, just as you do in Luke 4:19. Why would Jesus stop in the middle of a sentence, just before the conjunction *and* as He was reading? Why did He suddenly stop?

Luke says that Jesus closed the book. When He said, "This day is this scripture fulfilled in your ears," He was finished. It would be approximately two thousand years before the Holy Spirit would reopen the book and begin to bring revelation from the unread portion of that scripture to make it relevant to a generation of believers at the very end of this age. He is doing that today!

We see that those specific words, "to preach the acceptable year of the Lord," were all that Jesus was allowed to declare to be fulfilled in that particular time. "This day is this scripture [and only this portion of scripture] fulfilled in your ears" is evidenced by "and he closed the book."

VENGEANCE TO COMFORT!

Leaving Luke 4 and going back to the actual place in Isaiah where Jesus chose to read, we get a more detailed accounting.

The Spirit of the Lord GOD is upon me; because the LORD hath anointed me to preach good tidings unto the meek; he hath sent me to bind up the brokenhearted, to proclaim liberty to the captives, and the opening of the prison to them that are bound; To proclaim the acceptable year of the LORD [Isaiah places a conjunction where Jesus closed the book], and the day of vengeance of our God; to comfort all that mourn; To appoint unto them that mourn in Zion, to give unto them beauty for ashes, the oil of joy for mourning, the garment of praise for the spirit of

> heaviness....But ye shall be named the Priests of the LORD: men shall call you the Ministers of our God: ye shall eat [Heb., "consume, devour"] the riches [Heb., "riches, wealth, goods, substance, means, men and other resources"] of the Gentiles, and in their glory shall ye boast yourselves.
>
> —ISAIAH 61:1–3, 6

No longer Gentiles

> Wherefore remember, that ye being in time past Gentiles in the flesh, who are called Uncircumcision by that which is called the Circumcision in the flesh made by hands; That at that time ye were without Christ, being aliens from the commonwealth of Israel, and strangers from the covenants of promise, having no hope, and without God in the world: But now in Christ Jesus ye who sometimes were far off are made nigh by the blood of Christ.
>
> —EPHESIANS 2:11–13

Many years ago in Des Moines, Iowa, we were blessed to be in a Kenneth E. Hagin ministers' conference. He chose as his nightly text 1 Corinthians 10:32, "Give none offence, neither to the Jews, nor to the Gentiles, nor to the church of God." He masterfully clarified that in the above scripture, Paul made a distinction between the division of the classes of humanity in the Old Testament and that of the New Testament church. In this scripture the apostle gave the church of God a separate, unique national distinction.

In the past, there were just the Jews and Gentiles. We read in the prior Ephesians reference that we were Gentiles in times past. Brother Hagin showed us in 1 Corinthians 10:32 that we are distinguished from both the Jews and the Gentiles. Some were Jews prior to Christ, some were Gentiles, but as believers in Jesus Christ all are now one in Him.

> There is [now no distinction] neither Jew nor Greek [Gentile]...for ye are all one in Christ Jesus.
>
> —GALATIANS 3:28

Are there still Gentiles in the world? Are there still Jews? Yes, of course! With great respect to the Jewish nation of Israel, God has prophetic plans for them. In fact, they play a major role in the earth following the catching away of the church in the Rapture event. But if you have accepted Christ Jesus as Lord and Savior, as Messiah, then you have been brought out of your former place among the two ancient classes (Jew and Gentile), and as a part of the body of Christ you are now the church of God.

It is important to keep this truth in mind when reading from the Old Testament prophecies concerning the end of this age. In fact, in the next referenced verse we see the church appointed as a new nation, a new holy nation. Who makes up this new nation? And who are named the "priest of the Lord"? Who are called the "ministers of our God"?

> But ye [the New Testament body of Christ] are a chosen generation, a royal priesthood, an holy nation, a peculiar people; that ye should shew forth [Greek, "publish, minister, celebrate"] the praises of him who hath called you out of darkness into his marvellous light; Which in time past were not a people, but are now the people of God: which had not obtained mercy, but now have obtained mercy.
>
> —1 Peter 2:9–10

Praise God! Isaiah's prophecy identifies the church as the people of God in line to receive this prophecy. Israel as a nation is never named in Scripture as the priests of the Lord, nor the ministers of our God. This is a very important point in recognizing who Isaiah's prophecy is identifying. The Jews have never been allowed to partake of the priesthood except for only one tribe, that of Levi. As a nation, they are never given the privilege of boldly coming before God's throne as priests and ministers. Even after the Rapture, when God again visits Israel to take a remnant for Himself, even then the ancient priesthood will be reestablished from the one tribe set apart for priesthood, the Levites. But we, the body of Christ, all have that right and privilege in Christ Jesus.

As you can see, Jesus was unable to claim the fulfillment of the rest of the scripture for the people in the synagogue that Sabbath day. It was for a generation in the Last Days that were yet to be established and birthed into the earth. And to that generation He declared, "Ye shall eat [Heb., 'consume, devour'] the riches [Heb., 'riches, wealth, goods, substance, means, men, and other resources'] of the Gentiles [nations], and in their glory shall ye boast yourselves" (Isa. 61:6).

Isaiah called it a conversion of the world's wealth into the hands of God's people. Isaiah 60:5 says, "Then thou shalt see, and flow together, and thine heart shall fear [Heb., 'tremble in awe; be made to shake'], and be enlarged [Heb., 'be made larger, make room for more']; because the abundance of the sea [Moffatt Translation, 'rich sea trade and wealth of nations'] shall be converted unto thee, the forces ['riches, wealth, goods, substance, means, men and other resources'] of the Gentiles shall come unto thee."

We can see from these scriptures that God speaks of a prosperity phenomenon for His people!

THE ANGEL OF GLORY GOES OUT AFTER THE PLUNDER

In our assignment to bring the revelation of Jehovah Tsaba and a great prosperity phenomenon to the body of Christ, we have shared that Jehovah Tsaba, the King of glory, the Lord strong, mighty in battle, is arising in these latter days of time to fulfill a great pre-Rapture event.

In selected portions of Zechariah 2:8–13, we see that an angel of God was sent to Zechariah. The angel speaks in the name of Jehovah Tsaba with a prophetic announcement.

> For thus saith the LORD of hosts [Jehovah Tsaba]; After the glory hath he sent me unto the nations which spoiled you: for he that toucheth you toucheth the apple of his eye. For, behold, I will shake mine hand upon them, and they shall be a spoil to their servants: and ye shall know that the LORD of hosts [Jehovah Tsaba] hath sent me. Sing and rejoice, O daughter [Heb., figuratively, "branch"] of Zion: for, lo, I come, and I will dwell in the midst of thee, saith the LORD. And many nations shall be joined to the LORD in that day, and shall be my people: and I will dwell in the midst of thee, and thou shalt know that the LORD of hosts hath sent me unto thee.... Be silent, O all flesh, before the LORD [Jehovah Tsaba]: for he is raised up out of his holy habitation.
>
> —ZECHARIAH 2:8–11, 13

We are told that God has sent a great angel. The angel declares that Jehovah Tsaba (the King of glory, the Lord strong, mighty in battle) has sent him out with a mission in pursuit of the glory of the nations! The angel declares that he will shake his hand upon them, and they (the wicked Gentile nations) will be plundered of their individual wealth. This is representative of the angel going out "after the glory."

Haggai 2:4–9 joins together with Zechariah to fill in the prophetic picture:

> Yet now be strong, O Zerubbabel, saith the LORD; and be strong, O Joshua, son of Josedech, the high priest; and be strong, all ye people of the land, saith the LORD, and work: for I am with you, saith the LORD of hosts [Jehovah Tsaba]: According to the word that I covenanted with you when ye came out of Egypt, so my spirit remaineth among you: fear ye not. For thus saith the LORD of hosts [Jehovah Tsaba]; Yet once, it is a little while, and I will shake the heavens, and the earth, and the sea, and the dry land; And I will shake all nations, and the desire of all nations shall come: and I will fill this house with glory, saith the LORD of hosts [Jehovah Tsaba]. The silver is mine, and the gold is mine, saith the LORD of hosts [Jehovah Tsaba]. The glory of this latter house shall be greater than of the former, saith the LORD of hosts: and in this place will I give peace, saith the LORD of hosts [Jehovah Tsaba].

Is there any doubt on whose behalf the prophet has spoken? Between Zechariah and Haggai, God is declaring war on the glory and wealth of the secular nations of the world.

JEHOVAH TSABA APPEARS AT THE END OF THE AGE IN NEW TESTAMENT SCRIPTURE

After making these great prophetic statements in the name of Jehovah Tsaba, the Bible becomes silent regarding it. The Scriptures seem to be waiting until the end of the age to revive and begin its fulfillment.

In the New Testament, God does not reveal Himself by the name of Jehovah until suddenly in James 5:1–8 when the Scriptures break precedent. We begin to hear the same familiar theme of Isaiah, Haggai, and Zechariah.

> Go to now, ye rich men, weep and howl for your miseries that shall come upon you. Your riches are corrupted, and your garments are motheaten. Your gold and silver is cankered; and the rust of them shall be a witness against you, and shall eat your flesh as it were fire. Ye

have heaped treasure together for the last days. [*Thayer's New Testament Greek Lexicon* gives this definition: "'the last days,' a term used in the New Testament Greek only for 'the end of the age,' an end of time event. See also Acts 2:17; 2 Timothy 3:1; 2 Peter 3:3."] Behold, the hire [Heb., "wages, currency system"] of the labourers who have reaped down your fields, which is of you kept back by fraud [debt-based world currency system not backed by real worth], crieth: and the cries of them which have reaped are entered into the ears of the Lord of sabaoth [Greek transliteration for the Hebrew "LORD of hosts," Jehovah Tsaba]. Ye have lived in pleasure on the earth, and been wanton; ye have nourished your hearts, as in a day of slaughter. Ye have condemned and killed the just; and he doth not resist you. Be patient therefore, brethren, unto the coming of the Lord. [Notice how long we must be patient for the fulfillment of this prophetic word—until the end of this age!] Behold, the husbandman waiteth for the precious fruit of the earth, and hath long patience for it, until he receive the early and latter rain. [He lets us know that the delay is so that the wealth conversion will be used for the end-time harvest, to get in the last great mass of souls.] Be ye also patient; stablish your hearts: for the coming of the Lord draweth nigh.

—JAMES 5:1–8

As with Job, the latter will be greater than the former. The end of the Lord is very, very, good!

WORLD TRADE CENTER TOWERS: NOT A CATHEDRAL, NOT A USA LANDMARK—AN ICON OF A GLOBAL GROUP OF THE WICKED RICH!

Now, you may be still asking, "But what does all of this have to do with the attack upon the World Trade Center complex on September 11, 2001, in Manhattan, New York?"

To understand, you will need to keep fresh in your mind the economic fraud that has been forced upon the citizens of the United States, along with all of the civilized nations of the world.

We will begin by looking at the birth of a disastrous economic event triggered by the 9/11 World Trade Center attack. Things were definitely happening with lightening speed behind the walls of the Federal Reserve to gain an incredible financial opportunity, one that would within a decade prove to be at the expense of the U.S. labor force and tax-paying citizens.

Within hours after the horrible occurrence of the 9/11 attack, Alan Greenspan, then chairman of the Federal Reserve Board, issued a statement as follows: "The Federal Reserve will immediately release whatever liquidity it deems necessary in order to guarantee that our financial system remains secure." His announcement was carried by all of the leading TV news agencies, as well as the Associated Press and newspapers across the nation. By "liquidity" he was referring to the issuance of new, additional currency that would be flooded into both the government and banking sectors. It would appear that Mr. Greenspan stepped up to serve the nation.

Did anyone ask the right question?

How could the destruction of one building create an instant need to flood our economy with over $300 billion (which has since grown to several trillion dollars) of new inflationary currency? Over the period of a week, immediately following 9/11, the Federal Reserve issued approximately a quarter of a trillion dollars in new currency. Government bonds backed by future taxes (to be paid by its U.S. laborers) were signed by our Treasury Department, a debt that immediately began to incur interest to the betterment of the owners of the privately held Federal Reserve Banks. At that point distribution of funds began to flow through massive government spending, as well as through the "discount windows" of the regional Federal Reserve branches, to the local banks, followed by more recent massive bank and investment house bailouts.

So, I address the question concerning the events of 9/11!

Here would be the practical solution: given that the building is insured, and the companies inside the building have insurance for their employees, bury the dead, have a period of grieving nationally, scrape off the site, and rebuild it like it was originally built. End of story. We would never forget it, a hard lesson learned about extremist terrorism, but that is all that would have changed in our lives. The fall of that building could not possibly have created the need for a quarter of a trillion dollars of new money being spread liberally to all the banks throughout the nation! It made no sense.

When Mr. Greenspan made that announcement, its significance went right over the heads of almost every U.S. citizen and most government officials as well. You must understand, most people think the Federal Reserve Bank is a federal agency, an authorized branch of the government of the United States. What they don't know is that, in reality, the Federal Reserve Act of 1913 delegated constitutionally given authority to a privately held, for-profit banking institution that pays out dividends on the enormous interest-bearing profits that inure from the inevitable increasing income taxation of U.S. citizens, which eventually finds its way into the pockets of the Federal Reserve's privately held stockholders.

THE ORIGIN OF THE FEDERAL RESERVE BANK

> I believe that banking institutions are more dangerous to our liberties than standing armies. Already they have raised up a money aristocracy that has set our government at defiance. That issuing power should be taken from banks and restored to the government to whom it constitutionally belongs.
>
> —THOMAS JEFFERSON

As we have already learned, the Federal Reserve Bank, our national central bank, was originated by a group of descendants of family heads of the world's most powerful European banks, many of whom have, over the past two hundred years, gravitated to (perhaps a better term would be *infiltrated*) the United States through marriage and naturalization into American governmental and banking institutions. As previously discussed, these families, the owners of our nation's most powerful banks and financial institutions, are also the owners of the Federal Reserve Bank. They are the directors of not just a bank, but a central banking system. History records that they come from family banking cartels originating from the European family heads of the Rothschilds (Banks of England and Berlin); Warburgs (Banks of Hamburg, Amsterdam, Swiss Bank);[1] Lazard Brothers Banks of Paris; Seiff Banks of Italy; Chase Manhattan Bank of New York (owned by the Rockefeller family); Lehman Brothers of New York; and Kuhn, Loeb, and Co. of New York; the Morgan Banks; along with their brokerage houses and other offspring subsidiaries.

Paul Warburg, of Hamburg, Germany, was born into a wealthy banking

---

1 Note: The founder and first chairman of our Federal Reserve Bank was Paul Warburg.

family. He was sent to the London headquarters of the Rothschild banking empire. Two years later, sufficiently connected to the Rothschilds, he married Nina Loeb, the daughter of one of the Rothschild dynasty family members. In 1901, they moved to New York, where he was immediately offered a partnership in his father-in-law's firm of Kuhn and Loeb, one of New York's most prestigious firms. (At the time of the 9/11 attack, this firm had their offices in the New York World Trade Center.)

It is widely believed that Paul Warburg was sent to the U.S. for the express purpose of finding a way to establish a Central Bank of the United States, to be formed by the heads of the European banking families under the control of the Rothschild banking dynasty. After negotiating the help of Senator Nelson Aldrich, the maternal grandfather of John D. Rockefeller, Paul Warburg and a group of men representing all of the Rothschild dynasty members were able to get Congress to pass the Federal Reserve Bill. This bill, passed in a hurried-up session called on December 23, 1913, while many of the legislators were already home for Christmas, brought into creation the Federal Reserve Bank system. Congress transferred the power of the nation's banking and currency into the hands of a private, for-profit institution completely controlled by a select, very secretive group of men.

It seems that the House of Rothschild is directly connected through blood descendants to Brown-Harriman; the Rockefeller family; Kuhn, Loeb, and Co.; J.M. Schroeder; Jacob Schiff Co.; and Goldman Sachs. These families make up the actual owners of what the American people and government know as the Federal Reserve Bank. Only through a long, often boring historical review can the reader fully understand the origin of our banking system as we know it today.

Powers of the Federal Reserve Board

When Alan Greenspan spoke on 9/11, he was not a government official, elected, or held accountable for his actions to the American public. In fact, the Federal Reserve Bank holds the distinction of being completely outside the jurisdiction of outside audits, government agency oversight, or congressional committees, of which one congressman, Rep. Rand Paul, has for years pressed to find a way to force an audit. To date, however, the Federal Reserve remains outside their jurisdiction. I am sure that Mr. Greenspan was accountable to his employers, the private owners of the Federal Reserve Bank, yet he made decisions that brought overwhelming consequences to the nation. Still, he does not officially have to account to any elected or duly appointed government official or agency.

The Federal Reserve Bank, along with all of the central banks of the nations of the world, is owned by the same families that control our banking and currency system. The same names appear over and over again as principals of major central bank throughout Europe, along with the World Bank and its subsidiaries, such as the International Monetary Fund (the IMF). The World Bank serves nations in the same sense that your local bank serves you. They come to the rescue when nations reach a critical point in their economy.

Typically when the World Bank or the IMF steps in, it requires the nation it is bailing out to turn over all banking controls. Once on the hook to the World Bank the nation must act in a subservient manner to its new lenders. As bizarre as it might seem, the IMF prints at will and issues its own private currency, called Special Drawing Rights (SDRs), to the nations needing the IMF to bail them out of trouble. The participating nation's bankers must then pay for the SDRs in full-face principal plus interest with their own national currency, ultimately at the expense of its citizens through taxation. Meanwhile, the World Bank merely goes to the printing presses and prints out its own private currency. Don't try that yourself in your office or den at home. They would arrest you.

The World Bank is the banker to the nations. It is extremely powerful and unlike any other banker you know. With its power, it no longer needs to trade in (lend or mortgage to) the wealth of individuals or local, national, and international corporations! It now trades in the wealth of individual sovereign nations.

Alan Greenspan's announcement the week of September 11, 2001, after the WTC attack should have alerted our citizenry to the amount of power wielded by him. More recently, his successor, Mr. Benjamin Bernanke, along with the Obama Administration's Treasury Secretary, Mr. Timothy Geitner, has openly wielded the power possessed by the system to amass huge amounts of debt, as these individuals single-handedly opened the currency printing presses to virtually anyone in high places needing it. At the time of the printing of this edition, it is estimated that they have distributed almost $16 trillion in a matter of less than four years. Although Mr. Geitner, as Treasury Secretary, must go to the Congress for authority, Mr. Bernanke and the Federal Reserve Bank, which actually has carte blanche access to new U.S. currency creation, does not answer to any government body. They have the power to issue credit in the form of dollar currency to anyone they deem appropriate. It is widely reported in the news that they have issued additional trillions in loans to banks and investment houses both in the US and abroad. Where do they get their money to loan? They turn on the printing presses.

Who else in the nation has the kind of power allowing him or her to personally make a major national decision—without interacting with any government officials—to authorize the printing of $300 billion and in the process demand that the U.S. Treasury, on behalf of our citizens, sign a debt instrument to be repaid to the Federal Reserve Bank with interest without asking the United States Treasury or its citizens if they would like to borrow the money? The Federal Reserve Bank system is sovereign, answering to no one regarding its activities. They are not subject to congressional or civil subpoenas, and they have never had to answer any involuntary inquiry.

Not the president, not any branch of Congress, not the Supreme Court judges, nor any other ruling body have that kind of power. Our elected or appointed officials are empowered through processes involving (either directly or indirectly) the people of the United States. Mr. Greenspan was the chairman of the Federal Reserve Board, accounting only to the private owners of the Federal Reserve Bank System for his actions.

Since we know that the Federal Reserve System, consisting of its headquarters and twelve Federal Reserve Banks, is a private, for-profit, (European family owned) entity, how is it that the decision and announcement came from Mr. Greenspan? It would seem that any announcement of the issuance of new U.S. currency should come from the Treasury Secretary, or at least from some government official. You would never give over that kind of power to the insurance companies of the world or to the phone companies or some other privately held institution.

However, immediately following the September 11 terrorist attack the government leaders all had to look to the Fed (Federal Reserve Bank) in light of a possible national or international economic panic and ask, "What are you going to do to see that we are secure?" Mr. Greenspan, in return, stepped up to his own personal national podium in an unprecedented move. As CNN, FOX News, and all of the major TV networks pointed their cameras at him, he declared, "We are going to 'pump' into the system whatever currency is necessary in order to protect 'our' nation's system." I wonder who the "our" actually was in reference to? Who actually controls and owns our nation today? The answer seems to be, those who control the supply of gold and silver, which was many years ago taken from the then-bankrupted United States of America.

That day a new precedent was clearly set, one that has now begun repeating itself, as our nation and the world reel in one financial shock after the other.

THE WORLD'S BIGGEST MONEY-LAUNDERING SCHEME

Gleaning from many historical sources as my reference, let me share, in a simplified manner, how the system works. This is what actually unfolded after the 9/11 attack as Mr. Greenspan and the Federal Reserve decided to increase the nation's debt owed to them by approximately $300 billion.

1. The Fed, through its board of governors and regional bank centers, instructed the Bureau of Printing and Engraving (an authorized government subsidiary) to supply it with a new issue of currency (over a period of several days) amounting to approximately $300 billion in Federal Reserve Notes. This was the amount of new currency issued over a five-day period immediately following the World Trade Center attack and subsequently entered into the U.S. economy. As would be learned, this would create the beginning of economic woes that would surface less than a decade later.

2. After the supply of $300 billion in Federal Reserve Notes was printed, the Bureau of Printing and Engraving forwarded the currency to the Federal Reserve Board of Governors.

3. The Fed chairman then informed the U.S. Treasury Secretary that the currency was on hand and ready for circulation through its regional Fed banks.

4. The Fed, however, did not release the Federal Reserve Notes until that amount was backed with U.S. government bonds, most of which would be purchased by China, in order to secure a debt owed in the amount of $300 billion plus future interest owed to the private owners of the Fed. The above amount actually seems trivial compared to the amounts created in a matter of months in the last quarter of 2008 and first quarter of 2009.

5. After the appropriate signatures were placed on them, the U.S. Treasury secretary, under authority of the president, then ordered the issuance of the money in bonds. At this point, these bonds of $300 billion became a government debt, secured solely by the personal assets and wealth of its U.S. citizens and taxpayers.

6. The Bureau of Printing and Engraving subsequently forwarded the newly printed U.S. government bonds to the Fed to be held against $300 billion of new currency to be issued.

How much was the cost to the Fed to secure $300 billion of new assets (bonds owed them) in this transaction? Only the cost of the ink and paper upon which the new currency was printed. Remember, if you aren't having to match what is being printed with anything of value, it costs approximately the same to print a one dollar bill as it does to print a one hundred dollar or one thousand dollar bill. Don't you wish you, or your company, had that kind of access to the nation's currency presses?

According to the official Federal Reserve Bank Web site's information pages, called Fedpoint, "The Federal Reserve orders new currency from the Bureau of Engraving and Printing, which produces the appropriate denominations and ships them directly to the Federal Reserve Banks. Each note costs about four cents to produce, though the cost varies slightly by denomination."

When the Fed speaks of its assets, which it holds to back

the currency it produces, it is speaking of bonds and other financial collateral (manipulated paper), all of which is held as assets, having been purchased by simply ordering more currency from the Bureau of Printing and Engraving. They literally have the power to create all the money they wish to use.

7. The Fed accepted the government bonds (U.S. debt) as a pledge against the new supply of currency and graciously distributed it into the U.S. banking supply. This process began within twenty-four hours of the World Trade Center attack, supposedly to restore the badly shaken economic stability of our nation. (Interestingly, immediately following the 9/11 incident, to keep the world economy from crashing, this identical process occurred in the international community.)

Was Mr. Greenspan responding patriotically when he appeared before the nation's TV cameras to make his reassurances? No! While I can not judge his actual patriotism, obviously, he was already figuring the Fed's European banking family shareholders' future windfall of profits from the virtual cost-free creation of what now amounts to trillions of dollars, plus the accumulating compound interest that would be earned on the U.S. national debt that would accrue, along with the already trillions of dollars owed to them for the prior cost-free printing of similar Federal Reserve Notes (dollar bills).

It is no wonder that Mr. Greenspan and the European-banking-family-controlled Fed were so quick to offer to "supply all the liquidity necessary to secure the financial stability of the American people." The Fed owns the system! The Fed totally controls the system! We, the people of the U.S., got ripped off to the tune of trillions of dollars with nothing to show for it except the immediate inflation and increase in future income taxes needed to pay the interest annually to the owners of the Fed! Neither we nor our elected officials had any say in the matter.

Did the government of the United States, its Congress, or any other government leader ask for, approve, or in any manner provide consultation about this occurrence? Although it affected every tax-paying citizen, every future young person who will be coming into the system in this century, yet the answer is no! No one had a voice in this matter. It was decided for us by those sitting in the shadows; an unelected, unappointed, and, to many, an unwanted group of economic dictators. We are seeing, today, more and more evidence of this as a current reality.

If only there had been no Fed (Federal Reserve System), no scandalous secret meeting on Jekyll Island in the days immediately preceding December 23, 1913. If only there had been no conspiracy to slip a vote through Congress the day before Christmas Eve, when most of our elected officials had already left or were hurriedly preparing to leave for their home states with no opportunity to read the bill shoved before them. What if none of this had occurred that gave the power to the Fed to use our government printing services to print their own private Federal Reserve Notes to be sold to us for full face value plus interest, though it cost them nothing to create it? If only.

Were it not for these conspiratorial events and their subsequent effect, we, and our children, would likely not owe trillions of dollars in national debt. The government would likely not have taken our gold in 1933 when President Roosevelt issued executive orders EO6073, EO6102, and EO6111. Without any national awareness, these infamous orders were in essence the declaration of bankruptcy for the United States of America, allowing the Fed to plunder our citizens of their individual wealth. Thus, on April 5, 1933, President Roosevelt issued the official executive order EO6260, proclaiming, "All persons are required to deliver, on or before May 1, 1933 [only 25 days notice], all gold coins, gold bullion, and gold certificates now owned by them to a Federal Reserve Bank, branch or agency, or to any member bank of the Federal Reserve System."

As Cliff Ford wrote:

> The confiscation of private gold was under the authority of a 1917 law, codified as USCA95a, which allowed for exceptional Presidential authority only under a "state of emergency." The 1917 law was entitled the 'Trading with the Enemy Act of the 65th Congress, October 6, 1917.' Who was the enemy? In order for this act to be lawfully applicable, the citizens of the United States became the enemy of the new "Corporation of the United States." The Corporation of the United States was the [officially appointed] replacement entity for the now bankrupt United States of America!

Just prior to the recalling of all gold coins, bullion and certificates, a prominent congressman, Louis T. McFadden, then a past chairman for ten years of the Banking and Currency Committee in U.S. Congress, was challenging the committee regarding the imminent crisis immediately ahead, at which President Roosevelt was forced to issue his infamous order EO6260.

The following, photographed from the congressional record of June 10, 1932, is an actual depiction of McFadden's speech. (See the opposite page for the Congressional record. The full text follows on the subsequent page.)

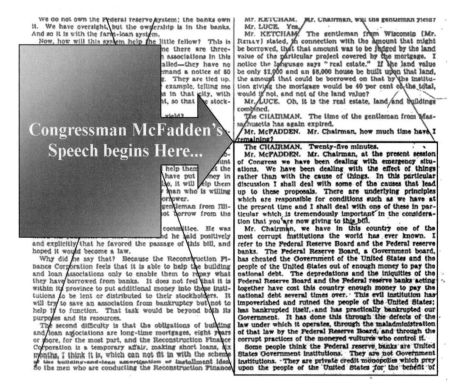

Congressman Louis T. McFadden Speech, June 10, 1932.

Here, in easy to read words, is a large section of Congressman McFadden's address to the Congress depicted above. You should find it revealing with regard to the Federal Reserve Banking system. In fact, if studied thoroughly, his speech could serve as a primer of what we are faced with in this present economic crisis. If you can weather a history lesson, he begins his speech as follows:

> Mr. Chairman, at the present session of Congress we have been dealing with emergency situations. We have been dealing with the effect of things rather than with the cause of things. In this particular discussion I shall deal with some of the causes that lead up to these proposals. There are underlying principles which are responsible for conditions such as we have at the present time and I shall deal with one of these in particular which is tremendously important in the consideration that you are now giving to this bill.
>
> Mr. Chairman, we have in this country one of the most corrupt institutions the world has ever known. I refer to the Federal Reserve Board and the Federal Reserve Banks. The Federal Reserve Board, a Government board, has cheated the Government of the United States and the people of the United States out of enough money to pay the national debt. The depredations and iniquities of the Federal Reserve Board has cost this country enough money to pay the national debt several times over. This evil institution has impoverished and ruined the people of the United States, has bankrupted itself, and has practically bankrupted our Government. It has done this through the defects of the law under which it operates, through the maladministration of that law by the Federal Reserve Board, and through the corrupt practices of the moneyed vultures who control it.
>
> Some people think the Federal Reserve banks are United States Government institutions. They are not Government institutions. They are private credit monopolies which prey upon the people of the United States for the benefit of themselves and their foreign customers; foreign and domestic speculators and swindlers; and rich and predatory money lenders. In that dark crew of financial pirates there are those who would cut a man's throat to get a dollar out of his pocket; there are those who send money into States to buy votes to control our legislation; and there are those who maintain international propaganda for the purpose of deceiving us and of wheedling us into the granting of new concessions which will permit them to cover up their past misdeeds and set again in motion their gigantic train of crime.

These twelve private credit monopolies were deceitfully and disloyally foisted upon this country by the bankers who came here from Europe and repaid us for our hospitality by undermining our American institutions. Those bankers took money out of this country to finance Japan in a war against Russia. They created a reign of terror in Russia with our money in order to help that war along. They instigated the separate peace between Germany and Russia and thus drove a wedge between the Allies in the [First] World War. They financed Trotsky's passage from New York to Russia so that he might assist in the destruction of the Russian Empire. They fomented and instigated the Russian revolution and they placed a large fund of American dollars at Trotsky's disposal in one of their branch banks in Sweden so that through him Russian homes might be thoroughly broken up and Russian children flung far and wide from their natural protectors. They have since begun the breaking up of American homes and the dispersal of American children.

It has been said that President Wilson was deceived by the attentions of these bankers and by the philanthropic poses they assumed. It has been said that when he discovered the manner in which he had been misled by Colonel [Edward M.] House, he turned against that busybody, that "holy monk" of the financial empire, and showed him the door. He had the grace to do that, and in my opinion he deserves great credit for it.

President Wilson died a victim of deception. When he came to the Presidency, he had certain qualities of mind and heart which entitled him to a high place in the councils of this Nation; but there was one thing he was not and which he never aspired to be; he was not a banker. He said that he knew very little about banking. It was, therefore, on the advice of others that the iniquitous Federal Reserve act, the death warrant of American liberty, became law in his administration.

Mr. Chairman, there should be no partisanship in matters concerning the banking and currency affairs of this country, and I do not speak with any.

In 1912 the National Monetary Association, under the chairmanship of the late Senator Nelson W. Aldrich, made a report and presented a vicious bill called the National Reserve Association bill. This bill is usually spoken of as the Aldrich bill. Senator Aldrich did not write the Aldrich bill. He was the tool, but not the accomplice, of the European-born bankers who for nearly twenty years had been scheming to set up a central bank in this country and who in 1912 had spent and were continuing to spend vast sums of money to accomplish their purpose.

The Aldrich bill was condemned in the platform upon which Theodore Roosevelt was nominated in the year 1912, and in that same year, when Woodrow Wilson was nominated, the Democratic platform, as adopted at the Baltimore convention, expressly stated: "We are opposed to the Aldrich plan for a central bank." This was plain language. The men who ruled the Democratic Party then promised the people that if they were returned to power there would be no central bank established here while they held the reigns of government. Thirteen months later that promise was broken, and the Wilson administration, under the tutelage of those sinister Wall Street figures who stood behind Colonel House, established here in our free country the worm-eaten monarchical institution of the "king's bank" to control us from the top downward, and to shackle us from the cradle to the grave. The Federal Reserve act destroyed our old and characteristic way of doing business; it discriminated against our one-name commercial paper, the finest in the world; it set up the antiquated two-name paper, which is the present curse of this country, and which wrecked every country which has ever given it scope; it fastened down upon this country the very tyranny from which the framers of the Constitution sought to save us.

One of the greatest battles for the preservation of this Republic was fought out here in Jackson's day, when the Second Bank of the United States, which was founded upon the same false principles as those which are here exemplified in the Federal Reserve act, was hurled out of existence. After the downfall of the Second Bank of the United States in 1837, the country was warned against the dangers that might ensue if the predatory interests, after being cast out, should come back in disguise and unite themselves to the Executive, and through him acquire control of the Government. That is what the predatory interests did when they came back in the livery of hypocrisy and under false pretenses obtained the passage of the Federal Reserve act.

The danger that the country was warned against came upon us and is shown in the long train of horrors attendant upon the affairs of the traitorous and dishonest Federal Reserve Board and the Federal Reserve banks are fully liable. This is an era of financed crime and in the financing of crime, the Federal Reserve Board does not play the part of a disinterested spectator.

It has been said that the draughtsman who was employed to write the text of the Federal Reserve bill used a text of the Aldrich bill for his purpose. It has been said that the language of the Aldrich bill was used because the Aldrich bill had been drawn up by expert lawyers and seemed to be appropriate. It was indeed drawn up by lawyers. The Aldrich bill was created by acceptance bankers of European origin in New York City. It was a copy and in general a translation of the statutes of the Reichsbank and other European central banks.

Half a million dollars was spent one part of the propaganda organized by those same European bankers for the purpose of misleading public opinion in regard to it, and for the purpose of giving Congress the impression that there was an overwhelming popular demand for that kind of banking legislation and the kind of currency that goes with it, namely, an asset currency based on human debts and obligations instead of an honest currency based on gold and silver values. Dr. H. Parker Willis had been employed by the Wall Street bankers and propagandists and when the Aldrich measure came to naught and he obtained employment with Carter Glass to assist in drawing a banking bill for the Wilson administration; he appropriated the text of the Aldrich bill for his purpose. There is no secret about it. The text of the Federal Reserve act was tainted from the beginning.

Not all of the Democratic Members of the Sixty-Third Congress voted for this great deception. Some of them remembered the teachings of Jefferson; and, through the years, there had been no criticisms of the Federal Reserve Board and the Federal Reserve banks so honest, so outspoken, and so unsparingly as those which have been voiced here by Democrats. Again, although a number of Republicans voted for the Federal Reserve act, the wisest and most conservative members of the Republican Party would have nothing to do with it and voted against it. A few days before the bill came to a vote, Senator Henry Cabot Lodge, of Massachusetts, wrote to Senator John W. Weeks as follows:

New York City, December 17, 1913

My Dear Senator Weeks:

Throughout my public life I have supported all measures designed to take the Government out of the banking business....This bill puts the Government into the banking business as never before in our history and makes, as I understand it, all notes Government notes when they should be bank notes.

The powers vested in the Federal Reserve Board seem to me highly dangerous, especially where there is political control of the Board. I should be sorry to hold stock in a bank subject to such domination. The bill as it stands seems to me to open the way to a vast inflation of the currency. There is no necessity of dwelling upon this point after the remarkable and most powerful argument of the senior Senator from New York. I can be content here to follow the example of the English candidate for Parliament who thought it enough "to say ditto to Mr. Burke." I will merely add that I do not like to think that any law can be passed which will make it possible to submerge the gold standard in a flood of irredeemable paper currency.

I had hoped to support this bill, but I can not vote for it as it stands, because it seems to me to contain features and to rest upon principles in the highest degree menacing to our prosperity, to stability in business, and to the general welfare of the people of the United States.

VERY SINCERELY YOURS,
HENRY CABOT LODGE

In eighteen years that have passed since Senator Lodge wrote that letter of warning all of his predictions have come true. The Government is in the banking business as never before. Against its will it has been made the backer of horsethieves and card sharps, bootleggers, smugglers, speculators, and swindlers in all parts of the world. Through the Federal Reserve Board and the Federal Reserve banks the riff-raff of every country is operating on the public credit of this United States Government. Meanwhile, and on account of it, we ourselves are in the midst of the greatest depression we have ever known. Thus the menace to our prosperity, so feared by Senator Lodge, has indeed struck home. From the Atlantic to the Pacific our country has been ravaged and laid waste by the evil practices of the Federal Reserve Board and the Federal Reserve banks and the interests which control them. At no time in our history has the general welfare of the people of the United States been at a lower level or the mind of the people so filled with despair.

Recently in one of our States 60,000 dwelling houses and farms were brought under the hammer in a single day. According to the Rev. Father Charles E. Coughlin, who has lately testified before a committee of this House, 71,000 houses and farms in Oakland County, Michigan, have been sold and their erstwhile owners dispossessed. Similar occurrences have probably taken place in every county in the United States. The people who have thus been driven out are the wastage of the Federal Reserve act. They are the victims of the dishonest and unscrupulous Federal Reserve Board and Federal Reserve banks. Their children are the new slaves of the auction blocks in the revival here of the institution of human slavery.

You can see from this glimpse at a past congressional record evidence for concern in the matter of the Federal Reserve System and the intent of its international investment-family owners.

All of this time we thought our government was doing business as the United States of America, the one founded in 1776, as our history books have taught us. But, alas! We, in reality, the citizens of the United States of America, are being governed as a reorganized corporation of the United States.

I believe our government in Washington, D.C., is actually doing its business as a corporation controlled and enslaved by a group, a conglomerate ("money cartel") consisting of the richest corporate families of the earth, a group of such vast wealth and power that no audit, no accounting of their wealth is required by any power on earth. It is a group so powerful that they remain invisible and unanswerable to anyone within our international community. Yet, they have the power to issue all of our money!

It is to this fact that the Scriptures address a great "vengeance... to comfort."

> Go to now, ye rich men, weep and howl for your miseries that shall come upon you [a prophetic promise]. Your riches are corrupted, and your garments are motheaten. Your gold and silver is cankered; and the rust of them shall be a witness against you, and shall eat your flesh as it were fire. Ye have heaped treasure together [Greek, "to amass a reserve, a conglomerate of wealth"] for the last days [Thayer's New Testament Greek Lexicon, "of the time nearest the return of Christ from heaven and the consummation of the divine kingdom, the following scriptures are so used: Acts 2:17; James 5:3; 2 Timothy 3:1]. Behold, the hire [Greek, "wages, currency"] of the labourers who have reaped down your fields, which is of you kept back by fraud [fiat money of no worth], crieth: and the cries of them which have reaped are entered into the ears of the Lord of sabaoth [Jehovah Tsaba].
>
> —JAMES 5:1–4

Within one decade of the creation of our central banking system and the control of it in the hands of the international banking cartel, they were able to plunder our total national and individual wealth of gold reserves, sending us into the Great Depression of the 1930s. Later on they accomplished the same with our silver reserves, finally replacing the "silver certificate" with unvalued dollars against the personal assets of the nation's citizens. Today, we are left with fiat currency and coinage of no value, as we will prove with no uncertainty.

There was a time in our national history when in order for the Federal Reserve Bank to issue currency it had to provide receipts confirming its equivalent in gold and silver to back the money issued. As previously stated, by definition of the U.S. Constitution with no subsequent amendment ever offered a dollar is "412 1/2 grains of 9/10 fine silver or its equivalent in gold bullion in store." Those issuing our paper currency had to supply the gold coinage or bullion of its equal value. For every dollar bill issued, there had to be its silver dollar coin counterpart in the nation's vaults.

Had this been the policy on September 11, 2001, and the week following, there would have had to been $300 billion of silver or its equivalent gold coinage and bullion placed on reserve in the vaults of the nation or Federal Reserve System. Then every citizen holding a Federal Reserve Note would have had something of real worth, something with real value behind it. Unfortunately, the system had much earlier stolen all real worth from us and left us with fiat money.

UNDERSTANDING THE EVOLUTION TO "FIAT MONEY"

Previously we have already looked at the following two quotes:

> This act [Federal Reserve Bill of 1923] established the most gigantic money trust on earth…when the President signs this act, the invisible government by the money power, proven to exist by the Money Trust Investigation [chaired by Mr. Lindbergh] will be legalized…The new law will create inflation whenever they want inflation to occur for their own monetary good."
> —CONGRESSMAN CHARLES LINDBERGH TO CONGRESS

> I am a most unhappy man. I have unwittingly ruined my country. A great industrial nation is now controlled by a system of banking. The real growth of our nation, therefore, and all of our activities are now in the hands of a few un-elected men. We have become one of the most controlled and dominated Governments in the civilized world — no longer a Government by the people, of free opinion, no longer a Government by conviction and the vote of the majority, but a Government by the opinion and duress of a small group of financially dominant men.
> —PRESIDENT WOODROW WILSON

I wonder? Where was this information in the history books when we studied our American history lessons? As a result of academia's treatment of these facts, until now it has been sometimes difficult to get educated friends to take the matter seriously.

A recent article from *Investor's Business Daily* examines the accuracy of our high school and college history books. William Chapman, an editor for *Investor's Business Daily*, a national newspaper in the U.S. published Monday through Friday that covers international business, finance, and the global economy, writes:

> Burton Folsom, a former college professor, now senior fellow at the Michigan-based Mackinac Center for Public Policy, found many textbook myths.
>
> One such myth is that laissez-faire capitalism caused the Great Depression and government spending cured it, says Folsom.
>
> "Almost every textbook misses on this," Folsom said. "Milton Friedman proved that the Federal Reserve caused it, and government programs didn't get us out of the Depression."
>
> Walter Williams, chairman of the economics department at George Mason University, agrees, "Some textbooks say that runaway capitalism caused the Depression, when it was the Fed and the Smoot-Hawley tariff that did it," Williams told IBD. "Friedman confirmed this."
>
> Among economists, only those of the Austrian School, such as Hayek and Ludwig von Mises, clearly predicted the '29 stock market crash and the Depression that followed.
>
> They both blamed the Fed's manipulation of the money supply, and interference in the investment markets, years before Friedman documented it. Yet the Austrian School rarely gets a mention in textbooks.

Thus, as you can see, you can't trust the fact-omission-riddled pages of the history books to give you accurate information, especially regarding "elite corporatists." No wonder, however, as they are published by foundations established and controlled by, among other elitists, the Rockefeller family.

So it has been for the average U.S. citizen, as he or she has for two centuries assumed the information at hand to be correct regarding our currency system.

The New York World Trade Center complex, at the time of the September 11, 2001 attack, housed the very international banking cartels representing all the banking families, the largest tenant being that of Morgan, Stanley, Dean Witter, and other family trading arms representing the trade of sixty-three nations of the world! Although located on U.S. soil, the New York World Trade Center was not an American establishment. It was symbolic of the world international banking and investment trading families. It was, in fact, the home of the rich men spoken of in James 5:3–4, "Ye have heaped treasure together for the last days. Behold the hire of the laborers [their wages]...which is of you kept back by fraud, crieth; and the cries of them...have entered into the ears of the Lord of sabaoth [Jehovah Tsaba]."

Let's take a closer look at this scripture. The phrase "heaped treasure together," when looked at in the Greek, *thesaurizo*, gives the picture of a financial conglomerate or banking/investment cartel. Nothing could better be used to describe the mission and purpose of the Word Trade Center.

Now we will examine the phrase "for the last days." The Greek word is *eschatos*, meaning "farthest, final (of place or time), ends of, last, latter end." According to *The Complete Biblical Library,* it is "used exclusively in prophetic scripture for the 'end of the age,' and is never used for the end of the span of a man's life. For that James would have used another word form, εσχατως eschatos—at the extremity of life—point of death." What we learn from this Greek word study is that James is not speaking of the end of the span of a specific rich man's life.

Later in that scripture James indicts a rich global financial cartel. He states, "The wages of the laborers which is kept back by fraud cries" (author's paraphrase). This addresses what we know as fiat currency, a form of fraudulent wages, of which James speaks. As we will show, the Federal Reserve has systematically and with clever deceit over a number of years transitioned our currency from that of redeemable worth to "worthless scrip," without any backing or foundation. Many economists today are recognizing this as the key factor in the financial meltdown of a system that was skillfully moved from an asset-based currency to that of a fiat, debt-based system.

For many years now, as citizens, we have been paid for our labor in Federal Reserve Notes. A note, of course, is a debt instrument. It is actually a receipt for a debt owed. When we cash in our paychecks, we are given, in exchange for our labor, a note, an "IOU." In other words, we are paid with a kind of debt instrument with no possibility of redemption. There is no promise on the note ever to be able to redeem it for its constitutionally protected value. It states on the face of it, "This note is legal tender for all debts, public and private." You traded your labor, or your hard assets, for a piece of paper good only for bartering in a debt system. Read the front of your own currency. You will see it is true.

"Legal Tender" statement.

An earlier five-dollar bill stated, "This certifies that there is on deposit in the Treasury of the United States of America five dollars…in silver payable to the bearer on demand." At that time, for every five-dollar bill, there had to be coinage in silver or its current equivalent in gold bullion for that exact amount. There was literally a silver dollar held in U.S. Treasury vaults for every dollar of circulated paper currency. You were promised that if you ever wanted to convert that certificate of receipt into the actual commodity it represented you could take your certificate of receipt to a local affiliate bank of the Federal Reserve System and exchange it ("payable to the bearer upon demand") for silver or gold coinage to place in your vault for safekeeping. At that time it was a legal note (debt), containing a promise of repayment upon demand.

Five-dollar bill "to the bearer on demand" statement.

During the past century a clever scheme was implemented to globally defraud an entire generation of its individual wealth. The aforementioned world renowned banking families have absconded with our gold and silver, leaving us with currency that no longer serves as a certificate of receipt of any backing. Rather, our money represents a worthless note, an IOU absent any promise or practical ability to ever redeem it.

In 1928, on a ten-dollar bill you would have read these words:

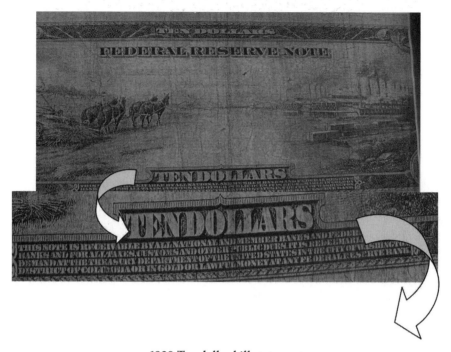

1928 Ten-dollar bill statement.

"Redeemable in gold on demand at the United States Treasury, or at any Federal Reserve Bank." As shown above it read in all capitals:

THIS NOTE IS RECEIVABLE BY ALL NATIONAL AND MEMBER BANKS AND FEDERAL RESERVE BANKS AND FOR ALL TAXES, CUSTOMS, AND OTHER PUBLIC DUES. IT IS REDEEMABLE IN GOLD ON DEMAND AT THE TREASURY DEPARTMENT OF THE UNITED SATES IN THE CITY OF WASHINGTON, DISTRICT OF COLUMBIA, OR IN GOLD OR LAWFUL MONEY AT ANY FEDERAL RESERVE BANK.

By 1934 you would have noticed a change in the wording. A smaller version would have been found in these words, "This note is legal tender for all debts, public and private, and is redeemable in lawful money at the United States Treasury, or at any Federal Reserve Bank." It is very important that you notice the words *lawful money*.

1934 reworded statement.

The Fed was not even attempting to hide the fact that the currency was itself not lawful money. It bore the declaration of such, the promise that the note could be redeemed for lawful money.

So, as an astute observer, what would be your only conclusion about the foregoing one-hundred-dollar bill? The only practical result you could possibly draw from this statement would be that paper currency issued is, by definition, not lawful money! Paper was conceived to serve as a note for convenience only, representing a hard asset (silver or gold) to be kept in safe-keeping and redeemable upon demand.

Every person reading this book should carefully consider what he or she is reading.

The small print is the legal declaration of the currency, a promise that it was redeemable for lawful money. That statement made it a promissory note, a Federal Reserve Note. This requirement is placed on the issuers of our money by the Constitution.

Interestingly, the founders of our nation made a great point of including in the framing of the U.S. Constitution what would qualify as lawful money, keeping in mind that it would take ratification of a Constitutional amendment (by all the states) to change what the founders deemed it to be. It is not something that Congress, or a particular political administration, has the power to alter. The Constitution declares "a dollar" to be 412 1/2 grains of 9/10 fine silver. That is the exact weight of every minted silver dollar.

In other words, there has never been a question legally as to what constitutes a lawful dollar. A lawful dollar is a minted silver dollar of the exact size and weight prescribed under the constitutional fathers. Nothing else qualifies. The only exception by the framers was "or its equivalent in gold weight." Our forefathers knew that gold would tend to be hoarded and therefore would not be practical to use in more common exchange. Therefore they chose a weight of 412 1/2 grains of 9/10 fine silver. Here is a constitutionally legal Morgan dollar, issued in 1891 (front and back):

Assayed, this silver dollar weighs the legal 412 1/2 grains of 9/10 fine silver.

Over time, without much public education on what constitutes a dollar, the Federal Reserve conspired with the United States Treasury to begin a deception on the American public. Over time they realized we were paying very little attention to our money. We have come to a point in that evolutionary process that neither our government, nor the Federal Reserve even bother any longer to hide it.

1891 Morgan dollar.

Next is a coin minted as "legal tender" in 1979 representing itself as one dollar (front and back). It only vaguely resembles what historically we could identify as a silver dollar, but it boldly declares itself to be one dollar (see enlarged insert):

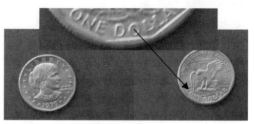

1979 coin.

Now let's compare what the Treasury issued as one dollar with the "real" Morgan silver dollar (Size good only for comparison purposes):

The little liberty "dollar" (left) is only a fraction of the size/weight of the Morgan silver dollar (right), and the smaller "dollar" is made of 75 percent copper and 25 percent nickel. (There is no silver metal in its composition.) On the other hand,

Liberty dollar, Morgan silver dollar.

the Morgan silver dollar contains 412 1/2 grains 9/10 fine silver. As you can see, the 1891 silver dollar is the real deal and qualifies as a lawful dollar.

The 1972 Eisenhower silver dollar was publicly called a silver dollar. It was the same height and weight as the Morgan silver dollar; however, its composition was 75 percent copper and 25 percent nickel. No silver was used in the creation of this fiat money.

In 1950, the Fed further reduced the size of the print on the face of paper currency, making it considerably more difficult to read the promissory note portion of the bill in preparation for the next step in the evolutionary process toward totally worthless "fiat money."

1972 Eisenhower silver dollar.

Finally, in 1963, the wording was shortened and limited to only two very hard-to-read lines, giving no promise of redemption: "This note is legal tender for all debts, public and private."

At this juncture in time, the principals of the international banking cartel had succeeded! There was no public outcry, no congressional investigations! Nothing! We were not paying attention to our currency certificates (receipts), and they pulled it off! The Fed removed any legal means to ever redeem the note for anything of constitutionally protected value.

Smaller text of promissory note statement.

With the knowledge of this, I want to reassert that I am a very loyal, patriotic citizen. I love our nation. I appreciate our government and its leaders. It is not our national leaders who forced this fraud upon our nation's wage earners. They were duped along with the rest of us. I'm speaking of a private international group who hide behind a government-sounding institution called the *Federal* Reserve Bank.

It sounds like government. Its headquarters looks like a government building.

Its chairman comes before Congress and speaks like a government official. But remember, when the Fed chairman appears before Congress, he never asks them for any counsel, he never asks them for authorization to act, he never asks them anything. They ask him what he and the Fed board is thinking of doing. No one knows for certain what they will do in their very secret sessions until they emerge to make their announcements. And whatever they decide, our nation of citizens and elected public officials, including our Senate, House of Representatives, and the executive branch of our government, go along with it!

Federal Reserve building, Washington DC

When the Federal Reserve leaders go into their secret meetings, the political leaders, the leaders on Wall Street, along with all venues of our nation, as well as the international community around the world, wait to see what they have decided to do. Our elected officials are not allowed present as they spin their economic webs.

This was most recently illustrated on March 18, 2009, in the testimony of Edward Libby, CEO of AIG, the giant insurance/investment company. He was discussing the $160 million in bonuses paid their investment traders. He was asked if any government representatives were present at the "secret meetings," as they were given instructions by the Federal Reserve regarding the distribution of those funds. (Keep in mind they were government bailout monies.) He stated under oath, "Only the Federal Reserve chairman was present. No one from the Treasury Department or Congress was involved." He went on to say, "The meetings were held at the Federal Reserve Headquarters."

They, the plunderers, are the same group who previously robbed us of our real individual wealth, who demanded we, our fathers, and our grandfathers, deliver the gold and silver that had been earned through a lifetime of hard and diligent labor. As individuals our nation had to give up our gold and silver or be fined ten thousand dollars and placed in prison for up to ten years, should we refuse to give it up.

On April 5, 1933, President Roosevelt issued the infamous Presidential Order 6102 enforcing the Fed's demand for the nation's gold:

> All Persons are hereby required to deliver on or before May 1, 1933, to a Federal Reserve Bank or a branch or agency thereof, all gold coin, gold bullion, and gold certificates now owned by them...Whoever willfully violates this executive order may be fined not more than $10,000 or may be imprisoned for not more than 10 years, or both.

Today, they hold our nation and the world's economies in their hands.

It's Not Judgment on a Nation–God Is About to Cause a Great Global Wealth Conversion

God says, "It is enough!"

It is true that these wealthy global corporate families think that they have succeeded without getting caught. Until now, perhaps this was so from the world's viewpoint. It stirs up activists, who cry out in underground magazines and books. Many become embittered by their knowledge of these things. From the standpoint of being without God, I can understand their anger and frustration.

But, if you are a believer, one who "overcomes evil with good," one who is in covenant with almighty God, then there is no need for despair. God watches over His Word to perform it! (See Jeremiah 1:12.)

> What then shall we say to [all] this? If God is for us, who [can be] against us? [Who can be our foe, if God is on our side?] [See Psalm

118:6.] He who did not withhold or spare [even] His own Son but gave Him up for us all, will He not also with Him freely and graciously give us all [other] things?

—Romans 8:31–32, amp

The international powers that be might have succeeded, had it not also affected God's elect, His people throughout the earth, those He dwells in the midst of who are the apple of His eye!

God has a great plan for Israel because of His friend Abraham. It does not diminish that fact when we declare an even greater love for His people, the body of Christ, the church. We are now also numbered as the heritage of God. We are now made part of the covenants and promises of Abraham. Galatians 3:29 (amp) says, "And if you belong to Christ [are in Him who is Abraham's Seed], then you are Abraham's offspring and [spiritual] heirs according to promise." Who shall separate us from the love of Christ? No weapon formed against the heritage of God's people will prosper! (See Isaiah 54:17.)

The Day of Jehovah Tsaba, a global shaking of all nations

Isaiah prophesies against a rich, wicked commercial cartel, and he speaks in the name of Jehovah Tsaba, the Lord of Hosts, whom the psalmist David declares to be the King of glory, the Lord, strong and mighty in battle. (See Psalm 24.)

In Isaiah 2:11–12, 19 we read, "The lofty looks of man shall be humbled, and the haughtiness of men shall be bowed down, and the Lord alone shall be exalted in that day. For the day of the Lord of hosts [Jehovah Tsaba] shall be upon everyone that is proud and lofty, and upon every one that is lifted up; and he shall be brought low.... For the glory of his majesty, when he ariseth to shake terribly the earth."

Later on, in Isaiah 6:5, Isaiah saw the glory of God and declared, "For mine eyes have seen the King, the Lord of hosts [Jehovah Tsaba]." In Isaiah 14:24, 26–27 he again prophesies, "The Lord of hosts [Jehovah Tsaba] hath sworn, saying, Surely as I have thought, so shall it come to pass; and as I have purposed, so shall it stand.... This is the purpose that is purposed upon the whole earth: and this is the hand that is stretched out upon all the nations. For the Lord of hosts hath purposed, and who shall disannul it? and his hand is stretched out, and who shall turn it back?"

It is in light of these scriptures that we move into a most startling scripture in Isaiah 23. I must warn you that in light of the September 11, 2001, World Trade Center attack this chapter proves to be quite graphic! To understand these passages, however, requires you to know some Hebrew word representations. In reference to these scriptures, the word *Tyre* (or *Tyrus*) means "economic system," and the word *Tarshish* means "the epithet of a merchant." *Zidon* represents "industry." With these representations in mind, read these verses with me.

> The burden of Tyre. Howl, ye ships of Tarshish; for it is laid waste, so that there is no house [building left standing], no entering in: from the land of Chittim it is revealed to them. Be still, ye inhabitants of the isle [Manhattan?]; thou whom the merchants of Zidon, that pass over the sea, have replenished [furnished]...She is a mart [marketplace] of nations....Howl ye inhabitants of the isle. Is this your joyous city?...Her own feet shall carry her afar off [a reminder that all of those present at the World Trade Center area were required to walk north off of the island of Manhattan; we watched in horror as they filled the wide streets and bridges with masses of stunned faces and stared gazes walking off the island]...

Tyre, Tarshish, and Zidon

The crowning city, whose merchants...whose traffickers [brokers] are the honourable of the earth. The Lord of hosts [Jehovah Tsaba] hath purposed it, to stain the pride of all glory, and to bring into contempt all the honourable of the earth....He stretched out his hand over the sea, he shook the kingdoms: the LORD hath given a commandment against the merchant city, to destroy the strong holds thereof.... They set up the towers thereof...and he [Jehovah Tsaba] brought it to ruin. Howl...for your strength is laid waste.

—ISAIAH 23:1–3, 6–9, 11, 13–14

This picture of God's character should not offend anyone. God is a God of love, power, wisdom, righteousness, mercy, justice, and judgment. You may have only seen Him as love or mercy, but He is all of these things all of the time! It is His sevenfold nature. All of His ways end in judgment. While God's mercy is always available all of the time, if the wicked refuse God's mercy, judgment is certain.

"They set up the towers thereof... and he [Jehovah Tsaba] brought it to ruin. Howl... for your strength is laid waste."

The wealth of the wicked converted into the hands of God's people

This is good news for the body of Christ and for the ministry of the church! The latter words of Isaiah 23 declare, "And her merchandise [profits of trade] and her hire [wages from labor] shall become holiness to the LORD: it shall not be treasured nor laid up [hoarded away, stored up]; for her merchandise [profits of trade] shall be for them that dwell before the Lord, to eat sufficiently, and for durable clothing."

The Living Bible Translation renders it this way, "Yet, the distant time will come when her business will give their profits to the Lord! They will not be hoarded but used for good food and fine clothes for the ministers of the Lord!"

The Amplified Bible states, "But her gain and her hire [the profits of Tyre's new prosperity] will be dedicated to the Lord [eventually]; it will not be treasured or stored up, for her gain will be used for those who dwell in the presence of the Lord [the ministers], that they may eat sufficiently and have durable and stately clothing [suitable for those who minister at God's altar]."

Finally, this judgment, this shaking of the nations, is more graphically explained in Ezekiel's prophetic parable of the same event. Although a part of these prophecies were local and thus fulfilled in part in ancient times, there are portions that point to being repeated on a broader, worldwide scale at a later time. Ecclesiastes 3:15 says, "That which hath been is now; and that which is to be hath already been; and God requireth [repeats] that which is past."

Engines (using sharp cutting instruments) crash into the World Trade Center Twin Towers

In Ezekiel 26:7, 9, 12, 14–18, 20 the following prophecy is given:

> For thus saith the Lord God; Behold, I will bring upon Tyrus [economic system]....And he shall set engines of war against thy walls, and with his axes [Heb., "sharp cutting instruments, knives"] he shall break down thy towers.... And they shall make a spoil of thy riches, and make a prey of thy merchandise....Thou shalt be built no more: for I the Lord have spoken it, saith the Lord God...Shall not the isles shake at the sound of thy fall, when the wounded cry, when the slaughter is made in the midst of thee? Then all the princes of the sea shall come down from their thrones...they shall clothe themselves with trembling...And they shall take up a lamentation for thee, and say to thee, How art thou destroyed...the renowned city, which wast strong in the sea, she and her inhabitants...Now shall the isles tremble in the day of thy fall; yea, the isles that are in the sea shall be troubled [terrorized] at thy departure....When I shall bring thee down...I shall set glory in the land of the living [the body of Christ who have been given eternal life will see God's glory come to them].

In Ezekiel 27:1, 3, 9, 12, 14–18, 20–22, 24, 27–28, 30–35, beginning with the first verse, the prophet continues:

The word of the LORD came again unto me, saying.... Say unto Tyrus, O thou that art situate at the entry of the sea, which are a merchant of the people for many isles. Thus saith the Lord GOD: O Tyrus, thou has said, I am of perfect beauty....

All the ships of the sea, with their mariners were in thee to occupy thy merchandise.... All kinds of riches; with silver, iron, tin, and lead, they traded in thy fairs... They... traded in thy fairs with horses and horsemen... Many isles were the merchandise of thin hand: they brought thee for a present horns of ivory and ebony... They occupied in thy fairs with emeralds, purple, and broided work, and fine linen, and coral, and agate... They traded in thy market wheat... and honey, and oil, and balm... in the multitude of the wares of thy making, for the multitude of all riches; in the wines of Helbon, and white wool... in precious clothes for chariots... in these were they thy merchants... They occupied in thy fairs with chief of all spices, and with all precious stones, and gold.... These

"For thus saith the Lord GOD; Behold, I will bring upon Tyrus [economic system]....And he shall set engines of war against thy walls..."

"Thus saith the Lord GOD: O Tyrus..."

were thy merchants in all sorts of things.... and in all thy company which is in the midst of thee, shall fall into the midst of the seas in the day of thy ruin. The suburbs shall shake at the sound of the cry of thy pilots....And shall cause their voice to be heard against thee, and shall cry bitterly, and shall cast up dust upon their heads, they shall wallow themselves in the ashes...

"...and shall cry bitterly, and shall cast up dust upon their heads, they shall wallow themselves in the ashes..."

they shall weep for thee with bitterness of heart and bitter wailing. And in their wailing they shall take up a lamentation for thee, and lament over thee, saying..."Thou didst enrich the kings of the earth with the multitude of thy riches and thy merchandise...thy merchandise and all thy company in the midst of thee shall fall. All the inhabitants of the isles shall be astonished at thee, and their kings shall be sore afraid [the horrible international fear of terrorism took root throughout the international community], they shall be troubled in their countenance.

I believe that the Day of Jehovah Tsaba, as shown in Isaiah 2, began with 9/11. I believe this to be where we are right now in the prophetic event, the Day of Jehovah Tsaba, the great judgment being sent to comfort God's people with a great wealth inversion. It is a period in which He said He would shake all nations and that they would become a "plunder," and the gold and silver will be supernaturally orchestrated into the hands of the righteous.

You will continue to see much volatility. Wall Street will go up and down, but it will go down with greater acceleration as the terror begins to take greater hold in the earth as God's judgment is allowed to be fulfilled.

Proverbs 13:22 tells us, "The wealth of the sinner is laid up for the just." Likewise, Job 27:13, 16–17 says, "This is the way of a wicked man with God.... Though he heap silver as the dust, and prepare raiment as the clay; He may prepare it, but the just shall put it on, and the innocent [righteous] shall divide the silver."

Today, we are beginning to see it fulfilled. With the fall of the World Trade Center the shaking began! Nevertheless, we shout with a great shout, "Let them shout for joy, and be glad, that favour my righteous cause: yea, let them say continually, Let the LORD be magnified, which hath pleasure in the prosperity of his servant" (Ps. 35:27).

Chapter Eleven

THE
"ALIVE AND REMAIN" GENERATION

Those who were once enlightened, and have tasted of the heavenly gift, and were made partakers of the Holy Ghost, And have tasted the good word of God, and the powers of the world to come.
—Hebrews 6:4–5

Just before Israel was to go over into the Promised Land, God sent twelve men over to bring back a sampling of what the land was like. These men were commissioned to reach over into the Promised Land and to partake of that glory! God is speaking the same thing to the church right now!

In Numbers 13:1–2 we read, "And the Lord spake unto Moses, saying, Send thou men, that they may search the land of Canaan, which I give unto the children of Israel." Then in verse 20 he reveals that they were to find out "what the land is, whether it be fat or lean, whether there be wood therein, or not. And…bring of the fruit of the land." They returned and "cut down from thence a branch with one cluster of grapes, and they bare it between two upon a staff.…And they told him and said, We came unto the land whither thou sentest us, and surely it floweth with milk and honey; and this is the fruit of it" (Num. 13:23, 27).

Later, in Numbers 14:7–9, Joshua and Caleb spoke to Israel, saying, "The land, which we passed through to search it, is an exceeding good land. If the Lord delight in us, then he will bring us into the land, and give it us; a land which floweth with milk and honey. Only rebel not ye against the Lord, neither fear ye the people of the land; for they are bread for us: their defence is departed from them, and the Lord is with us: fear them not."

I believe this to be analogous of where we are as the body of Christ. We have come to the end of this age, approaching the Rapture of the church! I believe God is going to allow a remnant of His people—those who are fearless, strong, and courageous and willing to receive God's goodness—to enjoy the powers of the world to come.

I am seeing things in Scripture that I have not seen in the past years of my life, although I have been studying God's Word since my earliest childhood. God has made provision for us through certain promises that, in the past, we have only seen in a measure of light. As we see these exceeding great and precious promises, we want to reach out and partake of them, much like Caleb and Joshua did when they went over into Canaan. Of course, there are others who, like the ten spies for Israel, may see what I am seeing and become afraid and intimidated by it. If you will let me, I will cut down a branch of the fruit of it and bring it back for you to enjoy. So just stay with me. I am not going to take you where the Word of God does not go!

A Phenomenon of Total Victory

Phenomenon: Something experienced by the senses as a remarkable thing; an experience in which something observed is said to be extraordinary.

You are a very special person! The fact that you and I have crossed paths through this writing lets me know that God has invited you to be part of a unique group upon the earth. (If you have not yet accepted Jesus Christ into your life, you may do so before finishing this book!)

God has strengthened me with might by His Spirit within me. For most of my life I have walked by faith in God's Word. I have lived my life during this period fully relying upon the laws of faith, patience, and the love of God. I know that He cannot and will not fall short of what He has promised, and I believe God has planned a pre-Rapture event exclusively for the church, a mass conversion of the wealth of the world. Those who use their faith and work the scriptural principles will be greatly blessed. It has been better described by some as "an inversion" of what the world has laid up in store. Everything will be turned upside down or rightside up. The wicked rich will become the non-rich, while the faith-believing righteous (the rich in faith) will become the rich of this world! You will see this in God's plan at the very end of this age. The greater wealth of the world will tumble into the laps of believers who are working the principles laid down for godly prosperity. This event that has begun in a measure will continue with ever-increasing force between now and the end of this age.

You will not receive it if you allow yourself to be captured by a selfish spirit. You cannot hang on to patterns and traits that might have prepared you for lack, for "just enough." You have to sever all of those ideas. Getting *my* house paid for, setting *myself* up for retirement, getting *myself* ready to adapt to a budget: while these things have their place in natural, human wisdom, none of these will be allowed if you want to step over into this new Promised Land of unlimited proportions, a place of the "no-budget anointing." Taking such steps will paralyze your entrance into the prosperity phenomenon. It will take a high level of possibility thinking, of total positivity regarding life, and an unusual measure of generosity relative to the needs of people around you.

God gave me an assignment regarding this phenomenon. He spoke prophetically to me out of Isaiah 62:10–12 and said, "Go through, go through the gates; prepare ye the way of the people; cast up, cast up the highway; gather out the stones; lift up a standard for the people. Behold, the LORD hath proclaimed unto the end of the world [speaking of the very last of the Last Days], Say ye to the daughter of Zion, Behold, thy salvation cometh; behold, his reward [Heb., "substance, wealth"] is with him, and his work before him. And they shall call them, The holy people, The redeemed of the LORD: and thou shalt be called, Sought out, A city not forsaken." God further explains in Isaiah 63:16 that Isaiah, known for his messianic prophecies for the church, is writing for the benefit of the body of Christ. "Doubtless thou art our father, though Abraham be ignorant of us, and Israel acknowledge us not: thou, O LORD, art our father, our redeemer; thy name is from everlasting."

God clearly said to me, "Go through, go through the gates!" He showed me that it was the gates of a prosperity phenomenon!

A REVELATION OF THE "DITCHES"

I have always enjoyed a particular portion of scripture found in 2 Kings 3:6–20, which details a miracle at the hand of Elisha. As the story unfolds, three kings, representing Israel, Judah, and Edom, were required to cross a desert area with their armies. After several days they and their animals were about to die from lack of water. Imagine how large a watering hole it would take to handle three armies of men and their beasts!

The kings went to Elisha, the prophet, for their answer. God subsequently used the prophet to bring water to them. As the anointing came upon Elisha, he proclaimed, "Thus saith the LORD, Make this valley full of ditches. For thus saith the LORD, Ye shall not see wind, neither shall ye see rain; yet that valley shall be filled with water, that ye may drink, both ye, and your cattle, and your beasts....And it came to pass in the morning, when the meat offering was offered, that, behold, there came water by the way of Edom, and the country was filled with water" (2 Kings 3:16–20).

As I was reading these verses, the Spirit of God quickened me and said, "Proclaim to the people to make their valley full of ditches for a great deluge of prosperity." He then reminded me of Psalm 126:1–4, "When the LORD turned again the captivity [Heb., 'reversed the prosperity toward'] of Zion, we were like them that dream. Then was our mouth filled with laughter, and our tongue with singing: then said they among the heathen [Heb., 'Gentiles'], The LORD hath done great things for them. The LORD hath done great things for us; whereof we are glad. Turn again our captivity [Heb., 'reverse the prosperity toward'], O LORD, as the streams [rivers] in the south [country]."

I was praying over these passages, and the Lord said, "Tell them that I am going to loose a flood tide of prosperity for the church. I will go into the world's system and cause the world's system to be shaken, and it will tumble. When this occurs, it will be for those who favor My righteous cause in the earth. It will tumble toward My people. Tell them that in order for it to come to them they will need to do like Elisha said: 'Make this valley full of ditches.'" God showed me how it is going to work. I want you to see it and get in on God's best with me.

Why did God tell Elisha they were to make the valley full of ditches? The word *ditches* in the Hebrew means "a canal for irrigation; a cistern." I remember that as a young boy back in Arkansas my family owned a mercantile store out in the country. All around us were cotton, soybean, and rice farmers. We would go down to the rice canals and play around. We would even go swimming in them. They were used to water the rice crops. Many farmers use very modern irrigation techniques that require them to crisscross their fields, making special furrows. These special ditches are designed with one purpose in mind. Somewhere close by there is an irrigation pump hooked up to a water well. That pump does not direct the flow of the water to the field. It only produces the water supply. As it flows forth as a deluge of water, the farmer determines where the water flows by making ditches connected to the main flow of water. As the water gushes down its main path, it is out of control. The ditches are necessary to determine its course. Suddenly, it crosses an intersection where there is an opening to a ditch. *Whoosh!* A portion of the water suddenly turns from its original destination and begins to flow down the path of that ditch. In Elisha's miracle, they supposedly made cisterns at the ends of the ditches to catch the water and give their cattle the ability to drink.

God said to tell you that every time you obey a promise of His Word connected to receiving material blessings from God, you make a ditch for this prosperity phenomenon! When you tithe or give anything in obedience to God or His Word, when you forgive, when you support the programs of your church, or do anything in faith, it is like making a ditch for this great material blessing! You are making your valley full of ditches!

Say with me now, "God takes pleasure in prospering those who favor His righteous cause!" Keep making those ditches, and stand with unwavering faith to receive what God has promised. As this deluge of prosperity is loosed towards the church, it will find you, and *whoosh!* It will flow right to your doors! Abundance of wealth will come to you!

Let me use Malachi 3:10–18 to demonstrate what God is saying to us. In the tenth verse God tells us that each time we bring in a tithe we get a blessing. We are told that just one of the blessings will bring so much that "there shall not be room enough to receive it." Say with me now, "A tithe, a blessing—so much that there will not be room enough to receive it!"

Imagine how many times you have given your tithe (a tenth) of your increase to God. It only takes one tithe to get the flow started, because the Word says, "Pour you out a blessing [singular], that there shall not be room enough to receive it [singular]"! You need to get hold of that promise accurately. Don't set your faith that you will have to prove and prove and prove and prove yourself until finally someday God will open the windows of heaven. No! Say it with me again, "A tithe, a blessing!" The very first blessing should be more than you have room enough to receive! Praise God for it, and don't ever turn loose of believing what is yours!

Let's look at the Hebrew on this subject. In Malachi 3:10 we have the phrase "that there shall not be room enough to receive it." In the Hebrew concordance that phrase consists of only one word. According to *Strong's Dictionary of Hebrew and Greek*, the words translated *that, not,* and *enough* are all one word in Hebrew, *dahee*. This is used as a Hebrew phrase meaning "able, more than enough, much as is sufficient, more than is containable, too much." As you can see, that one word means that when you bring in your tithe you make "a ditch" that will be "more than is containable, too much!" Praise God!

Remember that Jesus also measured a portion like that in Luke 6:38 when instructing us in the law of giving. He said, "Good measure, pressed down, and shaken together, and running over, shall men give into your bosom." Let me share how The Living Bible translation states it: "For if you give, you will get! Your gift will return to you in full and overflowing measure, pressed down, shaken together to make room for more, and running over. Whatever measure you use to give—large or small—will be used to measure what is given back to you." *Ditches! Ditches! Ditches!* I hear God saying right now, "Make this valley full of ditches!"

There are so many ways to make these "prosperity phenomenon ditches" that I cannot possibly share all of them with you. Just remember that if your faith and actions are connecting to one of God's promises of material blessing, then it is a ditch! I want to share one avenue that might have escaped you. Look at 1 Peter 3:9 with me: "Not rendering evil for evil, or railing for railing: but contrariwise blessing; knowing that ye are thereunto called, that ye should inherit a blessing." See! Another ditch is made! As this avalanche of prosperity is being poured out (it has already begun!), *whoosh!* It will suddenly turn toward you. It will head straight for your door!

I want you to get hold of this. You will need to put a guard on your mouth. You must know how to use your faith for this phenomenon prophesied in the Bible. God has taught you some things about faith. Many of you have been going from paycheck to paycheck, struggling with your bills, perhaps living in the land of "just enough." Some of you have been in the land of "not enough"! But you can do this! Receive right now into your spirit that you can do it by saying out loud, "I can do it! I can use my faith for this prosperity phenomenon!" Take the anointing for it right now. Reach up into the air, make a fist, and pull it back to you and say, "I'm taking that anointing that was upon Israel when they spoiled Egypt of its silver and gold!"

TWO KINDS OF TITHERS

In our prior tithe scripture in Malachi, God makes mention of two kinds of tithers. I call them "good tithers" and "bad tithers." With these terms I am referencing those who tithe using faith principles and those who tithe but refuse to stand on God's promise concerning the tithe.

God says to those who gave their tithe but wavered in their faith, "Your words have been stout against me, saith the LORD [Jehovah]. Yet ye say, What have we spoken so much against thee? Ye have said, It is vain to serve God: and what profit is it that we have kept his ordinance [of the tithe], and that we have walked mournfully before the LORD of hosts [Jehovah Tsaba]? And now we call the proud happy; yea, they that work wickedness are set up; yea, they that tempt God are even delivered" (Mal. 3:13–15).

Then God addresses those who tithed in faith. They stood on God's promises relating to the tithe. They used faith principles, described in the next verse: "Then they that feared the LORD spake often one to another [You see, they spoke faith's words and made faith's confession]: And the LORD hearkened, and heard it, and a book of remembrance was written before him for them that feared the LORD, and that thought upon his name" (Mal. 3:16).

I am declaring to you that God is preparing to pour out, in this very hour, those blessings that have been set to your account from your tithe! His "book of remembrance" will reveal what is yours, and the blessing will flow to your door! God goes on to say, "And they shall be mine saith the LORD of hosts [Jehovah Tsaba], in that day when I make up my jewels [Heb., 'to appoint; an appointment for distribution of wealth']; and I will spare [Heb., 'have compassion upon'] them, as a man spareth [has compassion on] his own son that serveth him" (Mal. 3:17). Let me make one additional note about this verse. The word translated *jewels* is, in the Hebrew, defined as "wealth," while the phrase *make up* means "to appoint the distribution of; or to bestow."

The last verse of this passage in Malachi is very exciting: "Then shall ye return [Heb., 'to turn and look again'], and discern [Heb., 'be able to tell the difference'] between the righteous and the wicked, between him that serveth God and him that serveth him not" (Mal. 3:18).

The prosperity "ditches" you make and guard to keep open with your faith in God's Word will keep you abundantly connected to this prosperity phenomenon that is now underway in the earth. Praise God!

A Revelation of Life Is Coming to Light!

> Who hath saved us, and called us with an holy calling, not according to our works, but according to his own purpose and grace, which was given us in Christ Jesus before the world began, But is now made manifest by the appearing of our Saviour Jesus Christ, who hath abolished death, and hath brought life and immortality to light through the gospel.
>
> —2 Timothy 1:9–10

I believe we are rapidly approaching the Rapture of the church. It is to take place at the very end of this age. Many serious theologians agree that all signs point to this fact. We believe the generation currently living will experience the great event of the church as it is caught away to meet the Lord Jesus in the air. To fully understand this message, you will need to think accordingly.

You may not want to think the way that many of our Christian fathers of past generations did. We have been blessed by these great men and women of faith, yet they have often demonstrated what I would call a Christian death mentality. What I mean is that they have incorporated into their faith an expectancy of physical death. They have prepared for it. They have preached it, exhorted, and declared to everyone, "You are going to die!" They say, "Death comes to all, and there is no escaping it!"

It is understandable that they would think this way since the only alternative was to achieve immortality, as Enoch did. None apparently considered that a viable possibility. The event of Enoch being caught up to heaven that can be found in Genesis 5:21–24 has remained a great mystery to the Church Fathers.

I am of a new breed, a new-generation student of the Bible. When I see something clearly pronounced in God's Word, I believe it is possible. If you believe the Bible, you cannot say that death comes to all men. Enoch did not die! Elijah went up alive into God's chariot. God does not give special respect to certain individuals. It may look like He does, but what He is doing is having special respect for certain principles of faith. I believe if a man or woman meets the same criteria that Enoch did, he or she will see the same results. Hebrews 11:5 tells us that "by faith Enoch was translated that he should not see death." You might ask, How did Enoch achieve immortality and never see death? He did it by using certain faith principles.

To use faith in God, you must have a word from God. Faith comes by hearing the Word of God! (See Romans 10:17.) So how did Enoch get a word from God that could cause his faith to produce such a great blessing? Well, you know if we search the Scriptures we'll find out! If we find that he had a unique and personal word from God that was exclusive to him, then we cannot use it. If we find that his revelation was not unique to him but included every believer, then we too have the right to claim the same promise that Enoch received.

The Bible declares that no promise of the Scripture is unique to just one person. (See 2 Peter 1:20: "Knowing this first, that no prophecy of the scripture is of any private interpretation.") So how did Enoch get his word from God? You will find the only clue in Jude 1:14, "And Enoch also, the seventh from Adam, prophesied of these, saying, Behold, the Lord cometh with ten thousands of his saints." We see here that Enoch had a revelation of Jesus! What was Jesus's great mission? It was to give His life and die for us. He saw Jesus! That is always the key to life's questions! As the songwriter said, "Turn you eyes upon Jesus," and as the lyrics say, the things of the world will seem to fade when we gaze upon the Savior.

Our spiritual Fathers did not seem to make any connection with Enoch's revelation. They obsessed in a mind-set that all men must physically die. I find no fault with them. However, please understand what I am saying. I have always found that God's plan, while given entirely from the beginning in Scripture, was designed to be progressively revealed by the Holy Spirit. In other words, the Bible contains all the truth of God's will, but the Holy Spirit reveals it progressively to complete its ultimate fulfillment by the end of this age. While our past spiritual Fathers acknowledged the possibility of the coming of Christ during their lifetime, they had no real assurance that it would occur that quickly.

The signs were not as clear as they are today. Without an imminent Rapture of the church facing them during their lifetime, they could conceive no alternative but to face death. Otherwise, they would be forced to live on to be so old that they would become tired of life on earth. They would be trapped. After all, there develops in a Christian believer a natural and progressive desire to see Jesus. We can get homesick for heaven and our closest loved ones who have already gone.

Therefore, our ministers of the faith (and consequently, believers who followed in their steps) have universally told us things like: "One thing is certain: everyone is going to die. You will surely face death." Typical Christian confessions have been, "I'll serve Him till I die" or "'till death do us part." One old beloved hymn proclaims that when we die we'll "fly away." Until now anyone who stood up and attempted to question dying and death from a scriptural standpoint was deemed a heretic and booed off the platform of ministry. Because of this persecution within the church, no one was motivated to really approach the subject for a foundation of faith. Without revelation there is no preaching and without preaching there is no hearing and without hearing there is no faith!

Apostle Paul's goal was not to die

Few know or understand the meaning of a scripture found in the Pauline Epistles. The verses themselves are not unfamiliar to the church. But no one has ever really made them a part of the aspiration of the Christian walk. They are found in the Book of Philippians.

> [For my determined purpose is] that I may know Him [that I may progressively become more deeply and intimately acquainted with Him, perceiving and recognizing and understanding the wonders of His Person more strongly and more clearly], and that I may in that same way come to know the power outflowing from His resurrection [which it exerts over believers], and that I may so share His sufferings as to be continually transformed [in spirit into His likeness even] to His death, [in the hope] That if possible I may attain to the [spiritual and moral] resurrection [that lifts me] out from among the dead [even while in the body].
>
> —Philippians 3:10–11, AMP

Did you catch that? "[That lifts me] out from among the dead [even while in the body]." Paul was looking at a possibility. He wasn't just fantasizing. He declared this as his "determined purpose" in life.

Why is it that when someone attempts to explore this realm in the church today he or she is often discredited as being "off the deep end" of ministry, accused of having "crazy faith," or labeled with some other innuendo to dissuade them in their believing.

I want to tell you that I have a word from God for this generation. It is a word that comes from God's Word, the Bible! I want to tell you that you do not have to have a mind-set of death. Why not? Because you are living during one of the most strategic and unique periods of history, comparable only to the Creation and the birth of Jesus. We are a chosen generation. If you will walk in God's best, you may choose to remain until the Rapture of the church and never see death! And as part of this generation, by using your faith in God's Word and working His principles, you may also live a lifestyle greater than the world and its kings have ever seen. That is the real purpose of this book.

I do not want you to mistake my motivation. It is not to satisfy your fear of death. It is not to entice you into a lifestyle of lasciviousness or covetousness. You must qualify to get in on this divine life and lifestyle. You will need to learn contentment, along with a true revelation of what God wants you to do with the great wealth He has planned to give you. You will learn to never "trust in uncertain riches, but in the living God, who giveth us richly all things to enjoy." You will need to learn that "it is more blessed to give than to receive," as Jesus stated (Acts 20:35).

You should also have absolutely no fear as a believer in Christ. God's promise to supply all of your need is connected to your learning His principles of sowing and reaping (giving and receiving). (See Philippians 4:15–19.) To live this life to the fullest you must exercise your authority over death. Death has no power over you. If you were to physically die as a Christian, you would go immediately into the presence of the Lord. Heaven becomes your home! Why should you be afraid of death? Why should you be frightened of going to a place with streets of gold and mansions for everyone, a place where many of your family members are waiting for your arrival? It is a place of utter rest and peace.

I am a card-carrying "alive and remainer"! I believe that I will "be alive and remain unto the coming of the Lord." Throughout this writing, my motivation for you to escape death and remain until Jesus returns for the church is not out of some morbid fear of death. Likewise, you will see that my reason for wanting you to get in on God's redistribution of the world's wealth is not for covetous purposes. I will show you that it may be better for you to remain until Jesus returns for His people. The best thing for past believers was to go on to be with the Lord. Because of the shortness of time and God's plan for His glory at this special time, I believe that it may be God's will for you, as a believer, to remain. You may say, "But I am of the older generation. My body is almost worn out. Maybe I should just plan to go on." That is the purpose of this writing: to inspire you to remain until He comes.

You will need to adjust many areas of your thinking. Did you know that I have a scripture that entitles you to get younger than you are right now? If need be, you can be physically rejuvenated and renewed by God's promise and power. It will be necessary that you renew your mind to what God says about this generation to make the appropriate transition. Say with me aloud right now, "I am part of a chosen generation destined to see the coming of the Lord! I believe I receive right now all of the supernatural benefits afforded this generation!"(In this section, I will frequently ask you to repeat things aloud. Please do it! It serves a very important purpose. Spoken words are spiritual containers. A word must be spoken to be a spiritual force. I do not have the space here to write a book on words, but others have done much writing on the subject. Writing is the physical mechanical representation of words. That is the way we get it to your mind! You read it, and it goes into your mind. To get them into your heart and out into your lives they must be spoken. You see, the moment words are spoken and subsequently heard, they become spiritual forces that (1) go into your heart and (2) have the ability to be released through your mouth. Then faith becomes a force in your life. Your mind will be affected as you read this, but it will do you no good until you get it into your heart and release it into your life. That is why I urge you to speak these things with me.)

We are going to experience the revelation of God's plan to transfer the wealth of the nations of the world into the hands of the righteous. That is right! That is us! Say, "That is me! I am one of God's righteous ones in the earth! I favor God's righteous cause in the earth!"

As a believer alive at this time you are to participate in a prophetic event. It was planned by God to grant you great temporal blessings of wealth, riches, honor, and long life. You need to get familiar with those words. Say, "Wealth, riches, honor, life!"

Proverbs 3:16, speaking of God's principles, says, "Length of days is in her right hand; and in her left hand riches and honour." The promise has always been there, but I believe that you may tap into a greater anointing today! Say aloud with me right now, "A greater anointing than Solomon's is here!"

As you read you will also see that God has ordained this last generation to experience the glory of the Lord in a way previously unknown to us. He has planned to come upon His people to bless them with the glory (wealth and honor) of this world.

For the most part, Christians are afraid of the glory of this world. It is the same glory that Satan tempted Jesus with during His wilderness experience. The scripture says, "Again, the devil taketh him up into an exceeding high mountain, and sheweth him all the kingdoms of the world, and the glory of them; And saith unto him, All these things will I give thee, if thou wilt fall down and worship me" (Matt. 4:8–9). All the things the nations of the world are seeking after was what Satan used to try to tempt Jesus. Yet Jesus promised in Matthew 6:32–33, "(For after all these things do the nations seek:) for your heavenly Father knoweth that ye have need of all these things. But seek ye first the kingdom of God, and his righteousness; and all these things shall be added unto you." You should not be afraid of having all these things.

Heaven, where God lives, holds an untold splendor unlike anything the earth has to offer. In other words, it is impossible to describe the glory reserved for us there. The church has majored on that. But the glory ordained for you here on this earth, while it has been ignored, has been described in greatest detail. In other words, I cannot tell you all that God has for us in heaven, but I can tell you exactly what God has for us here on earth. He knew that you would need to use your faith for it in order receive it. That is why He described it in such detail in the Scriptures. To really enjoy it you will need to adopt all of the principles included in God's Word for this end period.

I want to introduce you to what, for me, is a most startling revelation brought to light in the Bible. It is a revelation of life—for this life! God's best for your supernatural prosperity includes your being here to use and enjoy it.

You'll see your kids, grandkids, and possibly great grandkids reap the blessings for believers of this last Christian generation.

I want you to become aware of something. God spoke to me that we will see many of our great men and women of God go on to be with the Lord. He told me that this is His will if they are unable to receive this revelation of truth. They may receive the promises of wealth and riches but then die and go on to be with the Lord without enjoying wealth's benefits to the fullest end. He told me to tell you, "You can receive the revelation of prosperity without receiving faith to overcome physical death. But when faced with an enemy, if you don't overcome it, you can count on it overcoming you!" He wants you to receive it. I think as you read you will see its benefits and come to rest in the tremendous added blessing for you and your family.

The appointment

It is appointed unto men once to die, but after this the judgment.

—HEBREWS 9:27

We have heard or seen these words countless times: at church altar calls, funerals, in witnessing tracts, and in Christian sermons. "It is appointed unto men once to die." There is no question that the Bible reveals that when Adam sinned humanity received an appointment to die!

When Jesus came on the scene, He began to speak in revolutionary terms. One such statement is, "Verily, verily, I say unto you, If a man keep my saying, he shall never see death" (John 8:51). Of course, this statement declares (in some sense) that every believer is free of death. As Christians we know that death no longer holds power over us. Even if physical death comes, it has no power over you because you received the benefits of eternal life at the time you accepted Jesus Christ as your Savior. In John 5:24 Jesus declared, "Verily, verily, I say unto you, He that heareth my word, and believeth on him that sent me, hath everlasting life, and shall not come into condemnation; but is passed from death unto life."

We understand from the Scriptures that at the moment of death every believer's spirit and soul go to be with the Lord!

Therefore we are always confident, knowing that, whilst we are at home in the body, we are absent from the Lord: (For we walk by faith, not by sight:) We are confident, I say, and willing rather to be absent from the body, and to be present with the Lord.

—2 CORINTHIANS 5:6–8

Past Christian generations have held closely, as we do, to this very blessed truth. As believers we have much assurance that physical death is not the end for us. We have held to our belief that at the point of physical death we simply make a transition out of the physical realm into the spiritual atmosphere of heaven. We know this is true according to God's Word. Those who die, live with the Lord until the Rapture of the church. At that time they receive their resurrected, immortal bodies. Later, they return to this earth for a millennium, during which Jesus rules with all of His family on earth. Praise God for this wonderful truth! Every believer has this assurance of ultimate victory! Of course, we comfort bereaved loved ones with this truth when our Christian family members die and go to be with the Lord.

Those who sleep (through physical death) (1 Cor. 15:51–52: "We shall not all sleep, but we shall all be changed, In a moment, in the twinkling of an eye, at the last trump: for the trumpet shall sound, and the dead shall be raised incorruptible, and we shall be changed") will be caught up into the air with those who remain. We know that this refers to the physical body of the believers who have died. In 1 Thessalonians 4:14–17 the scripture explains, "Even so them also which sleep in Jesus will God bring with him. For this we say unto you by the word of the Lord, that we which are alive and remain unto the coming of the Lord shall not prevent them which are asleep. For the Lord himself shall descend from heaven with a shout, with the voice of the archangel, and with the trump of God: and the dead in Christ shall rise first: Then we which are alive and remain shall be caught up together with them in the clouds, to meet the Lord in the air: and so shall we ever be with the Lord." So whether we remain or whether we physically die, we will be together on that day.

Notice that by placing these two prior scriptures together we see that during the Rapture event prophesied, those who have died in Christ come with Jesus in the air, but their physical bodies are resurrected out of the earth. They are not just being raised from the dead, as some have been in this life. Their bodies change as they come out of the grave and become incorruptible.

The spirit and soul reunite with the physical body, transformed from corruption, and the result is immortality. Whether we sleep or remain, we change and become immortal.

As I began to be led by God into an in-depth study of what the Bible says about life, I concluded that the church has built doctrines on the lines of both physical life and physical prosperity around pieces of Scripture. How often have they warned us not to accept a part of a Scripture out of context. Yet in both the cases of authority over physical death and of prosperity for the believer I believe the church has done just that. I also believe that while Jesus knew that the church would not immediately receive His words in their fullest sense, He released them as He did because of the Father's plan for this last generation.

You will find that much of what Jesus said was to progressively come to its fullest and richest understanding at the very end of this age. All other generations would receive illumination of them only in a measure, but those of us who live in this last generation will receive them in their greater light. We have much yet to learn, but we are seeing many scriptures in the greatest light yet of any previous generation. This must come in order for the glory of God to increase in these last days.

Let's deal with the scripture found in Hebrews 9:27: "And as it is appointed unto men once to die, but after this the judgment." You will notice that this verse begins with a conjunction, suggesting that it connects with another thought. To understand what the writer is attempting to tell us, we would need to back up to the beginning of the thought rather than start in the middle. Notice the context of this verse in light of other verses around it in Hebrews 9:24–28:

> For Christ is not entered into the holy places made with hands, which are the figures of the true; but into heaven itself, now to appear in the presence of God for us: Nor yet that he should offer himself often, as the high priest entereth into the holy place every year with blood of others; For then must he often have suffered since the foundation of the world: but now once in the end of the world hath he appeared to put away sin by the sacrifice of himself. And as it is appointed unto men once to die, but after this the judgment: So Christ was once

offered to bear the sins of many; and unto them that look for him shall he appear the second time without sin unto salvation.

Let's add a scripture from Romans 5:6–8:

For when we were yet without strength, in due time Christ died for the ungodly. For scarcely for a righteous man will one die: yet peradventure for a good man some would even dare to die. But God commendeth his love toward us, in that, while we were yet sinners, Christ died for us.

Notice the context of Hebrews 9:27. Please allow me to paraphrase these scriptures for emphasis only: "The high priests had to offer their sacrifices of animals often, because it was not the perfect final sacrifice. But Christ offered Himself once. He did this because He was dying for humankind, who had only one appointment with death. Therefore He was able to keep our one appointment with His one death."

In other words, "one appointment to die" was met by "one appointment with death." Most Christian believers use Hebrews 9:27 as their basis for Christian death. They mostly quote it out of context like, "Well, you know the Bible says it's appointed unto man once to die." If they kept this verse in its context, it would not sentence them to die but rather loose them from their appointment of death. Romans 5:8 says, "Christ died for us." I believe the totality of the revelation of this has been held under wraps by the Holy Spirit until now.

You say, "But I believe in the mouth of two or three witnesses every word should be established." OK! I agree with you! When something is really scriptural, there will be several confirmations. Let's look at Psalm 102:18–21: "This shall be written for the generation to come: and the people which shall be created shall praise the LORD. For he hath looked down from the height of his sanctuary; from heaven did the LORD behold the earth; To hear the groaning of the prisoner; to loose those that are appointed to death; To declare the name of the LORD in Zion, and his praise in Jerusalem [His church]." This has to refer to the Christian believer. Adam and Eve were created, but since then the only people created are those who have accepted Christ. By being "born again" (John 3:3) they become a new creation (2 Cor. 5:17).

That makes three scriptures that provide confirmation: Romans 5:6–8, Hebrews 9:24–28, and Psalm 102:18–21. In each of these we have held to the accurate context of Scripture, namely that we are set free from the appointment of death. Now we have a basis for our faith. Now we can use this as a foundation to safely build upon. But because this may be a hard case to convince the average believer, I will give you one other basis of truth for believing this.

It is found in 2 Timothy 1:9–10, "Who hath saved us, and called us with an holy calling, not according to our works, but according to his own purpose and grace, which was given us in Christ Jesus before the world began, But is now made manifest by the appearing of our Saviour Jesus Christ, who hath abolished death, and hath brought life and immortality to light through the gospel."

Let's approach it from yet another standpoint. In Hebrews 2:8 there is a statement regarding the authority of the believer. It states, "Thou hast put all things in subjection under his [man's] feet. For in that he put all in subjection under him, he left nothing that is not put under him. But now we see not yet all things put under him."

Here is where faith in the Word will bring you a provision of God that is not yet universally seen. A good example is Enoch, one of the Old Testament heroes of faith mentioned in Hebrews 11:5. It states that "Enoch was translated that he should not see death." This would be difficult to understand, were it not for the principles of faith. You see, I left out the very first two words of the verse in order to place greater emphasis upon it now: "*By faith* Enoch was translated that he should not see death" (emphasis added).

I am not asserting that death for every believer will be destroyed prior to the Rapture of the church. We will continue to see Christian funerals until the very end of this age. But notice something unique here. First Corinthians 15:25–26 declares death to be an enemy: "For he must reign, till he hath put all enemies under his feet. The last enemy that shall be destroyed is death." Remember in Hebrews 2:8 we read that God did not leave anything that was not under our feet. He stated, "But now we see not yet all things put under him." Here is where faith comes into play! Faith is the "substance of things hoped for, the evidence of things not seen" (Heb. 11:1). In other words, faith has the ability to reach out and take the things promised but not yet seen, and possess them as a personal reality. Let's look at that verse from the Amplified Bible: "Now faith is the assurance (the confirmation, the title-deed) of the things [we] hope for, being the proof of things [we] do not see and the conviction of their reality [faith perceiving as a real fact what is not revealed to the senses]."

You can see that this is how Enoch escaped death, how he put it under his feet! It appears that Enoch walked with God to the point that God revealed to him the triumph of the Lord Jesus over death. We catch a glimpse of what Enoch knew in Jude 14: "And Enoch also, the seventh from Adam, prophesied of these, saying, Behold, the Lord cometh with ten thousands of his saints." It would appear from this scripture that Enoch was seeing the day when the enemy of death would be seen under the feet of every believer. We know, of course, that this was accomplished through the death and resurrection of Jesus. It is a finished work and available (through faith) for all who will grasp the revelation of it!

God brought to my mind, relative to remaining until the Rapture of the church (being an "alive and remainer") an account of a man in Luke 2:25–30. Mary and Joseph had brought Jesus to be dedicated to the Lord. We pick up the story in verses 25–26.

> And, behold, there was a man in Jerusalem, whose name was Simeon; and the same man was just and devout, waiting for the consolation of Israel: and the Holy Ghost was upon him. And it was revealed unto him by the Holy Ghost, that he should not see death, before he had seen the Lord's Christ.

I can just imagine what people were saying to him. "Simeon, you're gettin' old. Don't you know that you have no assurance of another day to live?" Simeon would reply, "I'll not die today. I will not die early. God has revealed to me that I will live until the coming of Messiah." You see, Simeon knew he would live out his life until he had seen Jesus come as a baby.

Verses 27–30 continue as follows:

> And he came by the Spirit into the temple: and when the parents brought in the child Jesus, to do for him after the custom of the law, Then took he him up in his arms, and blessed God, and said, Lord,

now lettest thou thy servant depart in peace, according to thy word: For mine eyes have seen thy salvation.

I, too, have a revelation from the Holy Spirit. It is very similar to that of Simeon. God has revealed to me that I will be an "'alive and remainer' unto the coming of the Lord." First Thessalonians 4:17 states, "Then we which are alive and remain shall be caught up together with them in the clouds, to meet the Lord in the air." Likewise 1 Corinthians 15:51 explains, "Behold, I shew you a mystery; We shall not all sleep [see death]."

A Periodic Recharge with Life!

The body is dead because of sin.

—Romans 8:10

Two essentials to being successful in this life are health and prosperity. That is God's best! Ecclesiastes 5:19 declares, "Every man also to whom God hath given riches and wealth, and hath given him power [health] to eat thereof, and to take his portion, and to rejoice in his labour; this is the gift of God." Ecclesiastes 2:24 also says, "There is nothing better for a man, than that he should eat and drink, and that he should make his soul enjoy good in his labour. This also I saw, that it was from the hand of God." Ecclesiastes 6:2 shows the flipside of this: " A man to whom God hath given riches, wealth, and honour, so that he wanteth nothing for his soul of all that he desireth, yet God giveth him not power [health] to eat thereof, but a stranger eateth it: this is vanity, and it is an evil disease."

Deuteronomy 28 is the best example of a summary of the blessing of Abraham and of the curse of the Law, which are referred to in the apostle Paul's writing in Galatians 3:13–14: "Christ hath redeemed us from the curse of the law, being made a curse for us…That the blessing of Abraham might come on the Gentiles through Jesus Christ." Deuteronomy 28 clearly states that our redemption includes both the blessing of health and the power to get wealth. This is why it is so hard for me to approach this subject without bringing these two blessings together. True prosperity has many ingredients, but Deuteronomy 28 prioritizes health and wealth at the very top. God said it like this to me: "You can have money and health without prosperity, but you can't have prosperity without money and health!" Both are essential, along with other things, such as love, joy, peace, long-suffering, gentleness, goodness, faithfulness, meekness, and temperance, in completing a prosperous life. Third John 2 says, "Beloved, I wish above all things that thou mayest prosper and be in health, even as thy soul prospereth."

Say with me right now, "I am *not* putting aside love, joy, and peace. I am *not* forgetting about the other aspects of godly living. I *am* adding supernatural ability to abundance (ability to operate in the earth) and divine health!" Most folks have a problem seeing what old age may really be like under God's provision. I am going to help straighten that out if you'll follow closely with me. Most see old age as being more dependent upon others, perhaps ending in a nursing home or other retirement facility. They will say, "That's not for me!" Well, I'll just tell you, that's not for me either! For most, however, death is the only alternative to an extension of life. But I want to declare to you that there is something better. There is another alternative. It is God's best for you!

God's best is that you live and be supernaturally renewed in both your soul and your body. Your spirit is automatically renewed daily through the flow of eternal life provided to it since the time of the new birth. (See 2 Corinthians 4:16.) But your physical body is constantly in a state of change. If something does not come to its rescue, it contracts physical diseases and goes through stages that place it in danger of perishing. Day by day the cells need rejuvenating, and the body weakens ever so slowly until death eventually comes. So what is the answer?

The answer is the same as it was for Enoch. Learn to walk with God! I believe from Genesis 5:24, Jude 1:14, and Hebrews 11:5 that as Enoch walked with God, God revealed to him the purpose and plan for Jesus.

God must have said to him, "Enoch, it is My will that mankind be loosed from their appointment with death." He then must have shown him the future in a great vision. We know He gave Enoch a vision, because Jude 1:14 makes reference to it: "And Enoch also, the seventh from Adam, prophesied of these, saying, Behold, the Lord cometh with ten thousands of his saints." Of course, this scripture seems to reveal only a small portion of the vision. I believe God must have shown Enoch the whole event of Jesus coming, preaching, healing, working miracles, suffering, dying, being raised from the dead, ascending to the Father, rapturing the church at the great resurrection, and finally (concerning the Jude 1:14 passage) returning at the end of the Great Tribulation period to defeat all of His enemies on earth and begin His one-thousand-year reign from Jerusalem.

As he experienced all of his divine vision, I think Enoch came to believe with his heart the message of redemption. Faith came to reside when he received it into his heart. Because he now had faith in God's victory over death through Christ Jesus, Enoch was the first man to be loosed from the appointment of death. He did not die.

Until recently I did not understand this "translation" business. Why did God choose to take him? As I meditated day and night on these promises and as I prayed for guidance from the Holy Spirit, I came to understand. God had a situation on His hands: Enoch was not going to die (he had already been loosed, by faith, from his appointment). It was going to perhaps be another six thousand years or so before God would take the church out of the world. It obviously didn't seem right for God to spend those six thousand years walking on His streets of gold surrounded by inconceivable luxury while He rewarded (or punished) Enoch by sentencing him to be this six-thousand-year-old man living his life out as some bizarre antique of the human species who stood out among mankind as unable to die. The only merciful, compassionate, and just action to take would be to translate him, spirit, soul, and physical body, to heaven to live out the six thousand years remaining in this age there, enjoying the luxuries of heaven with the Father.

Wow! I believe that as you think on these scriptures, you will come to the same conclusion—that Enoch did not escape death by being translated, but rather he first escaped death and then at some point after 365 years of life, God took him.

Romans 8:11 says, "But [the way the scripture begins denotes that the phrase about to be spoken has met a specific challenge of something previously addressed and has successfully met that challenge with the answer] if the Spirit of him that raised up Jesus from the dead dwell in you, he that raised up Christ from the dead shall also quicken your mortal bodies by his Spirit that dwelleth in you." That is the answer to the yet-to-be addressed challenge that preceded it.

So let's go back to the previous verse and look at the challenge: "And if Christ be in you, the body is dead because of sin; but the spirit is life [or alive with life] because of righteousness" (Rom. 8:10). What was the challenge in verse 10 that was successfully met in verse 11? "The body is dead" is the challenge, thus suggesting that the answer is, "He that raised up Christ from the dead shall also quicken your mortal bodies by his Spirit that dwelleth in you." If you still have not grasped an understanding of this, go back and study through it again! It is important to understand this point.

So, we have already found out that at the time of the Rapture our mortal bodies are not just "quickened." They are changed, or transformed incorruptibly, and have become immortal. They are no longer mortal bodies that need quickening.

The word *mortal* can be described best as "death-bound." Our bodies, during this life, are just like a car battery. Every car battery is death-bound. Unless it receives periodic "quickening," it will continue to get weaker with every use. That is the purpose of a generator while the car engine is running. As the generator turns from the rotation of the engine, it produces outside energy back into the battery to charge it (or quicken it) with life. If your generator goes out, you end up eventually with a dead battery. Like me, you too may have had to raise your car battery from the dead! You may have let it go dead by leaving the lights on and then, like me, had to call the auto club. When they came out, they gave your battery a quick charge (hence, to "quicken") and brought life back into it.

That also describes perfectly why those who have gone on to be with the Lord had to leave their bodies. Their bodies continued to weaken until they died. It is sometimes the will of God for us to lay our hands on a dead body through the power of the Spirit to quicken it with physical life, much like we do a battery. The same power that raised Jesus from the dead enters the body of the one who has died, empowering it with a "quick charge" of resurrection power. Romans 8:11 declares, "But if the Spirit of him that raised up Jesus from the dead dwell in you, he that raised up Christ from the dead shall also quicken your mortal bodies by his Spirit that dwelleth in you."

Jesus was first raised from the dead, then later received His resurrected body. He was first quickened with life as He came forth from the grave. He did not come out of the grave with His resurrected, immortal body. He said to Mary, "Touch me not; for I am not yet ascended to my Father" (John 20:17).

Following this event, Jesus, the Word made flesh, would bring His quickened human body into the Holy of Holies of heaven: "But Christ being come an high priest...Neither by the blood of goats and calves, but by his own blood he entered in once into the holy place, having obtained eternal redemption for us" (Heb. 9:11–12). There He would offer the blood of sprinkling. He would offer Himself so that those who received Him would have their conscience purged from guilt and condemnation. That which was brought upon them by the sin of Adam—and, like Adam, through their own sin—would be made clean by the blood of the spotless Lamb of God.

Later Jesus would return to Mary and to all of the disciples. But He would return to them with a totally different body. When one of us gets a new automobile or a new house, we want to show it off to our most intimate friends. You know what I mean? Your demeanor with your closest friends is different than when you are with others. Jesus told Mary to run and tell the disciples (His closest friends) that He would see them shortly. He told them that when He did, their sorrow would be turned into joy!

Let's pick up the story of the Resurrection in John 20:19, 27, "Then the same day at evening, being the first day of the week, when the doors were shut where the disciples were assembled for fear of the Jews, came Jesus and stood in the midst...Then saith he to Thomas, Reach hither thy finger, and behold my hands; and reach hither thy hand, and thrust it into my side."

It was early in the morning on the first day of the week when Mary saw Jesus, and He said to her, "Touch me not; for I am not yet ascended to my Father" (John 20:17). But on the same day at evening Jesus said to Thomas, "Thrust it [your hand] into my side."

We know that by the time Jesus began appearing to His disciples He had His immortal, resurrected body, because instead of traveling wherever He went, He would simply appear and then later vanish from the scene. When doing this, He would seem to want to show off His new form and manner of life to His friends. He desired that they see that His body, though still flesh and bone, was now immortal, with inherent supernatural powers. During His earlier earth walk, He relied upon the power of the Holy Spirit, upon God's anointing Him to accomplish His supernatural ministry. Jesus often declared, "It's not Me doing the work, but it is the power of Him that sent Me!" In Acts 10:38 we have this explanation, "How God anointed Jesus of Nazareth with the Holy Ghost and with power: who went about doing good, and healing all that were oppressed of the devil; for God was with him."

Just as Jesus's final phase of resurrection was a separate operation from His being raised from the dead, even so, there is a great difference between someone being raised from the dead and entering into the resurrection. We see that the resurrection of the dead at the Rapture is God's ultimate and final answer to sin's challenge. He changes the body from mortal to immortal, giving it the ability to have life within itself. There will never again be the need to be quickened with life. But for this life there is a quickening power available if we will receive it by faith in the promises from God.

Someday you will be embodied with resurrection power. During this time, however, you can walk in His resurrection power through faith in the living promises of God's Word, empowered by the Holy Spirit, just as Jesus did in His earthly ministry.

GOD'S PROVISION FOR LIFE

> According as his divine power hath given unto us all things that pertain unto life and godliness, through the knowledge of him that hath called us to glory and virtue: Whereby are given unto us exceeding great and precious promises: that by these ye might be partakers of the divine nature, having escaped the corruption that is in the world through lust.
>
> —2 PETER 1:3–4

God has given us certain promises that are beyond normal comprehension. Except for the Bible, we would never accept them as logical or even possible. They defy all reason. Only because they are contained in God's Word do we take hold of them as a viable, workable resolution to life's questions. As we believe them and act on them, we find that they perform what God said they would—but only as we believe and act upon them. In John 7:16–17 Jesus states, "My doctrine is not mine, but his that sent me. If any man will do his will, he shall know . . . whether it be of God, or whether I speak of myself." Again in John 8:31–32 Jesus says, "If ye continue in my word, then ye are my disciples indeed; And ye shall know the truth, and the truth shall make you free."

In 2 Peter 1:3–4, God speaks of "exceeding great and precious promises." Of those who receive them, He declares that they have the power "to [escape] the corruption that is in the world through lust." We know, of course, that He is referring to Adam and Eve, as they were tempted by the devil. They began to lust after the forbidden fruit in the garden. Corruption came by the actions of one man (Adam) after Eve came under the power of lust for the forbidden fruit.

> And when the woman saw that the tree was good for food, and that it was pleasant to the eyes, and a tree to be desired to make one wise, she took of the fruit thereof, and did eat, and gave also unto her husband with her; and he did eat.
>
> —Genesis 3:6

Notice that corruption (the law of sin and death) entered the picture through lust, just as 2 Peter 1:4 reminds us. He says that we escape the corruption by these exceeding great and precious promises, so the cycle can be broken for those who have believed upon Jesus. You can escape the corruption!

Now let's define corruption as it applies to us in our everyday lives. We get understanding from Romans 8:21–23, "Because the creature [creation] itself also shall be delivered from the bondage of corruption into the glorious liberty of the children of God. For we know that the whole creation groaneth and travaileth in pain together until now. And not only they, but ourselves also, which have the firstfruits of the Spirit, even we ourselves groan within ourselves, waiting for the adoption, to wit, the redemption of our body."

This event, exclusive to the church, the body of Christ, will take place for every believer at the Rapture of the church at the end of this age. We believe this event to be upon us now. But I believe that it would be a mistake for you to discount the "exceeding great and precious promises" granting you immediate benefits of health and life!

The corruption mentioned in 2 Peter 1:4 manifests in a very real way in our everyday lives. But God gives us a remedy for it. There is a provision for those who are waiting for the redemption of the body. It comes by exercising faith on a daily basis in God's exceeding great and precious promises. We become partakers of His divine nature through the promises of God and escape the corruption that is in the world. What a concept of faith! We can escape the corruption that is in the world!

Remember, we found out that our body is dead because of sin, but our spirit is alive through Christ. When we accepted Jesus, in one uncommon event God brought divine life to our spirits. It is our body and our unrenewed mind (or impure soul) that must find its answer through faith and obedience in God's promises.

Concerning the soul area, including the mind, God gives us His answer in two verses: "Put off concerning the former conversation the old man, which is corrupt according to the deceitful lusts; And be renewed in the spirit of your mind" (Eph. 4:22–23). "And [ye] have put on the new man, which is renewed in knowledge after the image of him that created him" (Col. 3:10).

Also, we read in 1 Peter 1:22, "Seeing ye have purified your souls in obeying the truth," and in James 1:21, "Receive with meekness the engrafted word, which is able to save [deliver] your souls." These are but some promises for deliverance for the soul, the intellectual, reasoning, and emotional realm.

What about the physical body? It is not enough that we escape death. It is not enough that our mind can find a place of peace and safety. Longevity has its place, but life eventually becomes unfavorable once the discomforts of disease, feebleness, loneliness, and so forth begin to take their effect upon the human body. Without "exceeding great and precious promises" to deliver us from these ill fates, the blessing of extended length of life could become a curse.

That is what God meant in Genesis 3:22 when He said, "Behold, the man is become as one of us, to know good and evil: and now, lest he put forth his hand, and take also of the tree of life, and eat, and live forever: Therefore the Lord God sent him forth from the garden of Eden."

You see, God in His mercy acted for the betterment of Adam by barring him from living forever. Long life, in this instance, would ultimately prove to be a curse. Remember, God has told the man, "Cursed is the ground for thy sake; in sorrow shalt thou eat of it all the days of thy life. . . . In the sweat of thy face shalt thou eat bread, till thou return unto the ground" (Gen. 3:17, 19). In the face of this judgment upon humanity, long life eventually becomes a curse!

Without a cure for the corruption that came in through Adam's sin, without a remedy for the sorrow that would increase from growing tired and weak in the advanced years of life, and without the solution to this challenge, man would not have a motivation to remain until the Rapture of the church. Many faith-filled believers have succumbed to death because they grew weary of the journey of life! Who could blame them for going on to be with the Lord? They need rest from the weariness of life.

This is the reason for this revelation from God! It takes knowledge from God's Word to know how to live out the rest of this age until the coming of the Lord Jesus without these flaws. Faith gives us certain promises that we will explore to enable those of us who will believe and receive it to live in total victory for the remaining time ahead. You are invited in on God's best.

Preserved Flawlessly Until Jesus Comes

> And the very God of peace sanctify you wholly [Heb., "complete to the end, i.e. absolutely perfect"]; and I pray God your whole [Heb., "complete in every part, i.e. perfectly sound in body: entire, whole"] spirit and soul and body be preserved [Heb., "to guard from loss or injury (by keeping an eye upon)"] blameless [Heb., "to be flawless, without fault, imperfection, or impairment"] unto the coming of our Lord Jesus Christ. Faithful is he that calleth you [Heb., "bid to, call out to"]. who also will do it."
>
> —1 Thessalonians 5:23–24

God promises in this scripture text to "sanctify you wholly...spirit...soul and body," to preserve you flawlessly until Jesus comes. He says that He will keep His eye on you to guard you from loss or injury (in spirit, soul, and physical body). He states that He will set you apart from all evil, harmful things (whether spiritual, soulish, or physical). He says that He will do this complete to the end, absolutely perfect. Furthermore, He says that He will be faithful to do this unto the coming of the Lord Jesus. That is why I say that I am a card-carrying "alive and remainer" until the coming of the Lord!

In John 17:15 Jesus prayed to the Father, "I pray not that thou shouldest take them out of the world, but that thou shouldest keep them from the evil." The words "keep them from" are the same as the Hebrew word *sanctify* seen in 1 Thessalonians 5:23. The Word is saying to you, "And the very God of peace keep you from evil wholly unto the coming of the Lord Jesus."

Perhaps we should also deal with the word *evil.* in John 17:15. The Hebrew word is *poneros*, which means "hurtful; calamitous; ill, i.e. diseased; also bad, evil, grievous, harm, malicious, wicked." God wants your body, as well as your spirit and soul, preserved flawlessly from that which is hurtful, calamitous, ill, diseased, bad, evil, grievous, harmful, malicious, or wicked. He says that He has called you and that He also will do it complete, absolutely perfect unto the coming of the Lord Jesus. Now we just have to find someone willing to claim that exceeding great and precious promise. It is so exceedingly great that you will have to challenge and win over all reason. Say with me right now, "I'm willing! I will not be denied God's best for me!"

My wife, Olene, makes a daily confession concerning this great promise. She repeatedly states, "I am strong, healthy, and pain free in every way and will be so all the days of my life until Jesus comes at the Rapture. And I am totally (wholly) positive." She knows that both the physical and psychological person must be preserved if we are going to productively remain until the Rapture of the church. As she confesses this promise, her faith deepens in her heart and raises her life to the level of that confession in God's Word.

God says in Hebrews 10:23, "Let us hold fast the confession of our faith without wavering; (for he is faithful that promised)." Hebrews 11:11, speaking concerning Abraham and Sarah, states, "Through faith also Sarah herself received strength to conceive seed, and was delivered of a child when she was past age, because she judged him faithful who had promised." Notice that she attained strength when she was past age through a promise. Yes, we can remain strong, healthy, pain free, and productive until the coming of the Lord Jesus. We are of that group that believe that once we see it in the Word of God we can declare what is rightfully ours and fully receive it! He is faithful who promised!

YOU ARE WHAT YOU EAT

And ye shall serve the LORD your God, and he shall bless [Heb., "to bless God (as an act of adoration) and (vice-versa) bless man (as a benefit)"] thy bread [Heb., "food, bread or grain for making it: eat, food, fruit, loaf, meat, victuals"], and thy water; and I will take sickness [Heb., "disease, infirmity, sickness"] away from the midst [Heb., "center, bowels, inward parts, midst, within self"] of thee. There shall none cast their young, nor be barren, in thy land: the number of thy days I will fulfill [Heb., "to fill, overflow, fulfill, replenish, satisfy, have wholly"].

—EXODUS 23:25–26

They tell us these days that we are what we eat. They (the so-called experts of the day) act as if they've only recently discovered this principle. Here in Exodus 23:25 we find God giving us a promise based upon that same concept: He says in effect, "Your food and drink will be blessed to be a benefit to your body. You will then take it into your body, and the results will be that I will take sickness, disease, and infirmity out of the inward parts of your body." Again, *wow!* How much clearer can a promise be? If we eat "a blessing," our bodies are blessed. If we eat "a curse," our bodies are cursed. God declares, "I will send My angel, and he will bless what you eat." Don't ever call cursed what God has blessed!

We have health gurus all of the time explaining their holistic views of care for the body. At the top of the list is what you eat. Secondly, they tell you if you already have poisons built up within your bodily organs you can purge them with certain herbs, foods, and so forth. God goes one better than that. He says, "I'll take whatever you eat or drink, bless it to benefit you as you ingest it, and take sickness away from the midst of you—if you will serve Me."

I do not trust in any natural ability to eat right. I watch what I eat with a degree of moderation. However, the challenge I have with the natural approach to healthy eating is that it is impossible to know for certain that you are eating healthy food. I'm not finding fault with the concept of developing a healthy lifestyle of eating. It is just that as hard as you may try it is virtually impossible to do so. There are so many unknowns regarding what poisons and harmful chemicals are loosed into our environment. Additionally, you can never be certain that the nutrients you really need are in the food you are eating. Popeye's spinach may not be worth too much if it is grown in soil that has been robbed of its original minerals.

But God has given us His way! It is simple! He says, "Serve me, pray, and give thanks for it to be blessed. I'll send my angel to you. Beware of him. He will bless your bread and your water. Through this means I'll take sickness out of your bowels, out of the midst of you."

You will need to develop faith for this to work in your life. It requires that you believe it. Remember, in Hebrews 4:2 the Word says, "For unto us was the gospel preached, as well as unto them: but the word preached did not profit them, not being mixed with faith in them that heard it." You will need to extend your knowledge of how this works. I am going to help you by walking you through exactly how God does it.

To accomplish this, we will need to back up to Exodus 23:20–23, 25. Follow me closely:

> Behold, I [God] send an Angel before thee, to keep thee in the way, and to bring thee into the place which I [God] have prepared. Beware of him[the Angel], and obey his [the Angel's]voice, provoke him [the Angel]not; for he [the Angel]will not pardon your transgressions: for my [God] name is in him [the Angel]. But if thou shalt indeed obey his voice [the Angel's], and do all that I [God] speak; then I [God] will be an enemy unto thine enemies, and an adversary unto thine adversaries. For mine Angel shall go before thee....And ye shall serve the LORD your God, and he [the Angel] shall bless thy bread, and thy water; and I [God] will take sickness away from the midst of thee.

You can see through this scripture that the angel has the power to bless whatever God has placed in him to bless. God says, "For my name is in him." Angels do not have inherent rights to use this power, except when they have been given instructions from God. God says in effect, "If you'll serve Me, I'll put My name in an angel for the purpose of blessing your food and drink!"

To understand the process through which God blesses your food, performs this supernatural purging from harmful contaminants, and causes it to purge out disease-causing poisons from your organs or "inward parts," allowing healing and strength to your body to be maintained, you must understand the first and second person of these verses. You simply have to apply some common sense English. If you just presumptuously quote verse 25 out of the entire context of these five verses, you will miss the important role of your angel in this process. Accurate usage of your faith is always the result of precise, accurate knowledge of God's Word.

God did not say that He would bless your bread and your water! Get this now! He said that He would send His angel, and that he [your angel] would bless your bread and your water. God said that through this process He [God] would take sickness out of you. You see, the angel comes from the presence of God to perform his task for you. I am aware of how radical it sounds, but it is truth! God sends him to you in fulfillment of the promise.

> But to which of the angels said he at any time, Sit on my right hand, until I make thine enemies thy footstool? Are they not all ministering spirits, sent forth to minister for them who shall be heirs of salvation?
> —HEBREWS 1:13–14

You must see the importance of angels if you want in on the things that are yours between now and the Rapture of the church. You must never worship angels. Nevertheless, you must become aware of the angels. Get to know them! Jehovah Tsaba is the Lord of Hosts (angelic armies)!

I want to cover other scriptures that will confirm what you have just learned. Again, in the mouth of two or three witnesses, let every word be established.

Go with me to Psalm 103 for more insight into these great promises. We'll begin at the beginning of the chapter:

> Bless the LORD, O my soul: and all that is within me, bless his holy name. Bless the LORD, O my soul, and forget not all his benefits: Who forgiveth all thine iniquities; who healeth all thy diseases; Who redeemeth thy life from destruction [this is speaking of the corrupting influence upon our bodies as a result of the sin of Adam]; who crowneth thee with lovingkindness and tender mercies; Who satisfieth [Heb., "to render to perfection"] thy mouth with good things; so that thy youth [Heb., "youth, the state (juvenility) or the persons (young people): childhood, youth"] is renewed [Heb., "to be new again, cause to rebuild, repair, renew"]like the eagle's.

Now notice very carefully in verse 7 these words, "He made known his ways unto Moses, his acts unto the children of Israel." What did we just learn about the way God took care of Israel? What did God reveal to Moses about their supernatural provision where His promise was concerned? He said, "I will send my angel." Through much of Psalm 103, God lists the various characteristics of His goodness, "To such as keep his covenant, and to those that remember his commandments to do them" (Ps. 103:18).

How does He do it? What is one method that God uses to bless us? "The Lord hath prepared his throne in the heavens; and his kingdom ruleth over all. Bless the Lord, ye his angels, that excel in strength, that do his commandments, hearkening unto the voice of his word. Bless ye the Lord, all ye his hosts; ye ministers of his, that do his pleasure" (Ps. 103:19–21). Remember, the Hebrew word for "hosts" is *tsaba* ("saw-baw") and is always used when describing God's angelic hosts.

One other area of physical provision is necessary to keep you from harm from now until the Rapture of the church: protection from accidental harm or death. For that we will go to Psalm 91:7–12 for a summary of God's way to accomplish this for you: "A thousand shall fall at thy side, and ten thousand at thy right hand; but it shall not come nigh thee. Only with thine eyes shalt thou behold and see the reward of the wicked. Because thou hast made the Lord, which is my refuge, even the most High, thy habitation; There shall no evil [Heb., *poneros*: 'hurtful; calamitous; ill, i.e., diseased; also bad, evil, grievous, harm, malicious, wicked'] befall thee, neither shall any plague come nigh thy dwelling. For he shall give his angels charge [Heb., 'appoint, give a charge to, send with a command'] over thee, to keep thee in all thy ways. They shall bear thee up in their hands, lest thou dash thy foot against a stone." You can see that God has already provided everything you will need to set your course.

You can walk in complete spiritual, physical, social, and financial freedom and victory if you choose to believe to remain and live prosperously and in health until the coming of the Lord. You are not left to yourself. You are not left on your own. You are God's property!

In Hebrews 13:5–6 the Amplified Bible states, "For He [God] Himself has said, I will not in any way fail you nor give you up nor leave you without support. [I will] not, [I will] not, [I will] not in any degree leave you helpless nor forsake nor let [you] down (relax My hold on you)! [Assuredly not!] So we take comfort and are encouraged and confidently and boldly say, The Lord is my Helper; I will not be seized with alarm [I will not fear or dread or be terrified].

What can man do to me?" I want you to say with me right now, "I am God's property! He will not leave me without supernatural support!"

You now have the keys to a great end-time prosperity phenomenon. You also hold the truth of how to be a part of this great final generation of victory. As you take these truths and put your faith into action, as you reach into that cloud of anointing that remains unspoiled since Israel took back Egypt's gold and silver, you too can be living victoriously when the great trumpet sounds and we leave this earth as the glorious church triumphant!

HOW THE PROSPERITY PHENOMENON ANOINTING WILL FLOW TO YOU!

You can see by now that this God-planned event is very real, although it may seem like a dream yet to come true. You have learned about doing your part by giving, being obedient to the Word of God, and by following the leading of the Spirit. Many of you have already developed highly in these areas as well as in *agape* love and forgiveness. But still you may wonder, *How*? It is no problem with your faith to approach this question. It is wrong to question the occurrence of what God has spoken, but it is OK to ask God, *How is this going to occur?*

In Luke 1 we have a perfect example of this: Zacharias, the father of John the Baptist, questioned God's angel, saying, "Whereby shall I know this? for I am an old man" (v. 18). You can see that he was questioning that God would do it. The result was that he offended the angel of God: "And, behold, thou shalt be dumb, and not able to speak, until the day that these things shall be performed, because thou believest not my words, which shall be fulfilled in their season."

On the other hand, in that same chapter we have Mary, the mother of Jesus, approached by an angel declaring, "Fear not, Mary: for thou hast found favour with God. And, behold, thou shalt conceive in thy womb, and bring forth a son, and shall call his name Jesus" (vv. 30–31). Her reply was a simple: "How shall this be?" (v. 34). The angel answered her question by saying, "The Holy Ghost shall come upon thee, and the power of the Highest shall over-shadow thee" (v. 35).

So, how is this prosperity phenomenon anointing going to come upon you? To understand the answer to this question you must also understand how the anointing works to bring to pass these occurrences.

How does God take an anointing, spoken of in ancient times, and get it to you? First, God promised a prosperity phenomenon to Abraham. This was the beginning of this anointing. In Genesis 15:9–14, Jehovah invited Abram to cut a covenant.

> And he said unto him, Take me an heifer of three years old, and a she goat of three years old, and a ram of three years old, and a turtledove, and a young pigeon. And he took unto him all these, and divided them in the midst, and laid each piece one against another: but the birds divided he not. And when the fowls came down upon the carcases, Abram drove them away. And when the sun was going down, a deep sleep fell upon Abram; and, lo, an horror of great darkness fell upon him. And he said unto Abram, Know of a surety that thy seed shall be a stranger in a land that is not theirs, and shall serve them; and they shall afflict them four hundred years; And also that nation, whom they shall serve, will I judge: and afterward shall they come out with great substance.

As Jehovah made His covenant with Abram, an event unfolded that did not come to pass for approximately 420 years.

The anointing rests upon the seed

We've had the mistaken idea sometimes in the past that God anoints events. If that were the case then we would spend the anointing set forth for that event. Then when the event was over the anointing to accomplish what had happened would be no more.

Have you ever heard someone say, "That church service (or that crusade) surely was anointed"? Folks sometimes misunderstand and are therefore tempted to try and recreate a particular meeting in order to get the same results. "Let's see. Now, what songs were sung? How many fast or slow ones?" As we study out the Word we find it was not the event that was anointed. Rather, someone with a promise from God received an anointing upon them to fulfill God's will and plan.

When God spoke the words of His covenant with Abram, an anointing was released through those words. They came to rest upon Abram and upon his seed. The part about "great substance" was not to Abram (himself), but rather it was to occur to his seed many years later. So how did it get from where Abram was then to where Israel was (in Egypt) at the time it actually occurred? The answer, as you will see, is that the anointing for the event flowed through the seed. The anointing was upon the seed!

In Genesis 15:13, God said to Abram, "Thy seed shall..." At that moment the anointing to fulfill this prophetic event was directed to and began to rest upon Abram's seed until the appointed time. Abram had children, who had children, who had children. As this occurred, the anointing flowed down the line of Abram's descendants until the promised event.

Had the anointing been upon the event itself, God would have needed to wait until time for the event to occur, then release it at that time upon the event. But God released the anointing upon Abram for the event to occur 420 years prior.

Since the anointing to cause the event to occur was upon the seed and not upon the event itself, once it had occurred the anointing continued to remain upon Abram's seed. This can be proven out through the Word of God.

We see proof of this in Haggai 2:4–5, "For I am with you, saith the LORD of hosts [Jehovah Tsaba]; According to the word that I covenanted with you when ye came out of Egypt, so my spirit [residue of power and anointing] remaineth among you." The event had occurred approximately one thousand years earlier from an anointing that had been released four hundred years prior to the occurrence. Yet, God is telling us in Haggai that the same anointing still remains upon the seed! He was encouraging them to continue to believe in the promise of God's great substance. He was letting them know that the power and anointing released during the cutting of that covenant with Abram was still as powerful and available as ever.

Now, let me ask you a question. If it was there when Abram cut the covenant, if it was there 420 years later when God raised up Moses for Israel to come out of Egypt, and if it was still upon Abraham's seed one thousand years later, where do you suppose it is today? Perhaps it finally just became worn out from use? Maybe God's supernatural power is like our human strength? The answer, most assuredly, is *no*! God's power is everlasting.

Let me show you that it still remains here today for one—and only one—more event to occur out of that same anointing! This time, however, the event itself is even greater than what Israel experienced when God judged Egypt, causing the Israelites to spoil Egypt of their riches. Instead of God judging a nation and giving its spoils to His people, this time God will judge all nations and, as you will see later in this chapter, the desirable and precious things of all nations will be loosed and flow into the hands of God's covenant people, the seed of Abraham! We will show you that the anointing of that covenant of great substance still today is resting upon and flowing right where it always has, upon the seed of Abraham.

> Now to Abraham and his seed were the promises made. He saith not, And to seeds, as of many; but as of one, And to thy seed, which is Christ....And if ye be Christ's, then are ye Abraham's seed, and heirs according to the promise.
>
> —GALATIANS 3:16, 29

Abraham's seed (his natural seed) became a nation. The anointing remained upon them generation by generation. They were the ones entrusted with that anointing. They were "carriers," infected, you might say, with that anointing released upon Abraham through the covenant cut between God and him, much like a person can be a carrier of a disease, having been infected yet not actually contracting the disease himself, so that anointing continued to flow down through the Hebrew lineage.

They continue to be carriers until it came ("flowed") to the seed for whom it was intended: *Jesus!* When Jesus went to the cross, something changed. When that anointing flowed upon Him, when it had come to the Seed for whom it was intended, it ceased to be carried by the natural seed of Abraham any longer! All of the blessings of Abraham had come to Christ as His possession. This would be the basis of a new covenant established upon better things than the blood of bulls and goats and heifers! Now Jesus's own blood would become the surety. Abraham had obtained the promises with a debt instrument, the blood of animals, used to temporarily attest to the surety of the covenant. That debt instrument would remain in force until the payment (of Jesus's own blood) was paid in full.

The anointing left the natural seed of Abraham, attested by the fact that the veil of the temple was torn open from the top to the bottom when Jesus fulfilled His sacrifice upon the cross. The anointing had come to the Seed for whom it was intended. No longer did it dwell upon Israel. Jesus was, at that moment, the only carrier upon whom the anointing rested. He became the possessor of the blessing of Abraham!

But He did not remain the only carrier for very long. On the Day of Pentecost something wonderful occurred. A new nation was born who would continue carrying that anointing of Abraham. This new nation is called the church of God, the body of Christ in the earth today. Read again with me from Galatians 3:16, 29:

> Now to Abraham and his seed were the promises made. He saith not, And to seeds, as of many; but as of one, And to thy seed, which is Christ....And if ye be Christ's, then are ye Abraham's seed, and heirs according to the promise.

Only those who are partakers with Christ are now the seed who carry that anointing!

The importance of Haggai's prophecy

Let's go back to Haggai 2:5–9:

> According to the word that I covenanted with you when ye came out of Egypt [remember that the covenant itself was made 420 years earlier with Abraham, not with Moses at the time of Israel's deliverance], so my spirit [supernatural power and anointing] remaineth among you: fear ye not. For thus saith the LORD of hosts [Jehovah Tsaba]; Yet once, it is a little while, and I will shake the heavens, and the earth, and the sea, and the dry land; And I will shake all nations, and the desire [spoils, riches] of all nations shall come: and I will fill this house [family, God's people of this time] with glory, saith the LORD of hosts. The silver is mine, and the gold is mine, saith the LORD of hosts. The glory of this latter house shall be greater than of the former, saith the LORD of hosts: and in this place [in time] will I give peace, saith the LORD of hosts [Jehovah Tsaba].

God is letting Haggai know that the same anointing that came upon Israel when they spoiled Egypt of its riches will one more time be used for an even greater event, for the desirable and precious things of all nations to come to His family at some future time. "It is a little while" (v. 6)!

Yet once, it is a little while...

Haggai's prophecy was recorded approximately 520 years prior to Jesus's appearance on the earth as a baby. It is clear that the way this prophecy is to be fulfilled is through the exercise of the same anointing that caused Israel to spoil Egypt of its wealth. We know that this anointing began with the covenant made between God and Abraham. God had said to him, "And I will bring them out with great substance." (See Genesis 15:14.)

When God sent Moses to deliver Israel, Moses drew upon the anointing of the words of that covenant. God spoke to him and said, "I will give this people favour in the sight of the Egyptians: and it shall come to pass, that, when ye go, ye shall not go empty. But every woman shall borrow of her neighbour, and of her that sojourneth in her house [Egyptian house guests], jewels of silver, and jewels of gold, and raiment: and ye shall put them upon your sons, and upon your daughters; and ye shall spoil the Egyptians" (Exod. 3:21–22).

So, as Moses prepared the people to leave Egypt, he told them to act upon what God had said. We read that "the children of Israel did according to the word of Moses; and they borrowed of the Egyptians jewels of silver, and jewels of gold, and raiment: And the Lord gave the people favour in the sight of the Egyptians, so that they lent unto them such things as they required. And they spoiled the Egyptians" (Exod. 12:35–36).

The importance of Haggai 2:5–9 is that God said, in essence, "I will use that same anointing to do yet a greater work just one more time. It will be a little while before I do it, and it will not just affect one nation this time. But, I will cause all nations to be shaken until the desirable things of all nations are shaken loose and come to My house or family in the earth."

"Yet a little while." Time passes down through the ages. The Book of Hebrews records the prophecy of Haggai as a promise still not yet fulfilled. The writer speaks of it as a future event yet to come: "Whose voice then shook the earth: but now he hath promised, saying, Yet once more I shake, not the earth only, but also heaven" (Heb. 12:26). Clearly here the writer is making a reference to the prophecy of Haggai. While he does not quote all of the prophecy, notice that it is still spoken of as an unfulfilled prophecy and that it is to occur only "once more."

Haggai gives the details missing in the Hebrews reference. When the event occurs, Haggai says that as God shakes all nations, the desirable and precious things (Moffatt's translation renders the word "treasures") of all nations shall come to us for whom this promise was given, the seed of Abraham in Christ Jesus!

Just as the silver and gold and the other riches were taken from the nation of Egypt and given to Israel, even so all nations will give up their treasures to us as God shakes His hand upon them once again. As it shakes loose and flows to us, He will fulfill a word that He has spoken of over and over again in these passages of Scripture.

An angel appeared to Zechariah and spoke of this event, saying, " For thus saith the Lord of hosts [Jehovah Tsaba]; After [in pursuit of] the glory hath he sent me unto the nations which spoiled you: for he that toucheth you toucheth the apple of his [Jehovah's] eye. For, behold, I will shake mine hand upon them, and they shall be a spoil…and ye shall know that the Lord of hosts [Jehovah Tsaba] hath sent me….And many nations shall be joined to the Lord in that day, and shall be my people" (Zech. 2:8–9, 11).

The anointing for this event is now being released through this writing and through the ministry as it goes forth to proclaim one of the greatest events in the church. Your past and present faithfulness is allowing it to flow to you. Shout boldly and declare it! Make your boast of what God is now doing in the body of Christ and in your life.

Begin confessing these great truths! Say, "The King of glory, Jehovah Tsaba, has come in! He is strong and mighty, mighty in battle! His glory is upon us and shall be seen upon us! The wicked Gentile world will see the brightness of our rising! We'll begin to sparkle with their glory, their silver and gold, their treasures. The rich sea trade and the wealth of nations will be converted. It will tumble from their hands and flow to us! A multitude of burden-bearing labor to bring goods will overwhelm us! Our gates will be open continually. They will not be shut day nor night to allow for continual (twenty-four-hour) employment, so that men may bring to us the forces (riches, wealth, goods, substance, means, men, and other resources) of the Gentile world! We are the priests of the Lord! We are the ministers of our God! We will consume the riches of the Gentile world, and in their glory will we boast (exchange, change place with and boast) ourselves of it! And our seed (children) will be known among the Gentile world, and all who see them will acknowledge them, that they are the seed which the Lord hath blessed!"

Chapter Twelve

SO WHERE ARE WE HEADED?

N O MATTER WHERE you are now in terms of material wealth, God has a plan for you to become a part of this end-time prosperity phenomenon. You may be reading this in the poorest of financial conditions, but you can immediately turn your face away from the lifestyle that you have contended with. You do not have to continue to go from paycheck to paycheck, from bill to bill, or even from handout to handout. No more! Say it with me right now, "No more!"

God recently spoke to me and said, "In the past you have put the foot of your will down, and it has worked only in a measure. But when you put your spiritual foot down and declare My eternal Word on it, My foot will be placed on your circumstances, and they will change!"

It is important that you understand that God has promised to take you from level to level to level—until you see the fulfillment of the promises that I have shared with you. Make the decision to receive it for you and your family. Boldly announce to them, "We'll never be broke again another day in our lives. We've been delivered out of the land of 'not enough,' out of the land of 'just enough,' and into the land of 'more than enough'! We'll always have it, all sufficiency in all things and abound to every good work!"

God promises that there is a place in Him where you will wind up working independently of any earthly source. He will direct you and be the total Source of all of your supply. He will take you from level to level to level!

In Isaiah 60:17 God declares to you, "For brass I will bring gold, and for iron I will bring silver, and for wood brass, and for stones, iron: I will also make thy officers [Heb., 'those in charge, officials'] peace, and thine exactors [Heb., 'taskmasters (employer)'] righteousness." Imagine someone asking, "Who do you work for? Who is paying you all of this money? Where is your wealth coming from?" You can reply, "Peace and righteousness is what is bringing all of this wealth to us in the body of Christ!" You explain to them that God ordained of old that "the wealth of the sinner [finds its way eventually] into the hand of the righteous" (Prov. 13:22, AMP). You declare to them, "He that by usury and unjust gain increaseth his substance, he shall gather it for him that will pity the poor" (Prov. 28:8). You remind them of the powerful promise in Job 27:13, 16–17: "This is the portion of a wicked man with God, and the heritage of oppressors, which they shall receive of the Almighty.... Though he heap up silver as the dust, and prepare raiment as the clay; He may prepare it, but the just shall put it on, and the innocent [Heb., from a root meaning 'to be made clean, held guiltless, blameless, be free, be acquitted'—clearly, only those who have been made righteous by the blood of Jesus qualify for this category of mankind] shall divide the silver."

Praise God! Righteousness and peace will not treat you like your old employers. They found ways to keep the wealth and keep you on a short string. They were willing to give you a plaque, to give you a special parking place for the month, or some special title, but they were not willing to make you rich! The rich, wicked Gentile world has found a way to make a stronghold of all of the wealth. God is now going to do something about it in order to comfort His people and allow them to play a chief role in His end-time harvest of souls. We will be able to finance the gospel out of our prosperity instead of from our financial sacrifices while struggling to find a way to meet the needs of our family.

Make these confessions with me right now:

God's glory is coming upon me and my family. I will come to the light of the Gentile world around me. They will see and take special notice of the brightness of my rising. God declares that I am the head and not the tail, above only and not beneath!

The same anointing that came upon Israel when they spoiled Egypt of their silver, their gold, and their fine apparel remains here among us now.

I am reaching for that anointing! God, as Jehovah Tsaba, is causing the rich sea trade and the wealth of nations to come to me. I will begin to sparkle like the sheen of a running stream.

As Jehovah Tsaba sends His angel out to the wicked, rich Gentile world in pursuit of their glory, and as He begins shaking His hand upon them, their desirable and precious things will tumble into my hands like the rushing of a stream in the desert. It will be like a dream as I am overwhelmed with a multitude of burden-bearing labor to bring goods.

My gates will be open continually. They will not be shut day nor night, that men may bring to me the riches, wealth, goods, substance, means, men, and other resources of the rich Gentile world. I will consume the riches of the Gentiles, and in their glory I will change places with and boast myself.

My profits from employment and trade will be turned to holiness unto the Lord. It will not be hoarded, treasured, and stored up but will be used for those who minister for the Lord, that they may have a sufficient amount and so that they might have durable and stately clothes and abundant supply, suitable for those who minister the gospel. I will be a part of those who will favor God's righteous cause.

I will give my tithe to my local pastor, and I will greatly support the work of the ministry of the gospel and partner with those who are taking the life of Christ into all of the earth.

I will walk in humility and meekness. I will walk in love with long-suffering and gentleness and goodness.

I will not be afraid or intimidated by the world, and I will not be impressed by the appearance of their power and influence. They will not impress me. I am the head. I am above only. I am the seed of Abraham and blessed in all of my doings. I will lift up those who are down.

I will remember that it is the Lord who gives me the power to get wealth, that He may establish and totally fulfill all of His covenant promises to all generations.

A PRAYER TO RECEIVE JESUS

THE GOSPEL IS for all who will receive it!

Dear Lord Jesus, I come to You because I want You to be the Lord of my life. At this moment, I make the decision to trust in the fact that God raised You from the dead. I choose today to accept that You died for me to pay the price of the sin. I understand that You will accept me and make me a child of God. I confess You now with all of my heart as the Lord of my life! Recreate in me a new heart, a new spirit, and fill me with Your own life and Spirit. Jesus, You are now my Lord! Use me throughout the remainder of my life here on earth. I will yield to You and to the direction of the Holy Spirit. I will make Your words my words, Your thoughts my thoughts, and Your ways my ways. From now on, I will favor Your righteous cause in the earth. I will allow You to make me a greater blessing to humanity. I want to be a part of this great end-time harvest of other souls to be brought into Your kingdom. I thank You for eternal life and for a heavenly home with You throughout all eternity. Almighty God, in Jesus's name, You are now my Father God. Amen!

Behold, what manner of love the Father hath bestowed upon us, that we should be called the sons of God...Beloved, now are we the sons of God, and it doth not yet appear what we shall be: but we know that, when he shall appear, we shall be like him; for we shall see him as he is.

—1 JOHN 3:1–2

BIBLIOGRAPHY

Ford, Cliff. *Blood, Money, and Greed*. Beverly Hills, CA: Lion's Head Publishing, 2001. At the time of printing, every effort was made to contact publisher and author to obtain permission to quote. Please contact Creation House if you have further information on contacting author and/or publisher of *Blood, Money, and Greed*, by Cliff Ford.

Harris, Ralph W., ed. *The Complete Biblical Library*. Springfield, MO: Gospel Publishing House, 1991.

"How Currency Gets into Circulation." Federal Reserve Bank of New York Web site. Available at http://www.ny.frb.org/aboutthefed/fedpoint/fed01.html, June 2008 (accessed November 23, 2011).

Jamieson, Robert, A. R. Fausset, and David Brown. *Commentary Critical and Explanatory on the Whole Bible*, 1871. Public domain. Available at http://www.biblestudytools.com/commentaries/jamieson-fausset-brown/ (accessed November 23, 2011).

Merriam-Webster Online Dictionary. Available at www.m-w.com (accessed November 23, 2011).

Shanks, Hershel and Ben Witherington III. *The Brother of Jesus*. New York, NY: HarperCollins Publishers, Inc., 2003.

Thayer, Joseph Henry. *Thayer's New Testament Greek Lexicon*. Public domain. Available at http://www.biblestudytools.com/lexicons/greek/ (accessed November 23, 2011).

Thompson, Frank C., ed. *Thompson Chain-Reference Bible*. Indianapolis, IN: Kirkbride Bible Company.

Wesley, John. *Wesley's Explanatory Notes*. Public domain. Available at http://www.biblestudytools.com/commentaries/wesleys-explanatory-notes/ (accessed November 24, 2011).

ABOUT THE
AUTHOR

Dr. Don G. Pickney, with thirty-eight years full-time ministry, is well known for his gift for a special depth of insight into revelation of the scriptures with respect to faith and patience. As an anointed teacher, with sixteen prior books, he reaches into the "unsearchable riches" of Christ and His Word, always bringing forth divine secrets, hidden by God for the body of Christ.

Since beginning continuous full-time ministry in 1974, his prayer has been, "Father, I thank you for accounting me as a minister of Christ, and a steward of the mysteries of God. I pray that I may be faithful to that calling – that I may speak boldly, and make known the mysteries concerning Christ, unfolding them, and making the clear as is my duty. I thank you, Father, that your word will run its course, and be glorified and triumphant in this earth." In May, 2000 God gave him a prophetic anointing for a biblical revelation of things which would shortly come to pass. At that time, he unveiled an event found in scripture, giving almost every detail of the destruction of the World Trade Center that took place on September 11, 2001. He has devoted his ministry since receiving this special assignment, preaching and teaching an end-time prosperity phenomenon, reserved for the Church, which, he believers, began its global fulfillment, beginning with the historic 9/11 attack.

As he explains, "The World Trade Center was not an American enterprise, although it rested on United States' soil. It was a 'world-trade center,' the powerful financial trade headquarters for the financial cartels. It was the icon of global commercial trade." Dr. Pickney's current ministry vision is to explore and make more widely known to the Church, what is happening in the current events of the nations of the world in which, "everything that can be shaken, will be shaken!" Dr. Pickney says, "If God prophetically spoke that he would make war on all of the governments and economies of the world in one great event, designed to bring about a supernatural wealth transfer to the Church, what would be the most likely place to allow coming under attack."

He is convinced it was, indeed, the World Trade Center complex. He contemplates a startling reality, "How can the collapse of a group of buildings in a single day, fully insured, in one location, cause every industrialized nation of the world to enter an instant economic crisis, with each of their central banks forced to pump hundreds of billions of dollars into their respective banking systems during each consecutive twenty-four hour period for many days following the destruction of the buildings, an occurrence from which no nation, after a full decade, has been able to find any hope of recovery."

Dr. Pickney's ministry is dedicated to proving, that on the fateful day of 9/11, God in His name, Jehovah Tsaba (Lord of hosts), began the unfolding of a biblical prophetic event, revealed in scripture as the Day of Jehovah Tsaba, during which He would plunder the nations of their "created glory" – their wealth, goods, substance, means, men and other resources, converting it into the hands of the righteous, a happening already being widely forecasted in charismatic Christianity. He and his wife of almost 30 years, Olene, now make their home and ministry headquarters in Scottsdale, Arizona, where he currently conducts the "largest home Bible study in the world," globally webcasting each week, from his home, to thousands of regular viewers.

CONTACT
THE AUTHOR

DON PICKNEY MINISTRIES

PO BOX 26118

SCOTTSDALE, AZ 85255

WWW.DONPICKNEYMINISTRIES.ORG

COMING SOON...

The Prosperity Phenomenon: A Revelation of the Day of Jehovah Tsaba

The Final Chapter!